the Frugal Gardener

How to Have **More Garden**
for *Less Money*

Catriona Tudor Erler

To my husband, Jim, who had the idea,
and to my father, who taught me to be frugal

RODALE

WE **INSPIRE** AND **ENABLE** PEOPLE TO IMPROVE
THEIR LIVES AND THE WORLD AROUND THEM

Editor: **Sally Roth**

Contributing Editor: **Karen Costello Soltys**

Researcher: **Heidi A. Stonehill**

Cover and Interior Book Designer:
Nancy Smola Biltcliff

Layout Designers: **Keith Biery, Dale Mack, and Donna Rossi**

Interior Illustrators: **Robin Brickman, Michael Hill/Hillustration, and Reed Sprunger**

Cover Illustrator: **Reed Sprunger**

Copy Editors: **Nancy N. Bailey and Stacey Ann Follin**

Manufacturing Coordinator: **Patrick T. Smith**

Indexer: **Lina Burton**

Editorial Assistance: **Susan L. Nickol**

We're always happy to hear from you. For questions or comments concerning the editorial content of this book, please write to:

Rodale Book Readers' Service
33 East Minor Street
Emmaus, PA 18098

Look for other Rodale books wherever books are sold. Or call us at (800) 848-4735.

For more information about Rodale Organic Gardening magazine and books, visit our Web site at:
www.organicgardening.com

RODALE GARDEN BOOKS

Executive Editor: Kathleen DeVanna Fish
Managing Editor: Fern Marshall Bradley
Executive Creative Director: Christin Gangi
Art Director: Patricia Field
Production Manager: Robert V. Anderson Jr.
Studio Manager: Leslie M. Keefe
Copy Manager: Nancy N. Bailey
Manufacturing Manager: Eileen Bauder

**Library of Congress
Cataloging-in-Publication Data**

Erler, Catriona T.
   The frugal gardener : how to have more garden for less money / Catriona Tudor Erler.
         p.   cm.
   Includes bibliographical references (p.   ) and index.
   ISBN 0-87596-801-5 (hardcover : acid-free)
   1. Gardening.   2. Organic gardening.   I. Title.
SB453.E689   1999
635—dc21   98–58098

ISBN 0–87596–865–1 (paperback)

Distributed in the book trade by St. Martin's Press

2   4   6   8   10   9   7   5   3   hardcover
2   4   6   8   10   9   7   5   3   paperback

Rodale Press
Organic Gardening Starts Here!

Here at Rodale Press, we've been gardening organically for more than 50 years—ever since my grandfather J. I. Rodale learned about composting and decided that healthy living starts with healthy soil. In 1940 J. I. started the Rodale Organic Farm to test his theories, and today the nonprofit Rodale Institute Experimental Farm is still at the forefront of organic gardening and farming research. In 1942 J. I. founded *Organic Gardening* magazine to share his discoveries with gardeners everywhere. His son, my father, Robert Rodale, headed *Organic Gardening* until 1990, and today a fourth generation of Rodales is growing up with the magazine. Over the years, we've shown millions of readers how to grow bountiful crops and beautiful flowers using nature's own techniques.

In this book, you'll find the latest organic methods and the best gardening advice. We know—because all our authors and editors are passionate about gardening! We feel strongly that our gardens should be safe for our children, pets, and the birds and butterflies that add beauty and delight to our lives and landscapes. Our gardens should provide us with fresh, flavorful vegetables, delightful herbs, and gorgeous flowers. And they should be a pleasure to work in as well as to view.

Sharing the secrets of safe, successful gardening is why we publish books. So come visit us at the Rodale Institute Experimental Farm, where you can tour the gardens every day—we're open year-round. And use this book to create your best garden ever.

Happy gardening!

Maria Rodale

Maria Rodale
Rodale Garden Books

Contents

How to Be a Frugal Gardener

As you probably already know if you're reading this book, being frugal doesn't mean settling for less. You *can* have a beautiful, rewarding garden bursting with flowers and vegetables—no matter how small your gardening budget. Gardening frugally means gardening smart: saving your time and money wherever possible so that you can spend these valuable resources on the things that are most important to you. Shave a few dollars here, a few hours there, and you'll soon see that your wallet is the least important ingredient in the recipe for gardening success.

In this book, you'll find a multitude of commonsense ideas, all of them easy to apply and sure to bring results. Whether you're a new gardener trying to fill flowerbeds without spending a bundle or an old hand looking for ways to cut down on maintenance chores, you'll discover shortcuts and penny-pinching tips in these pages that are so simple you can put them into action right away. No special skills or new tools are needed—just a willingness to think creatively. And creative thinking is the hallmark of the frugal gardener.

IDEAS THAT INSPIRE

Once you start sampling, you'll learn lots of fast tricks you can use right away, plus plenty of ideas for the future that you can start thinking about now. Think about where the money leaks are in your gardening budget: If you know you can't visit a garden center without coming home with a trunkful of plants, read the sections on flowers, veggies, and herbs to learn how you can trim your out-of-pocket costs and have even more fun growing your own. And remember that frugal gardening can be a big time-saver, too. If you're tired of spending your precious gardening hours on weed pulling and lawn mowing instead of on the planting and picking that give you real pleasure, turn to the section on maintenance to learn how to slice the drudgery to a minimal amount.

Let your creative frugality go free as you read. I have no doubt that you'll come up with your own brilliant money-saving ideas, too, once you get started.

THINK THRIFTY YEAR-ROUND

Frugal gardening is a year-round way of thinking. In the pages that follow, you'll find practical suggestions you can use immediately, like quick tricks for getting rid of weeds. You'll also find long-range ideas that will help you make the most of your garden right through the year. The hundreds of bright ideas that fill these pages are arranged by general categories, such as plants, tools, maintenance, and furnishings, so you can turn quickly to what you need. But feel free to flip through the pages to find inspiration in any section. And make the index your friend—you can turn to it when you want to make sure you'll find all the tips on the subjects you're most interested in.

If price is important, finding the right raw materials for gardening can be tricky, unless you spend a lot of time comparison-shopping. So I've eliminated a lot of the work by supplying "Resources for Frugal Gardeners" on page 263. There you'll find sources for reasonably priced, good-quality supplies, from seeds to spring bulbs to sturdy tools.

Every time you put a frugal tip into practice, give yourself a pat on the back for restoring your garden to what it was meant to be: a partnership between you and your plants. Buying fancy toys or pricey plants may be fun, but the knowledge you gain from getting to know your plants and soil is the heart of gardening. When it comes to gardening, a green thumb beats a greenback by a mile.

CHAPTER ONE

GET THE GARDEN YOU WANT— THE FRUGAL WAY

YOU CAN HAVE BOUNTIFUL GARDENS and a beautiful land-scape—and save thousands of dollars in the process—when you start thinking like a frugal gardener. But there is a lot more to being a frugal gardener than just saving money. Being frugal means having fun, too. I love the challenge of thinking of ingenious substitutes for expensive plants, tools, and accessories. And I know you will, too!

What makes being a frugal gardener so much fun? It's because there are so many ways to go about saving money that it makes every day a new and exciting adventure.

As frugal gardeners, we're constantly on the alert for money-saving opportunities to make our gardens grow. A good place to start saving is on plants. Buy and plant healthy, well-rooted specimens. Keep an eye out for bargains, too, when plants go on sale at your local garden center. And don't forget visits to friends' gardens. You'll have earned your frugal gardener badge when you always have clippers and a plastic bag on hand in case you have the opportunity to take a plant cutting on the spot!

1

How to $ave Right from the Start

You'll save the most if you're frugal right from the start of your gardening project. (It's harder once you've already jumped in with blazing checkbook, *then* realized that you've made an expensive mistake.) And that means using sense instead of cents—whether you're planning your garden, choosing the best plants, or adding furniture and decorative features. Buy it in your head (or on your calculator) before you buy it on credit. You may be stunned at the price of that short list of perennials! But luckily, there are always lots of frugal choices for those high-ticket items, and I'll show you plenty of them.

Once you're finally at the nursery, follow the frugal gardener's first rule of plant buying: It costs no more to buy a healthy plant than it does to buy a sick one—and in the long term, it costs a lot less! The trick is knowing the "vital signs" of plant health.

Buying Healthy Plants Pays Off in the Long Run

When you're shopping for plants, the simplest way to save is to start off with healthy specimens. Restoring sick plants to good health can cost money for sprays or fertilizers or waste your time returning the failed plant for a replacement. Worst of all, an afflicted plant can spread trouble to the rest of your garden.

Examining the foliage and roots of the plants at your local garden center will tell you in a hurry whether or not a plant is healthy. Here's what to look for.

Aboveground Clues to Plant Health

Look for leaves with vivid, even coloring. Healthy foliage looks vigorous and fresh, whether it is green, gray, or variegated.

Look at both sides of leaves before you buy. Discolorations usually indicate that a disease or insect has been at work. Shun plants whose leaves or leaf stems are marred with light or dark spots or blotches or have shiny, clear spots or webbing.

Pass up wilted plants. Drought-stressed plants wilt and lose roots and leaves. Even if you shower them with water and kindness at home, their growth may be slowed or stunted. Seriously wilted plants may never recover. Don't take chances on wilted plants.

Underground Clues to Plant Health

Vital signs below ground are harder for you to evaluate than leaves and stems, especially if the plant is growing firmly in place in a clay or plastic pot. But if you can slip a plant from its pot, it's worth taking a peek.

Pale tan or white roots that are pliable and firm textured are signs of good underground health. The roots should fill one-half to three-quarters of the soil in the pot, without circling the pot walls.

Reject mushy, rotten, or black roots. And pass up plants that have too few or too many roots. Sparse roots, filling less than half the pot, may indicate a newly potted cutting or a plant that has lost roots to rot or drought stress. Roots that encircle the pot may be too tangled to

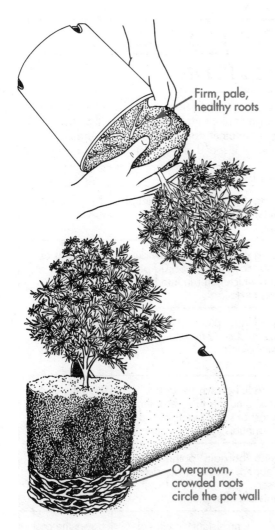

Firm, pale,
healthy roots

Overgrown,
crowded roots
circle the pot wall

Slip a plant from its pot to examine its roots. Look for firm, pale roots that fill one-half to three-quarters of the soil.

Look for clues to a strong root system. If you can't slip the pot off a plant, turn the pot on its side and look for a few roots escaping through the pot's drain hole. If the tips of those roots are still healthy and growing, your plant will establish quickly in the garden. If a mass of roots is clogging the drain holes, the plant is pot-bound and may never fulfill its potential in the garden.

After the plants are in your garden, you can save by keeping your plants healthy and eliminating the need to replace them. You'll find even more great money-saving tips on buying and growing plants in Chapter 2, "Save Money on Plants."

Fill Your Garden with Giveaways

A plant that multiplies beyond your needs—or your garden's boundaries—is an ideal candidate to divide and share with friends and neighbors, and sharing is one of the most joyful ways of frugal gardening. Get to know other gardeners, and you'll find your beds soon fill up with passed-along plants. As your collection grows, take cuttings, make divisions, or save seeds for plant exchanges (or just to give to your friends). Plant exchanges are great fun because everyone who participates goes home with new treasures.

I believe seeds are the most frugal source of new plants because they're so plentiful. When collecting seeds from your plants, keep enough for yourself and then share the rest—or trade them for seeds of plants that your friends are growing but that are new to you.

Exchanging seeds through the mail is a great way to stay in touch with and feel closer to your far-flung gardening friends. And seeds are ideal gifts for mailing to

unwind at planting time, stunting the growth of a plant or even killing it. Mushy roots indicate rot; black roots, in almost all cases, are dead roots. (A few plants, such as American persimmon, have black roots naturally; they will feel pliant and solid to the touch, not brittle or mushy like roots that have died and blackened.)

FRUGAL GARDENER'S GUIDE

Saving Big on Plants

When you start your own plants from seeds, cuttings, and divisions, you'll have the satisfaction of doing it "from scratch." You'll have healthier plants, too, because they'll be better adapted to your garden than plants shipped in from other parts of the country. And best of all, you'll save the big bucks that you would otherwise spend at a garden center or nursery!

FRUGAL METHOD	STORE-BOUGHT	SAVINGS*
Starting plants from cuttings using recycled pots and sterile soil medium; yields unlimited plants; costs pennies per plant	Buying 4-inch pots of individual plants; costs $2.50–$5.00 per plant	$2.50–$5.00
Starting plants from seeds, using recycled pots and sterile soil medium; yields ½ dozen to several dozen plants; costs pennies per plant; costs $1.40–$4.00 per seed packet	Buying 4-inch pots of individual plants; costs $2.50–$5.00 per plant, which can run into hundreds of dollars	Hundreds of dollars
Buying small, starter plants at a nursery; waiting one to two seasons for them to mature; costs ⅓ to ½ less than buying larger plants	Buying large plants at a nursery; costs at least 2 times the price of starter plants	Half (or more) the cost of larger plants
Mixing small perennials and shrubs with annuals for their first few growing seasons; filling gaps with annuals saves the cost of full-grown specimen plants	Buying full-grown specimen plants; amounts to several times the cost of small plants mixed with annuals	Half the cost of larger plants
Buying healthy nursery plants at full price; higher initial cost but no need to replace dead plants	Buying "bargain" potbound, damaged, wilted, or diseased nursery plants; savings lost if plants die after planting	Saves the cost of replacing plants
Buying disease-resistant varieties of ornamentals and vegetables; costs as much as or slightly more than most seeds and plants but reduces risk of plant loss	Buying nonresistant varieties of plants and seeds; results in minimal savings, but an increased risk of replacement cost if plants die	Saves the cost of replacing plants
Allowing plants to self-sow or collect seed; produces free plants for following seasons	Buying fresh seed or new plants each year; results in paying the ever-rising cost of seed packets and bedding plants	$1.40–$4.00 per seed packet; $2.50–$5.00 per plant
Growing vegetables from seed; costs pennies per plant	Buying vegetables at a grocery store or farm stand, often a day to a week old; cost per package is more than a seed packet	As much as $30 per week on grocery bills

*Costs may vary due to individual store prices and regional retail prices of products.

out-of-town friends because they're so small and lightweight—you'll share the fun of gardening with each other, and save on postage, too! Look for additional inspiring ideas for giving and receiving in Chapter 2, "Save Money on Plants."

Tooling Up for Frugal Gardening

Choosing from the hundreds of gardening tools available is enough to confuse even the most experienced among us. Save money and frustration by choosing a few basic, well-made tools that you'll use on a regular basis.

As a frugal gardener, I find I can do all my garden chores with just five essential tools: a good hand trowel, garden rake, hoe, shovel, and wheelbarrow. You can add more specialized tools, such as bulb planters and edgers, depending on the nature and design of your garden, as you find a need for them.

Thrifty Tips for Tool Shopping

Sometimes to be truly frugal, you have to spend a little money! You'll want to buy the best garden tools you can find. Poor-quality tools may be inexpensive, but they are no bargain. Look for the hallmarks of high quality: forged blades or tines of thick, durable steel, firmly attached to handles of hardwood, metal, or heavy-duty plastic. Tools of this quality can be pricy, but in the long run they're the best buy. Still, there are ways for a frugal gardener to cut tool costs.

Hunt for second-time-around tools. Good tools can last a lifetime—sometimes even two or three lifetimes. Look for

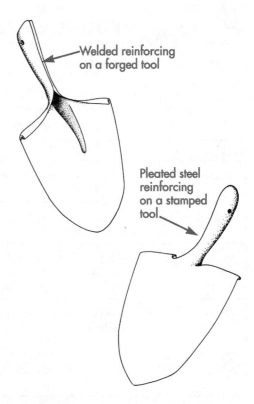

Welded reinforcing on a forged tool

Pleated steel reinforcing on a stamped tool

Forged tools are superior because they are made of thick, reinforced steel. Stamped tools are made of a sheet of thinner steel that is pressed into shape, typically with a "pleat" where it attaches to the handle.

hand-me-down tools at thrift shops, auctions, and yard sales. A little rust is only skin deep. With soap, sandpaper, and elbow grease, you can clean up used tools so they work like new. Keep them looking good by sticking the business end of the tool into a bucket of sand and linseed oil between uses to scour and rust-proof the blade.

Shop the sales. Take advantage of store clearance sales at the end of the season or whenever new models are

FRUGAL GARDENER'S GUIDE

Essential Garden Tools

Although there are many kinds of tools for sale in garden centers and mail-order garden catalogs, you'll save money and frustration by using the five basic tools described here on a regular basis.

TOOL	DESCRIPTION	USE
Garden rake	A long-handled rake with short, durable tines	For breaking up clods of soil, covering seeds, and smoothing planting beds
Hand trowel	A short-handled tool with a wide or narrow blade	For digging planting holes for bulbs or small plants
Hoe	A long-handled tool with a flat, sharp blade	For cutting weeds off below the soil line, breaking up clods of soil, and digging trenches for drainage
Shovel	A long-handled tool with a sharp, curved blade	For digging planting holes and trenches and for moving loose materials, like soil, gravel, and compost
Wheelbarrow	One- or two-wheeled carts	For hauling tools, plants, soil amendments, and garden debris

introduced. When it's time to make room for Christmas decor, garden tools are commonly marked down to giveaway prices. You may also find better-than-retail prices in mail-order catalogs that cater to professionals, like those listed in "Resources for Frugal Gardeners" on page 263.

Salvage broken-handle bargains. Create your own specialized tools, at great savings, by shortening the handles and narrowing the blades and tines of standard tools to meet your needs. Used tools and bargains that come with broken handles are the perfect candidates for tool makeovers. For dozens of other ingenious ideas for saving on tools, see Chapter 3, "The Frugal Gardener's Tools."

Save from the Ground Up

Put a little time and effort into building quality soil in your garden before planting, and you'll find the effort pays big dividends in healthy, vigorous plants. An abundance of organic material is the fastest way to fix any soil—wet or dry. Digging in compost, aged manure, or other amendments not only helps improve drainage in soggy soils, it also helps retain moisture in drier soils, saving you time and money on watering chores.

Most plants do best in soil with a slightly alkaline to somewhat acidic pH. If your soil's pH is either extremely acid or alkaline, it's easier—and less expensive—to choose plants that favor those conditions. However, you can also amend your soil to match the pH requirements of special plants you want to grow in your garden. Just keep in mind that you'll be spending more time and effort to change the pH level.

Free Soil Amendments

Many top-quality organic amendments and mulches are available at the frugal gardener's favorite price—absolutely free! You'll find free manure from riding stables, compost from municipal centers, bags of leaves donated by your neighbors or scrounged at the curb on trash pickup day, and of course, your own homemade compost. These and many more frugal ideas for improving your soil are described in detail in Chapter 4, "Save Money with Soil Amendments."

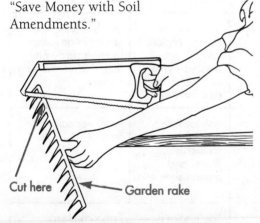

Cut here   Garden rake

A narrow rake is perfect for cultivating the soil between tightly spaced plants in intensive vegetable gardens and ornamental borders. It's easy to make a narrow-tined rake from a standard-sized garden rake, which has a handle connected directly to the line of tines, forming a "T." Use a hacksaw to cut off two or three tines from each end of the rake's head.

Make It Easy on Yourself with Low-Maintenance Techniques

Ingenuity makes caring for your garden more affordable—and less work! Instead of looking at the care and feeding of your garden as costly and time-consuming, you'll delight in discovering how simple the tricks of easy gardening can be. Not only will you save time and effort, you'll save cold hard cash, too, because your plants will be lush and healthy.

Stop Being a Slave to Weeds

Save a weekend of weeding by learning how to prevent weed problems and how to stop them in their tracks. Smother existing weeds and block new ones with mulch, newspapers, or plastic sheeting. Cheat weeds out of the space they need to grow by filling gaps in your perennial beds with potted annuals you started yourself. You'll discover more easy ways to wipe out weeds in Chapter 5, "Cutting Maintenance Costs."

Slow Down and Save on Watering

Water your lawn and garden plants the thrifty way, by applying water slowly and deeply and allowing the soil surface to dry out between waterings.

Give plants a deep drink. Plants watered deeply grow deep roots because they're not searching for water that just wets the surface of the soil. Shallow surface roots are vulnerable to drought damage because the upper few inches of soil are always at the mercy of the hot sun and drying winds. Deep watering provides a constant supply of moisture to those far-reaching plant roots.

FRUGAL GARDENER'S GUIDE

Organic Fertilizers

Organic fertilizers are gentle on the soil and good for your plants, but you can sometimes pay designer prices for these "specialty" products. Here is a rundown on the best organic fertilizers, how to use them, and how to get them on the cheap.

ORGANIC FERTILIZER	WHEN TO APPLY	NUTRIENTS SUPPLIED	HOW YOU SAVE	COMMENTS
Bloodmeal, dried blood	Apply in fall or spring; lasts 3–4 months; sprinkle lightly around plants to deter rodents	Readily available nitrogen	Call local butcher shop and offer to pick up waste material for free or at low cost	Add to compost pile to speed release of nutrients
Cottonseed meal	Apply in fall; lasts 6–12 months	Excellent source of nitrogen, phosphorus, and potassium	Mix with wood ashes when you apply to stretch fertilizer and neutralize acidity	Acidifies soil as well as adds nutrients
Fish meal or fish emulsion	Apply as soil drench in early spring and when plants need a boost; lasts 6–8 months	Excellent source of nitrogen and phosphorus	If you live in coastal region, call fish processing plants for free or low-cost fish meal	Apply diluted fish emulsion as foliar-feeding spray any time during growing season
Granite dust, also sold as granite meal or crushed granite.	Apply in fall; very slow-release; lasts up to 10 years	Excellent source of potassium and has 19 trace minerals; use the mica-rich type only	Ask for free granite dust at rock-crushing plants and paving sites	Improves soil texture
Chicken manure	Apply aged or composted manure in fall or early spring	High in nitrogen, phosphorus, and potassium	You'll save if you buy direct from egg or poultry farm	Fresh chicken manure can burn plants, so compost it before use
Earthworm castings	Apply as top-dressing any time, or use as soil amendment before planting	Excellent source of organic matter and trace nutrients	Raise your own earthworms in a bin indoors or out and harvest castings	Improves soil texture; great for houseplants

Mulch saves moisture. Mulch helps keep that precious water from evaporating, saving you time and keeping your water bill low because you won't have to water nearly so often. A couple of inches of loose, organic mulch, like bark chips, compost, or pine needles, will keep the soil moist much longer than if it were bare.

Frugal Ways to Thwart Pests and Diseases

Save your money—and your plants!—by inspecting plants closely and often to nip developing problems in the bud. Left to develop and spread in a garden, a few pests and diseases can turn into an epidemic.

Bring in the beneficials. Beneficial insects—such as lady beetles, praying mantids, and garden spiders—keep pest populations low. Some beneficials prey directly on pests, while others parasitize the pests with their larvae. Small-flowered plants with flat flower heads, including alyssum, dill, scabiosa, yarrow, and Queen-Anne's-lace, offer beneficial insects easy access to nectar, a high-energy food source to fuel their hunting activities. Plant these small-flowered nectar plants throughout your garden to put out the welcome mat for your beneficial buddies.

Try a trap crop. Your planting schemes to thwart pests frugally can also include "trap crops," like cabbage, which are

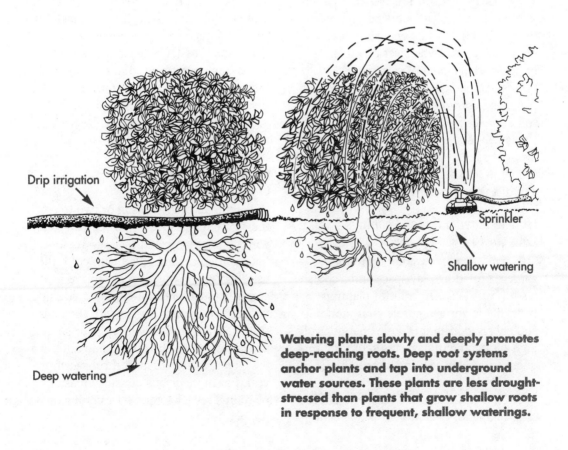

Drip irrigation

Deep watering

Sprinkler

Shallow watering

Watering plants slowly and deeply promotes deep-reaching roots. Deep root systems anchor plants and tap into underground water sources. These plants are less drought-stressed than plants that grow shallow roots in response to frequent, shallow waterings.

plants that certain pests find irresistible. Put these trap crops at the outer limits of your beds to lure pests away from your prized plants, and when they're infested, pull them up and dispose of them.

Get companionable. Companion planting is another way to combat pests. Mingle insect-repelling, pungently scented, or strong-flavored plants among your vulnerable plants. For a frugal approach to companion planting, I like to use pest-repelling plants that do double duty as culinary, medicinal, or potpourri herbs (garlic, rue, and lavender are three of my favorites). You'll find more information on defeating garden pests organically in Chapter 5, "Cutting Maintenance Costs."

Start with prevention. When it comes to disease, frugal gardeners take a preventive approach. Start by choosing disease-resistant varieties whenever possible. Fungal and bacterial plant diseases flourish among overcrowded and stressed plants, so head off problems by improving soil drainage, spacing plants so air circulates freely, and applying mulch to prevent drought stress and weed competition. More tips and secrets for penny-wise pest and disease control are in Chapter 5.

How to Have a Great-Looking, Low-Cost Lawn

Lawns are a lovely addition to the garden, providing play space and a cool, restful oasis between colorful planting beds. But lawns can guzzle your money and energy, consuming large quantities of high-nitrogen fertilizers and requiring frequent trimming, aerating, dethatching, and other high-maintenance treatments.

Keep the pleasure of a lawn and cut the costs and labor of caring for it by making

a few compromises. The biggest way to save is to cut back on the space you allot to the lawn. Plan your lawn for low maintenance by matching the type of grass you grow to your climate and the level of sunlight, the amount of rainfall, and the type of soil you have.

Save Backaches and Heartaches by Planning Ahead

Frugal gardeners think ahead. With a master plan in hand, it's easy to budget and develop your garden step by step. A scattershot approach ends up costing you more as you nickel-and-dime yourself into spending major money on your garden. Your initial master plan can be as simple as making up your mind to spend your first season's budget on permanent, sizable trees and shrubs. They make an instant visual statement and form the basic structure of your landscape.

Create an Instant Garden— On the Cheap

Perennials take a season or two to reach their potential, especially when you start with young plants. But that's no reason your garden can't be filled with color the very first year! Snuggle inexpensive seed-grown annuals and fast-climbing vines between your perennial plants for the first season. Then gradually fill in your garden, season by season, by buying and adding a few perennials, trees, and shrubs each year. For more details on frugal master planning, see Chapter 6, "Designing on a Budget."

Annual Plants for Fast Color

Enjoy a gratifying garden even the first year by filling spaces with long-blooming annuals. Try these easy-to-grow plants for quick growth and fast color.

Fast-Growing Annual Vines for Height

Climbing nasturtiums (*Tropaeolum majus*)
Common morning glory (*Ipomoea purpurea*)
Crimson starglory (*Mina lobata*) (syn. *Quamoclit lobata*)
Hyacinth bean (*Dolichos lablab*)

Annuals for Colorful Foliage and Flowers

Ageratum (*Ageratum houstonianum*)
Coleus (*Coleus* × *hybridus*)
Flowering tobacco (*Nicotiana alata*)
'Acapulco Silver' summer cypress (*Kochia scoparia*)

Fast-Growing Annual Groundcovers and Grasses

Creeping zinnia (*Sanvitalia procumbens*)
Lantanas (*Lantana* spp.)
Portulaca, moss rose (*Portulaca grandiflora*)
Quaking grass (*Briza maxima*)

Save with Do-It-Yourself Garden Art and Structures

A garden isn't complete without paths, a bench or two, and a few ornaments. With a little ingenuity and your own labor, you can locate low-cost materials and create money-saving garden art as well as paths, walls, and other permanent features, called "hardscaping" by landscape designers.

Make rustic garden seats and benches from such things as tree stumps, logs, and stacked flat stones. Create handsome plant supports and fences with recycled pillars and stair rails, which you can purchase from building materials warehouses. Or build trellises and fences from inexpensive stock lumber and salvaged logs and branches.

Garden Paths for Penny-Pinchers

Navigate your garden with paths that are inviting and practical. Grass paths are the most frugal way to get from here to there—you just lay them out and let nature take its course. But with minimal effort and cost, you can make a no-mow

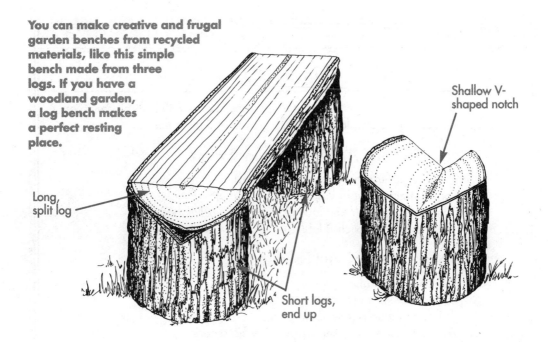

You can make creative and frugal garden benches from recycled materials, like this simple bench made from three logs. If you have a woodland garden, a log bench makes a perfect resting place.

Shallow V-shaped notch

Long, split log

Short logs, end up

path by covering the ground with a weed barrier of newspaper, plastic, or even old carpeting and disguising it with a topping of bark mulch or gravel. Make it easy on yourself by making your paths wide enough to roll a wheelbarrow along without mangling plants along the edge.

A beautiful brick path is pricey when installed by professionals, but do-it-yourself efforts will save your wallet. Shop around for the best buy on materials. You can sometimes get a great deal on used bricks at construction sites. Depending on the length of the path, the project may take a weekend or more to make, but you'll save a bundle by doing it yourself. And you'll enjoy your beautiful brick path for years to come!

Garden Shopping Smarts

It's not a sin to be extravagant once in a while, if in the end you achieve a beautiful garden that brings you joy. But you can

achieve many gardening goals by spending no money at all. And it's never too late to become a frugal gardener! Examine the dollar cost of the projects or purchases you have in mind, and look for parts of the project you can do yourself—or corners you can cut to keep costs reasonable.

Your time is always valuable, and after giving some thought to an idea, you may decide that the money you'd save making a project is not worth the time it would take. Or you may discover that it's too late in the season to start seeds indoors and that buying bedding plants may be the only way to enjoy a summer harvest of tomatoes or peppers.

Remember to think long-term when making purchasing decisions. The higher initial cost of high-quality tools or other permanent items, such as a drip irrigation system, can save you lots of money for many years—even a lifetime!

Garden Smart to $ave

Whether your garden is a vegetable bed, an herb garden, a flower border, or an entire landscape, tips and techniques for saving money are abundant—and fun to discover. Read on, and I'll show you how gardening smart can mean big savings.

Vegetable Garden Smarts

The frugal gardener's approach to vegetable gardening saves you money over storebought produce and gives you other bonuses besides. Growing your own vegetables organically is certainly a healthier alternative. And your vegetables will be more flavorful, too, because you can plant the best-tasting varieties and harvest them at their peak of perfection. Most veggies taste best when they're first harvested. Flavor, texture, and vitamins tend to deteriorate the longer vegetables are stored.

Save Money with Organic Gardening

Organic gardening is a great cost-cutter. Instead of buying expensive chemical fertilizers and pest-control products from garden centers, you'll be building rich soil for free by adding organic matter like shredded leaves, grass clippings, and homemade compost made from spent garden plants, weeds, shredded newspapers, and your recycled kitchen scraps and coffee grounds. As a frugal gardener, I'm always on the lookout for soil amendments I can collect for free, like leaf bags left on curbs. The more nutrient-rich your soil is, the healthier your vegetables are

likely to be, so they'll be less susceptible to the onslaught of pests and diseases.

When you use organic vegetable gardening techniques, you know that your produce is free from potentially harmful chemicals. And you'll enjoy the unmistakable pleasure of picking and eating the freshest possible produce. The taste of ripe, sun-warmed tomatoes, picked from the vine and eaten on the spot, can't be beat. And although newer corn hybrids maintain their sweet taste longer after picking than the old varieties, the flavor is still best when you cook corn as soon as you've picked it.

Grow Your Own and Save on Groceries

Growing your own vegetables can save serious money on your grocery bills. Bedding plants and seed are a fraction of the store-bought cost of even one week's supply of most veggies. By planting high-yielding varieties, you'll get even more bang for your buck. You'll save big, too, by devoting garden space to plants that are most expensive at the market. Grocery store or farmer's market prices for exotic vegetables like blue potatoes, 'Moon and Stars' watermelons, and mesclun can be astronomical, but these crops are as easy to grow as your basic tomatoes.

Grow Disease-Resistant Varieties

Shop smart by selecting disease-resistant varieties of susceptible vegetables. Melons, for example, are traditionally prone to fungal diseases such as mildew and fusarium wilt, but breeders have

Vegetables That Make Savings Add Up

If your tastes lean toward the unusual, you'll pay a premium price in supermarkets. Grow your own and save plenty—plus have hard-to-find veggies in easy reach right outside your door. High-yielding vegetables pay off, too, even though they're sold at lower prices. And if you freeze, can, or pickle the extras, you can enjoy your frugality in the winter, too!

Exotic Vegetables

Artichokes
Arugula and other specialty greens
Asparagus
Brussels sprouts
Cauliflower
Chinese cabbage
Melons, heirloom or specialty
   varieties
Mesclun
Peppers, unusual varieties
Potatoes, unusual varieties
Tomatoes, heirlooms

High-Yield Vegetables

Cucumbers
Eggplants
Leaf lettuces
Peppers, bell
Rhubarb
Summer squash
Tomatoes

developed several resistant melon varieties, including 'Athena', 'Ambrosia', and 'Classic'.

Many disease-resistant varieties of tomatoes have a series of initials after their name: V stands for resistance to verticillium wilt; F is for resistance to fusarium wilt; N is for resistance to nematodes; and T is for resistance to tobacco mosaic.

Rotate Plants to Foil Problems

Planting each crop in a different location each year is a great frugal gardening technique. You'll increase yields and savings by minimizing plant exposure to pests and diseases. Rotating is easy. Simply grow plants in the same families together, and move them to different locations in the garden periodically, trading places with unrelated plants, to remove them from plant-specific pests and diseases. Three-year rotations are ideal for most crops: After the third year in other locations, you can move your plants back to where they started.

Get a Jump on the Season by Sowing Indoors

Get more for your money by extending the vegetable-growing season. Early in the year, when it's still too cold to plant things outside, start seeds indoors. Time your planting so that the seedlings are big enough to set outdoors when the soil warms in spring. Sow the seeds according to the planting guidelines on the seed packets. For details on sowing seeds indoors, see page 70. You can use the same trick to extend the season in fall. Start seeds of cold-tolerant crops like kale and broccoli during the summer, and set them out in time for a fall harvest. You can also direct-seed a late crop of snap peas.

Protect Plants from the Cold for Extra Insurance

Spring weather can be iffy, and cold spells have a habit of sneaking up right after you've set out tender seedlings. Keep your tender plants thriving by tucking them in with portable covers, called cloches, that protect plants from killing cold temperatures. Cloches are valuable early in the spring to get a jump on the growing season and toward the end of the season to keep your garden going longer, when days are still warm but nights are frosty.

Cut your own cloches. Bell-shaped glass cloches are elegant but expensive, and frugal covers work just as well. Cloches will cost you nothing if you recycle translucent plastic gallon milk jugs or 2-liter soft drink bottles. Cut off the bases of these containers with an old pair of scissors. Place the bottomless containers, with caps in place, over your tender seedlings. Remove the bottle caps during the day to ventilate the cloches while still keeping the plants inside protected.

A Tomato-Cage Trick for Heat-Loving Plants

Keep tall, heat-loving plants like tomatoes and peppers cozy in spring and fall with protective plastic coverings. Set a wire tomato cage over each plant, and wrap clear plastic kitchen wrap over the top. Punch a few ventilation holes in it, then wrap plastic around the sides of each cage. When the plants grow tall enough to reach the tops of the cages or the weather warms, cut away the plastic "lids." When frosts threaten in fall, wrap plastic over the cages before sunset and remove it when the daytime temperatures rise. Re-cover each night.

Covering a wire tomato cage with inexpensive plastic wrap turns it into a frost-repelling shelter for tender plants, allowing you to stretch the season for heat-loving plants like tomatoes and peppers. When the plants reach the top of the cage, remove the plastic top. Once nights remain warm, remove the plastic from the sides of the cage.

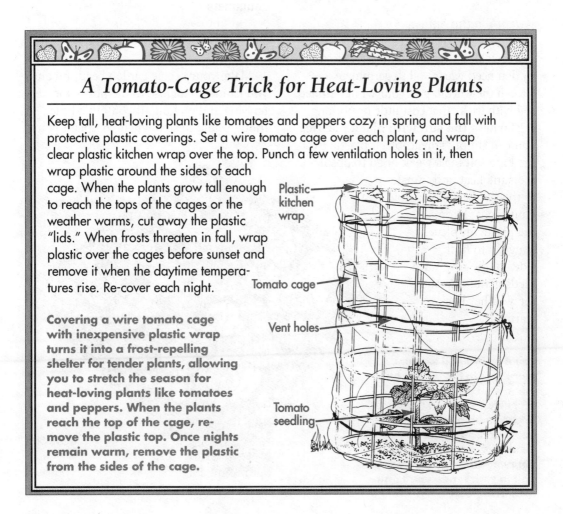

Plastic kitchen wrap

Tomato cage

Vent holes

Tomato seedling

Improvise with other plant protectors. As a frugal gardener, I enjoy the challenge of coming up with ingenious ways to protect my plants. Sheltering covers can be as small as a flowerpot, which I use for covering a single seedling, or as big as a bedsheet, which I stretch over a group or row of plants to protect them from nighttime frosts. I pull off the covers in the morning so the plants can bask in the sun. See Chapter 5, "Cutting Maintenance Costs," for many more frugal suggestions for extending your growing season.

Warm Up the Soil for Early Spring Planting

Vegetable seeds sown directly into the garden need warm soil to germinate. Hasten the warming of your winter-chilled soil with tricks that cost little or nothing.

Harness the sun with black plastic. You can simply spread black plastic over the bare soil for a week or so to absorb the sun's heat and transfer it to the soil before you sow your seeds. Keep the plastic in place, snugged to both sides of the row, until seeds germinate and the weather has warmed.

You'll be inclined to spend more time in the veggie patch when it's a pretty one, and that investment of time translates into bigger yields from better-cared-for plants. And instead of being an eyesore, your vegetable garden will add to your landscape's ornamental appeal!

Grow with what you mow. One of my favorite ways to get a jump start on the season is to use grass clippings to warm up my beds. Grass cuttings generate heat as they break down, warming the soil as well as adding nitrogen to it. When you start mowing in early spring, use the clippings to warm your beds. Mix clippings into the beds at a rate of 1 part grass clippings to 5 parts soil. If you don't have enough clippings to warm an entire bed, use what you have to get an early start on plants grown in containers.

Frugal Flash: Veggies Can Be Beautiful!

Make your veggie garden beautiful and you can keep it close to the house for easy tending and picking. If you put a little thought into design when you plant your

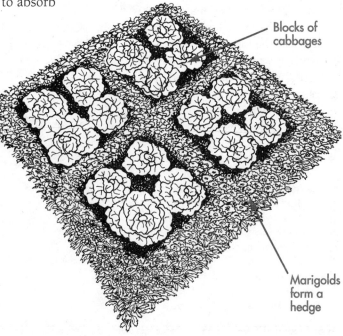

Blocks of cabbages

Marigolds form a hedge

vegetable garden, or when you slip peppers and other pretty veggie plants into your flowerbeds, these useful plants don't have to live as ugly ducklings anymore. No need to worry "What will the neighbors think?" when your vegetable patch is transformed from boring rows to an appealing ornamental design.

What's the secret of a beautiful veggie garden? The French, who have an unmistakable flair for design, plant vegetable gardens, which they call *jardins potagers*, that are just as attractive and appealing to look at as flower gardens.They arrange vegetable plants to create beautiful patterns, colors, and textures. Each bed becomes a picture, and each picture is framed with a miniature hedge. The hedge can be as permanent as boxwood or rosemary, or it can be made of annuals like marigolds, leaf lettuce, or low-growing herbs.

Go geometric. To create the French look, plant your vegetable beds in geometric shapes, such as squares or diamonds. Use colorful plant combinations, such as jade green carrot tops, blue-green cabbages and leeks, and red-leaved beets. Grow each kind of plant in a block of color so that the garden creates a pattern as appealing as a patchwork quilt.

Finish with a frame. One finishing touch makes your vegetable garden complete: a low border around each bed to frame your creation. A border of marigolds is simple, low-cost, and pretty, and it also repels harmful, parasitic root-knot nematodes.

Add some edibles among the flowers. If your garden space is limited or you just want to try new combinations, grow your vegetables and herbs among your ornamental flowers. Parsley and leaf lettuces, particularly the curly varieties, make delightful edgings for flowerbeds. Use rhubarb as a dramatic specimen plant, add 'Bright Lights' Swiss chard for its colorful stems, and grow peppers among flowers for their bushy, leafy foliage and colorful fruit.

Get Extra Space by Growing Vertically

Frugal gardeners take advantage of every inch of space. Sometimes that means looking up for the answers to space restraints. In small gardens, you can squeeze in more vegetables and save precious ground space by growing crops vertically whenever possible. In any garden, growing up means less soil to till, cultivate, fertilize, mulch, and weed! Peas, pole beans, cucumbers, melons, and vining varieties of tomatoes will quickly climb a trellis, wire fence, stake, or plant cage.

Trellis your tall crops. If you run a trellis along the center of a bed, you can plant a different crop on each side. Try peas on one side and beans on the other. The early summer harvest of peas will be finished about the time the beans need the space, so the two crops won't compete with each other for light.

Plant the "Three Sisters." Sturdy, tall-growing plants such as corn make admirable plant supports for climbing crops. This is not a new idea! First-rate frugal gardeners, Native Americans planted corn, squash, and pole beans together. They called the combination the "Three Sisters of the Cornfield." Try it yourself.

The vining beans quickly grow up the corn stalks, using them as living supports, and the squash plants trail along the ground, filling in the spaces between the corn and shading its roots. As an added bonus, the beans release nitrogen into the soil, providing additional nutrients for the heavy-feeding corn and squash plants. You'll enjoy showing off your ingenious idea—and your knowledge of history!

Make this frugal living trellis and see how easy it is to grow three crops in the space of one! Use a tall, sturdy plant like sweet corn to support a climbing crop like beans, and then shade the ground around them with a living mulch of squash or pumpkins.

The Frugal Gardener's Workshop:
A Simple-to-Build Fan Trellis

B UILD-IT-YOURSELF garden projects are both fun and frugal. Here's an eye-catching old-fashioned fan trellis that you can build in an afternoon for the cost of one 8-foot and one 4-foot length of standard, rot-resistant lumber (such as cedar) and a handful of bolts and nails.

Materials

8-foot-long 1 × 4 of rot-resistant lumber

4-foot-long 2 × 2 of rot-resistant lumber

Four $\frac{1}{4} \times 2\frac{1}{2}$-inch machine bolts, washers, and nuts

Fifteen 2-inch-long nails

Cut the Pieces to Size

1. Clamp a knot-free, 8-foot-long 1 × 4 board to a worktable. Using a power saw, cut it lengthwise (the woodworking term for making lengthwise cuts is *ripping*) into seven $\frac{3}{8}$-inch-thick pieces, which will eventually form the fan of the trellis. If you are not a practiced woodworker, ask your lumberyard to rip the board when you buy the wood.

2. Cut one of the 8-foot-long strips down to $51\frac{1}{2}$ inches long for the top crosspiece of the fan. Cut the remainder of the strip to 24 inches long for the lower crosspiece. Cut a second 8-foot-long strip down to 38 inches long for the middle crosspiece. Reserve the five remaining 8-foot-long strips to use as vertical fan pieces.

Fasten the Pieces Together

1. Clamp the five vertical fan pieces together. Drill a ¼-inch hole through them, 4 inches from what will be the bottom of the trellis. Drill a second ¼-inch hole 3 inches higher than the first one. Fasten all the vertical pieces together by bolting them with two ¼ × 2½-inch machine bolts, washers, and nuts.

2. Attach the crosspieces. Measure and mark the 51½-inch-long top piece at five equal intervals (one in the center, one at each end, and the other two spaced equidistant between center and ends). Drill a hole through the top piece at the markings to attach each vertical fan piece. Nail the top piece through the holes to each vertical fan piece. Measure down 16 inches from the top crosspiece, lay the 38-inch-long middle crosspiece on the fan, and mark holes for attaching each of the strips. Drill and nail together as for top piece. Repeat with the 24-inch-long lower crosspiece, positioning it 16 inches lower than the middle crosspiece.

Make and Attach the Stake

1. Cut one end of a rot-resistant 2 × 2 × 4 board to a point, and shorten it enough to easily drive into the ground. Hammer the stake into the ground where you want your trellis to stand, leaving 8 inches aboveground.

2. Hold the trellis against the stake and drill two ¼-inch holes through both, spacing them about 4 inches apart. Bolt the trellis and stake together with ¼ × 2½-inch machine bolts, washers, and nuts.

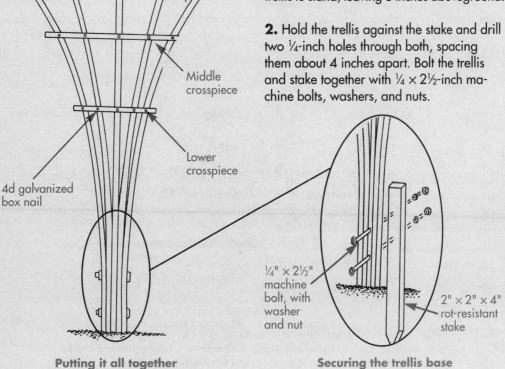

Top crosspiece

Vertical fan piece

Middle crosspiece

Lower crosspiece

4d galvanized box nail

¼" × 2½" machine bolt, with washer and nut

2" × 2" × 4" rot-resistant stake

Putting it all together

Securing the trellis base

Herb Garden Smarts

We all know how expensive a small bundle of fresh basil, oregano, or dill is in the grocery store! Yet even the smallest yard has room for a few plants or pots of these and many other herbs. Growing your own herbs means you can enjoy a continuous harvest throughout the growing season.

Even in winter, you can harvest a few sprigs of the hardy perennial herbs such as thyme and oregano—or grow them in pots indoors. Just bear in mind that indoor herbs need some extra coddling in the form of lots of light. In the dark of winter, even a south-facing window may not be good enough. You'll get the most from your indoor herb garden if you grow the plants in pots under growing lights, pinch (or harvest) them regularly, and fertilize biweekly with liquid seaweed or a dilute organic fertilizer. (Don't use fish emulsion in the house—it smells!)

Grow from Seed and Save

Many herbs grow readily from seed. Basil is one of the easiest—the seeds germinate in just a week, and the fast-growing plants will be ready for moderate harvesting a few weeks after that. Tuck ten basil plants into your garden, and you'll have more than enough for a summer's worth of fresh seasoning and a winter's supply of frozen pesto! Borage, calendula, catnip, chamomile, chervil, chives, coriander, dill, fennel, lemon balm, nasturtium, perilla, summer savory, and sweet marjoram are easy to grow from seed, too.

Plant as many seeds as you want plants, and save the rest for another year. (Or, for extra insurance, plant a few extras just in case—you can always give the seedlings away or swap them.) While the germination rate does decrease as the seeds get older, the same packet of seeds should last you two to three years—just sow more thickly each year to make up the difference.

Growing basil from seed is just as easy as growing marigolds or sunflowers. Try several different varieties. Large-leaved basil such as 'Large Green' is great for a fast batch of pesto.

Herbs That Plant Themselves

Some herbs are so eager to grow from seed, they'll self-sow—saving you planting time and money! Let the plants set seed and you'll have a garden that plants itself.

Some plants self-sow so generously they can become a nuisance. *Perilla frutescens*, a purple-leaved annual herb with a flavor that combines mint and cinnamon, for example, is apt to be overly enthusiastic about self-sowing. If perilla or any other self-sowing plant goes too far, snip off the flowers before they set seed.

Here are herbs that will save you money by self-sowing:

Anise hyssop	Feverfew
Borage	Foxglove
Caraway	Horehound
Catmint	Lemon balm
Chamomile	Mustard
Chervil	Perilla
Dill	Pot marigold
Fennel	Roman chamomile

Collect Dividends from Division

Increase your herb inventory at no cost with a swift slice of the shovel. Many herbs grow in ever-expanding clumps or by spreading underground rhizomes. Sever a mat of creeping thyme into quarter-size pieces and you can line a whole walkway. Divide a single clump of chives into scores of single bulblets, each with just one leaf, and by next year each flimsy single plant will develop into its own healthy cluster.

Super-fast spreaders like bee balm, mint, sweet woodruff, and tansy travel so readily they risk becoming pests. If you have limited space, grow these invasive plants in pots or decorative containers. If you want them to be at ground level, plant the pots in the ground, allowing 2 inches of rim to protrude above the surface as a barricade to traveling roots.

Root Cuttings for More Herbs in a Hurry

Get 20 plants from 1—now there's a deal that appeals to any frugal gardener! Many herbs, including rosemary and lavender, are easy and quick to propagate from rooted cuttings. This makes it possible to get 10 to 20 new plants from 1 mother plant. Water the plants thoroughly a few hours before you prune. Cut 3- to 4-inch stems just before a node (the swollen part of the stem where leaves or buds originate), and strip off the lower leaves.

Rooting in water is clearly simple. The simplest way to root cuttings is to stick a few stems in a glass of water. You can clearly see when the roots have developed and it's time to replant. Be prepared to offer a bit more TLC after planting than with soil-started cuttings; the rooted cuttings will appreciate liberal watering until they adjust to their new environment.

Root cuttings in potting mix. You also can root cuttings in a sterile, lightweight growing mixture. Enclose these cuttings in plastic wrap to keep them from losing

Herbs to Divide

After self-sowing, division is the easiest way to make new plants for free. Many herbs are easy to divide, including these:

Anise hyssop	Creeping thyme	Licorice	Sage
Bee balm	Horseradish	Lovage	Savory
Calamint	Hyssop	Mint	Society garlic
Catmint	Lemon balm	Oregano	Sweet woodruff
Chamomile	Lemongrass	Pennyroyal	

Dividing a plant gives you more of a good thing. Slice the roots of lemongrass or other obliging herbs into sections and replant. They'll recover quickly and grow robustly.

moisture, or mist them frequently. They may take several weeks to root. Be patient: As long as the cutting doesn't wilt or rot, it will eventually root. When you feel resistance when you give a gentle tug on the cutting, new roots have formed and the cutting is ready for transplanting to the garden.

Pick for Plenitude

The more you pick, the more you'll get is the rule when it comes to herbs. These generous plants respond to harvesting with a spurt of new growth. Each time you "prune" off the tip of a stem, the plant will send out two or three branches from each cut, more than

Herbs That Root Easily from Cuttings

Another easy way to get free plants is to start them from cuttings. Many herbs lend themselves to this simple technique. Here are some of the easiest:

Bee balm	Lavender cotton	Rosemary	Thyme
Borage	Lemon balm	Sage	Winter savory
Catnip	Lemon verbena	Scented geraniums	Wormwood
Hyssop	Marjoram	Sweet woodruff	
Lavender	Oregano	Tarragon	

Freebie plants give a frugal gardener great pleasure. Snip a few sprigs from your herb plants to start cuttings of lemon verbena, rosemary, scented geraniums, and other easy growers. Frequent misting keeps the cuttings fresh until they grow their own roots.

doubling the bushiness and productivity of each plant.

Frequent picking keeps herbs at their most flavorful, too. Basil, parsley, and other herbs lose some of their flavor once they set flowers. The longer you can delay flowering by pinching and pruning the growing tips, the tastier the herb will remain. Pinching and pruning also stimulate growth, generating larger, more succulent leaves.

Herbs Go beyond Cooking

Culinary herbs are excellent for adding lively flavor to food. But after you're done with dinner, you can use many of the same kinds of herbs to soothe your body. Herbal soaks, lotions, and teas are simple to make and wonderful pleasure to indulge in—and it feels even better when you know the herbs were tended by your own hands. Compare the cost of store-bought herbal lotions and teas with

Grow the World's Most Expensive Herb

Saffron, the world's costliest seasoning, is literally worth its weight in gold! Some say the bittersweet herb makes almost anything taste better, although most of us know its distinctive flavor from paella, bouillabaisse, and risotto. The vibrant yellow coloring it imparts to dishes is considered auspicious in India.

Native to Turkey and Persia and grown commercially in Spain's La Mancha region, saffron sounds exotic indeed. Not true! Saffron is actually an autumn-blooming crocus (*Crocus sativa*) that will thrive in gardens in USDA Plant Hardiness Zones 5 through 9 (the bulbs need some winter chill).

The reason saffron is so expensive is because harvesting it is extremely labor-intensive. Saffron "threads" are really the three bright red stamens of the crocus flower, which must be plucked out of the lavender flowers the day they open because the ephemeral blossom lasts only from sunrise to sunset. Once picked, the saffron is dried before storing in an airtight container. On a commercial scale, the labor is daunting. For the home gardener, it's fun.

Plant the bulbs 3 to 4 inches deep and 6 inches apart in well-drained soil; they like to stay dry through the summer. Make sure you plant plenty of saffron bulbs for an attractive display. Over time, the bulbs will divide, increasing your inventory. To maintain a high level of bloom, unearth the bulbs every two to three years and re-plant them farther apart.

Snip the deep orange stamens of pretty *Crocus sativus* to harvest saffron, the world's most expensive seasoning. Use a smidgen of the strong-flavored dried herb to add an intriguing taste to rice, stews, and other dishes.

your homegrown, homemade version, and you'll feel even better!

Soothe your body and brain with an herbal bath. Instead of buying expensive bath salts, bundle herbs in cheesecloth or a piece of nylon stocking and drop them into the water. Relax in a warm bath infused with fresh rosemary sprigs when you're feeling particularly tired. Bathe in mint to calm nervous exhaustion. (It's also used commercially as a natural disinfectant in face masks, facial steams, toothpaste, and herbal baths.) Steep your body in thyme-infused water to reduce swelling and sprains.

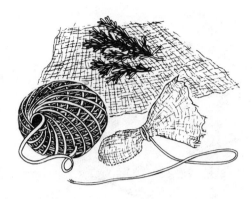

Let the rich balsamic scent of rosemary refresh your senses after a hard day. Bundle a handful of sprigs in a square of cheesecloth, tie with string, and hang from the faucet while you draw your bath. The steaming rush of water will release the fragrance and infuse your bathwater.

Refresh yourself with herbal teas. Herbal tea infusions, or tisanes, are another way to enjoy the health-giving benefits of herbs. Mint tea helps relieve indigestion. Rosemary tea is also believed to ease indigestion as well as rheumatic pain. Try an infusion of lavender to alleviate a tension headache. You can make these teas yourself with either fresh or dried herb leaves from your garden. Throw a handful of leaves into the pot, pour boiling water over them, and allow them to steep for several minutes.

Improve your garden's health with herbs. Not only are herbs good for you, they can be good for the garden as well. Chamomile has been dubbed the physician plant because it appears to have a positive effect on the health of nearby plants. Basil, which enhances the flavor of tomatoes in cooking, is reputed to do the

same for them in the garden. Sage is believed to make cabbages, broccoli, and other coles tastier as well as repel the white cabbage butterfly. Some gardeners plant rue near roses and raspberries to repel pesky Japanese beetles.

Practical Herbs Are Pretty, Too

An all-herb garden is appealing, but frugal gardeners like to make their plants do double duty. Herbs are perfect dual-purpose plants because many are as ornamental as plants grown solely as ornamentals. Chives, for instance, create a charming bouquet of round, lavender-pink flowerheads in late spring that are just as pretty in the foreground of a flowerbed as, say, dianthus. But the beauty of chives is more than skin-deep: After you admire how good they look, you can snitch a few flowers to add sweet oniony flavor and a dash of color to soups and salads!

Move herbs into the flower border. A prime candidate for a sunny flowerbed or herbaceous border is anise hyssop (*Agastache foeniculum*), also known as licorice mint or anise mint. A tall, upright plant, it produces showy spires of blue-violet flowers that are adored by bees and butterflies. But anise hyssop packs another punch: Its gray-green leaves add a delicious licorice flavor to teas and fruit salads. Other herbs that fit well in flower gardens include bee balm, calendula, calamint, pineapple-scented sage, lavender, creeping thyme, and Roman chamomile.

Choose herb foliage for a sophisticated palette. Don't overlook the ornamental qualities of herb foliage, such as the variegated leaves of tricolor sage with its pink, cream, and green leaves. Herbs with

Herbs can be as pretty as perennials in beds and borders. Let your edibles do double duty by using them as ornamentals. Tufts of cheerful chives perk up the front of this border.

golden foliage include 'Icterina' sage, golden feverfew (*Tanacetum parthenium* 'Aureum'), golden marjoram (*Origanum vulgare* 'Aureum'), and golden lemon thyme (*Thymus* × *citriodorus* 'Aureus'). For a palette of grays and silvers, look to French lavender, lamb's-ears, santolina, silver horehound, silver thyme, and southernwood.

Contain your herb gardens. Most herbs thrive as happily in containers as in the ground, which means that even if you have only a patio or balcony, you can enjoy the pleasures of herbs. Plant tall herbs in the middle, short ones on the outside, and cascading herbs such as silver or golden lemon thyme, marjoram, and prostrate rosemary around the edges. If you have only small patches of sun in a shady garden, you can plant a bouquet of different herbs in a large pot and place it where it will get the most sun. If you're

really dedicated, you can even move the pot in the afternoon to follow the sun.

Plant theme gardens for the fun of it. Have fun with theme-planted pots or herb gardens. Design a sunny-looking container full of herb varieties with golden leaves such as sage, feverfew, oregano, and thyme. Or combine lemongrass, lemon thyme, lemon verbena, lemon basil, and lemon-scented geranium for a citrus-flavor theme.

Keep Culinary Herbs Close at Hand

Save steps by keeping your cooking herbs within easy reach. If herbs are handy, you'll use them much more often than if you have to hike across the yard to pick them. When the scrambled eggs are in the pan, it's nice to open the door, snip a few spears of chives, and step back in before the eggs need stirring again.

Cook's Checklist of Culinary Herbs

Fill your close-at-hand kitchen garden with these popular culinary herbs.

Anise hyssop
Basil
Chives
Fennel
French tarragon
Lemon balm
Lemongrass
Lemon verbena
Lovage
Marjoram

Nasturtium
Oregano
Parsley
Peppermint
Rosemary
Sage
Sorrel
Spearmint
Summer savory
Thyme

No room for a garden outside the kitchen door? Plant it in a pot so fresh herbs are in easy reach for every meal. Rosemary, thyme, sage, and oregano are frequently used favorites that grow well together.

"Easy reach" means as close to the kitchen door as possible. If a dooryard herb garden doesn't fit your plans, at least keep a container garden of your most-used herbs near at hand.

Dry a Little, Save a Lot

Little jars of dried herbs will set you back plenty in the supermarket, but with a few minutes of picking and a bit of patience, you can fill little jars for free with your own garden herbs.

Collecting and drying a winter's worth of herbs may require more time than you want to set aside—and may yield more dried oregano than you know what to do with!—but drying a handful or two of herbs every few days is an easy task with a big payoff. Perfect for a frugal gardener! Here's how to do it:

1. Rinse off the plants in the garden with a fine spray of water either early in the morning or late in the afternoon.

2. When plants are dry, snip off the leafy tips of stems, collecting pieces about 2 to 4 inches long.

3. Spread the clean, dry herbs on a paper towel or clean cloth and leave them to dry on an unused part of your kitchen counter or other out-of-the-way place.

4. Your herbs will be ready for storage in a three to seven days, depending on how humid the weather is. When they are crisp to the touch, they're done.

5. Strip the leaves off the stems over a large bowl.

6. Funnel the dried, crumbled leaves into small jars. Attach the lids.

Handling Herbs for Drying

It's the foliage of herbs that carries the flavor you want, so you'll need to separate the leaves from the stems before storage. Here's how:

❖ Remove the leaves from stems of large-leaved plants, such as basil, before you dry them.

❖ For small-leaved plants, such as thyme and rosemary, run your hand along the stems to dislodge the leaves after they're thoroughly dry.

❖ Chop herbs with grassy foliage, like chives and lemongrass, before you set them out to dry.

Save a Bundle on Dried Arrangements

If you're the crafty type, you know that bundles of dried herbs can be a budget-breaker. Save your wallet by growing and drying your own herbs for arrangements and craft projects like herb wreaths and herb-ornamented garlic braids.

The Frugal Gardener's Workshop:
Convenient Screens for Easy Herb Drying

C OLLECT THE BOUNTY of your summer herb garden for winter use by drying herbs in quantity. Make these simple screens in a size to fit your storage area, and stack them to save space.

1. Make a square or rectangular frame of 1 × 3s in an overall size that will be convenient for your herb-drying area, which should be a dark, dry place such as a closet or attic.

2. Staple Fiberglas window screening to the bottom of frame pieces.

3. Nail 2 × 2 × 4-inch wood blocks to each corner of the frame for legs.

4. Spread herb clippings on the screen, allowing space between each stem of foliage.

5. Place the screen and clippings in drying area; stack screens if desired.

6. Check herbs every few days for dryness. When thoroughly dry, strip leaves and store in jars.

To dry bundles of herbs for arrangements, cut long stems and strip off the lower leaves. Then fasten small, loose bundles together at the base of the stems with rubber bands. (Stems shrink when they dry and tend to fall free from string.) Hang the bundles upside down in a dark, dry place where air can circulate. To make room for hanging lots of bundles, try clipping the bundles to a freestanding laundry rack, to coat hangers, or to a clothesline. Drying herbs hanging from wooden beams add a great—and free!—country decorating touch. The bundles of herbs add a pleasant, old-fashioned look to the room, and they smell good, too.

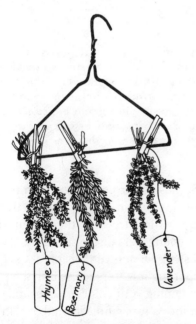

Frugal specialists take advantage of every inch of free space for drying herbs. A coat hanger full of fragrant bunches will slip into a few inches of dry, dark closet space—the perfect place to dry herbs like lavender and thyme. Use clothespins to clip the bunches of herbs to the hangers.

Flower Garden Smarts

A good-looking flower garden depends on reliable plants that fill beds with color from one season to the next. So thrifty gardeners look for flowering plants that will give the biggest return in garden presence and ease of care.

Perennial plants come back year after year, but most bloom for only a couple of weeks, so mix them with annuals that bloom nonstop from early summer through frost. Use spring bulbs for early color, and be sure to include shrubs and ornamental grasses to add stature and architectural form to the design as well as winter interest when most of the perennials have died back.

Make Perennial Beds That Last

Unlike beds for annuals or vegetables that can be refurbished and fed at the end of the growing season, perennial beds must last for years. If you're starting from scratch to create a perennial border, dig in lots of organic matter, such as aged manure or compost, to improve the soil. Good soil pays big dividends: Plants are healthier, grow faster, look more lush, and multiply more quickly.

Find the Flowers That Fit

Frugal gardeners don't waste time trying to fit in plants that are unsuitable for their climate or conditions. Choose plants that are happy with your soil and weather, and your life will be much simpler. Unless you must have a particular "prima donna," keeping a languishing or marginally hardy flower alive is usually not worth the trouble.

Use Water-Wise Plants

In dry climates where water is a precious—and expensive—commodity, opt for drought-tolerant flowering plants. Not only will you save money on your water bill, but the garden will take less time to maintain. Fortunately, there's a wide selection of flowering annuals and perennials that tolerate or even prefer dry conditions.

Go Native for Easy Care

Replacing plants that succumb to pests or diseases costs time and money. Save yourself frustration by selecting hearty, unfussy native plants. Many of our under-appreciated American plants are highly valued in Europe. Plant breeders on both sides of the ocean are hard at work to develop new varieties of native plants that have all the sturdy qualities that help them survive in the wilds as well as more refined qualities that we value in our gardens. "Half the plants in the flower borders at London's Kew Gardens are new varieties of American natives," says Phillip Watson, owner of Washington Gardens, a landscape design company based in Fredericksburg, Virginia. An all-American garden filled with plants that naturally thrive in your area is bound to be an easy-care success!

Pinch Pennies with Annuals

Annual flowers are eager beavers that fill your garden with a long-lasting splash of color for just pennies a plant. Enjoy them for their own beauty, but also use them to disguise your frugal gardening plan of starting with small, young (read "inexpensive") permanent plants that take one to two years to come into their own.

A few all-American native plants have become firm favorites among gardeners, like this purple coneflower (*Echinacea purpurea*), which blooms for months and attracts butterflies like a beacon. Many other deserving natives are waiting for smart gardeners to discover them.

Stand-ins for permanent plants. Annual vines can quickly climb a trellis to lend a vertical accent to the garden while your young clematis, for instance, gets established. Or annual flowers can play a supporting role to perennials in a border, maintaining your color scheme while you wait for your perennials to fill out. Instead of buying three of each pricey perennial, plant just one of each, and fill in the gaps with inexpensive, color-coordinated annuals. In a couple of years, the perennial plant will be big enough to divide, giving you the extra plants you want at no cost except patience.

Water-Thrifty Flowers

If drought stalks your garden or summer rains are naturally scarce, these plants will still look good without supplemental watering.

Annuals

African daisies (*Arctotis* spp.)
Cleome, spider flower (*Cleome hasslerana*)
Cosmos (*Cosmos* spp.)
Portulaca, moss rose (*Portulaca grandiflora*)
Scarlet flax (*Linum grandiflorum* 'Rubrum')

Perennials

Agaves (*Agave* spp.)
Artemisias (*Artemisia* spp.)
Basket-of-gold (*Aurinia saxatilis*)
Bearded iris (*Iris* cvs.)
Black-eyed Susans, coneflowers (*Rudbeckia* spp.)
Blanket flowers (*Gaillardia* spp.)
Blue flax (*Linum perenne*)
Butterfly weed (*Asclepias tuberosa*)
Candytuft (*Iberis sempervirens*)
Cinquefoils (*Potentilla* spp.)
Coreopsis (*Coreopsis* spp.)
Daffodils (*Narcissus* spp.)
Daylilies (*Hemerocallis* hybrids)
Dropwort (*Fillipendula vulgaris*)
Evening primroses (*Oenothera* spp.)
False dragonhead (*Physostegia virginiana*)
False indigo (*Baptisia australis*)
Gayfeathers, liatris (*Liatris* spp.)
Globe thistle (*Echinops ritro*)

Golden marguerite (*Anthemis tinctoria*)
Lamb's-ears (*Stachys byzantina*)
Lavender cottons (*Santolina* spp.)
Lavenders (*Lavandula* spp.)
Mallow (*Malva alcea*)
Moss pink, moss phlox (*Phlox subulata*)
Mountain bluet (*Centaurea montana*)
Naked lady (*Amaryllis belladonna*)
Purple coneflower (*Echinacea purpurea*)
Red valerian, Jupiter's beard (*Centranthus ruber*)
Rock cress (*Arabis caucasica*)
Rock soapwort (*Saponaria ocymoides*)
Rosemary (*Rosmarinus officinalis*)
Russian sage (*Perovskia atriplicifolia*)
Sea hollies (*Eryngium* spp.)
Sea lavenders, statices (*Limonium* spp.)
Sedums (*Sedum* spp.)
Sunflowers (*Helianthus* spp.)
Thymes (*Thymus* spp.)
Verbenas (*Verbena* spp.)
Yarrows (*Achillea* spp.)
Yuccas (*Yucca* spp.)

Ornamental grasses

Fountain grass (*Pennisetum setaceum*)
Japanese silver grasses (*Miscanthus sinensis* cvs.)

A bouquet of long-stemmed beauties.
Most of the annuals sold in garden centers
are low growers, making them good for
bedding plants but not for bouquets. If
you want flowers for cutting, grow your
own annuals from seed for fresh flowers
that aren't an extravagance!

Patience Is Rewarded with Perennials

Starting perennials from seed means
waiting a year before you see flowers. But
the savings are incredible, considering
that a single $2 pack of seeds may yield
two dozen plants! Take the long-term approach and start new perennials each year.
That way, you'll always have ready-to-
bloom plants filling the beds and a crop of
youngsters to look forward to next year. A
"nursery bed" for the seedlings will give
them the elbow room they need the first
year. For more about growing perennials
from seed, turn to Chapter 2, "Save
Money on Plants."

A Cut Flower That Lasts for Weeks

With their long blooming season in the
garden and flowers that last two weeks in
a vase, alstroemerias are a good value for
cost-conscious gardeners. Once limited to
mild-winter areas, hardy new cultivars like
'Redcoat', 'Freedom', and 'Sweet Laura'
have been introduced, thanks to the hy-
bridizing that Dr. Mark Bridgen and his
colleagues at the University of Connecticut
have done. Adaptable to many growing
conditions from USDA Hardiness Zones 6
through 10, these new cultivars offer lush
foliage and long-lasting flowers and will
grow in full sun or partial shade. 'Sweet
Laura', hardy to Zone 4, is named for its
spicy, carnation fragrance. "In a vase, it
will scent a whole room," Dr. Bridgen says

about this cultivar. (Don't know your hardiness zone? See the map on page 280.)

In Southern California, look for the
Meyer and Mojonnier hybrids developed in
San Diego County as well as the
Connecticut-bred hybrids. These plants are
readily available in local nurseries and
home centers and are frugal additions to the
flower garden because they readily self-sow
and their clumps spread quickly. Del Mar,
California, gardener Bill Teague reports that
a Meyer alstroemeria planted in the ground
from a 6-inch pot will grow big enough in
six months to divide into 7 to 24 plants!

**You can kiss the florist good-bye when
you grow your own alstroemeria, a
flower that lasts for weeks in water.
Once enjoyed only by gardeners in mild
climates, today's cultivars include cold-
hardy 'Sweet Laura' and her easy-to-
grow cousins.**

Landscape Smarts

Designing your landscape for frugal gardening starts with a realistic assessment of how much time you can give to the garden. Better to have a smaller garden you can easily tend than a monster that's always nagging for attention. If you have to hire help to maintain your garden, it's going to be expensive! Use low-maintenance tricks throughout the landscape so you can keep the garden workload to a minimum. You'll find plenty of other brainstorms in Chapter 5, "Cutting Maintenance Costs."

A Practical Plan Conserves Your Energy

Organize your garden so that everything is easily accessible. Put flowers and vegetables for picking near the house so you don't have to trek too far to get them. If beds need extra watering, make sure there's a hose nearby, or install an irrigation system. Make your paths wide enough for a wheelbarrow and other tools to fit comfortably. Design your beds so you can easily reach across for weeding and other maintenance chores.

Woody Plants Save Work

For the ultimate in low-maintenance gardening, fill your landscape with flowering trees and shrubs instead of annuals and perennials. But avoid the tendency to rush out in early spring and buy everything that's in bloom. Choose trees and shrubs that produce flowers or fruit over several seasons instead of one so your landscape stays appealing all year. And

---

Time Is Money: Cut Back on Pruning

Eliminate time-consuming pruning chores by choosing plants that have a pleasing natural shape and a size that's in proportion to the rest of your landscape.

- Select small trees like flowering cherries instead of towering silver maples if your front yard is modest in size.

- Keep foundation plantings naturally low by planting dwarf cultivars that won't need a crewcut every year.

- Look for conifers that have a natural conical or oval form that remains tidy without trimming. In the yew family, consider dwarf *Taxus baccata* 'Aurea', which grows as a golden-tinged cone to about 20 feet tall. The arborvitaes *Thuja orientalis* 'Aurea Nana' and 'Semperaurea' are two that also maintain a compact, tidy form.

- Some shrubs, such as the contorted hazel known as Harry Lauder's walking stick (*Corylus avellana* 'Contorta'), are so naturally eye-catching that they look better without their 'clothes' on in winter than they do when fully dressed in summer green.

don't forget to choose plants like maples and sweetgum with colorful fall foliage!

Replace Grass with Groundcovers

Groundcovers are a great substitute for grass: They add variety and interest in your garden, they often have colorful foliage, and they're a lot less work!

Give up the shade battle with lawn grass. In shady areas where you have to fight a battle continually to get the lawn to grow at all, groundcovers like ivy, pachysandra, vinca, sweet woodruff, *Mazus reptans,* ajuga, wild ginger, epimediums, lamiums, and a host of other attractive groundcovers will grow quite happily.

Don't overlook the allure of moss. Instead of spreading massive quantities of lime to kill moss, enjoy the lushness it adds to the lawn.

Trim your water bill. In dry climates where water bills are a significant budget item, opt for groundcovers that don't need much moisture, such as salt-bush (*Atriplex* spp.), euonymus, lantana, African daisy (*Arctotis, Dimorphotheca,*

and *Osteospermum* are three related genera that answer to that name), juniper, rosemary, star jasmine (*Trachelospermum jasminoides*), or germander. Ivy and vinca (periwinkle) take both shade and drought and still look great.

Minimize Lawn Care

A few simple strategies will keep you free from bondage to your mower. You'll find more bright ideas for saving on lawn care in Chapter 5, "Cutting Maintenance Costs."

Never edge again. To avoid the job of edging with hand clippers or a string trimmer, install a hard-surface border along the lawn at ground level so the mower wheel can run along the surface and the blades can reach right to the edge of the grass. By the same token, avoid planting grass against

Combine a groundcover with a mowing strip, and you'll never bang your head on tree branches again. One zip around the perimeter of the bed is a lot speedier than finagling the mower around the unprotected trunk, which risks injury to the tree, not to mention your head.

walls or fences where you'll need to trim; use a strip of mulch edged by a mowing strip instead.

Get out from under the trees. To avoid negotiating your mower around the trunks of trees and having to hand-trim where the mower won't reach, lay a circle of mulch around the trunk or plant a bed of groundcover. If the tree is young, extend the mulch or planted area to the tips of the branches (the "dripline"). If the tree is an old giant, make the size of the bed around it aesthetically appealing. If you must mow under trees, remove low-growing branches so you don't get snagged when you walk under the tree with the mower. You'll also let in more light, so the grass will grow better and healthier.

Place Plants for Privacy

When privacy is an issue, building a fence or wall around the perimeter of the property is a tempting solution—but not the most frugal one! Walls and fences cost a lot of money and take a lot of time to install. A hedge will be easier on your budget, and it will also get around any height restrictions your community may have for man-made structures. The green background of a hedge also makes any plants in front of it look even better.

Install a trellis for immediate privacy. There is one catch to the hedge thrifty solution: It can take several years to reach its full height. For immediate privacy with a frugal slant, invest a few dollars in a trellis along the patio or terrace to screen you from the neighbors. Inexpensive lattice framed in 2 × 4s will do the trick. Grow speedy annual vines up the trellis and create a cozy, private garden room where you can enjoy seclusion while your hedge grows at its own pace.

Disguise your chain-link fence with vines. If your property has a chain-link fence and you can't afford to remove or replace it, don't despair. Camouflage it with fast-growing annual vines like scarlet runner bean, grow perennial climbers like clematis and honeysuckle, or hide it completely with a dense, evergreen vine.

Create instant privacy with inexpensive prefab lattice and fast-climbing annual vines while you wait for your young shrubs to grow and fill in for a better barricade.

smart tips   25 SMART SHOPPING TIPS

1. Ask and you shall receive! Post a frank and friendly "Plants wanted free or cheap" note on the bulletin board at the library, the supermarket, and the laundromat, and you'll be surprised what comes your way.

2. The classified ads in your local newspaper are a treasure trove of bargains. Look for garden furniture, outdoor art, hand and power tools, plants, and even tool sheds.

3. Dickering over price is part of the game at garage sales. Find a piece of garden furniture you like? Ask the owner if the price could possibly come down a bit. Even a $2 shovel is worth negotiating. Get it for $1.50, and you have 50¢ to spend on something else!

4. Patronize plant sales given by local garden clubs, plant societies, or botanical gardens. Be first in line for the best choice of old reliables and rare finds.

5. Visit plant sales as late as possible on the last day. If there are leftovers, you can fill your backseat at marked-down prices.

6. Keep an eye out for surveyors' flags that indicate new construction. Often you can rescue perennials and even shrubs and young trees if you just ask.

7. Don't scorn the orphan corner of your garden center. A once-over with the pruning shears to improve form and encourage new growth can turn an ugly duckling into a garden-worthy swan.

8. Become a regular at your local garden centers and nurseries. Knowing the retail prices of plants will help you spot a bargain when you see it. Besides, many locally owned businesses like to give steady customers a break on price now and then.

9. If you're planning to buy more than $100 worth of plants from one place, ask if you can buy them at the price charged to landscapers and other professionals, instead of the retail price.

10. Assess your handyman abilities before you cart home outdoor furniture in need of repair. A wobbly bench you don't fix or use is no bargain. But metal furniture that just needs a coat of paint to spruce it up is a true find.

11. Compare prices of ready-made structures with the cost of materials before you do it yourself. Even without adding the value of your labor, it costs less to buy a sheet of lath at the store than it does to make one of the same quality yourself.

12. Delivery charges can eat up savings from smart shopping in a hurry. Negotiate for free delivery or buttonhole a friend with a pickup truck.

13. Take a list with you when you visit the garden center or nursery. It's a great way to control impulse buying, which can be mighty hard to resist if they're out of the shrubs you went for but stocked to overflowing with flowers in full glory.

14. Check the yellow pages to find architectural salvage yards, perfect for one-of-a-kind *objets d'art* that cost a tiny fraction of the cost of mass-produced stuff. A hefty chunk of carved limestone, even if it's missing a corner, is a lot more satisfying than a faux marble statue at ten times the price.

15. Estate sales and auctions are great places to find garden tools at rock-bottom prices.

16. Watch for advertised specials on plants, tools, and supplies, and get to the store early to have the best choice.

17. Big clay or ceramic pots are hard to ship and display without an occasional hard knock. Look for the less than perfect in the stack, point out the chip on the rim, and you're apt to get a discount. (Then hide the defect with a trailing plant!)

18. Looking for a sturdy garden bench? A chaise lounge? A hammock and stand? Post a note on local bulletin boards and run a classified ad; decorating tastes change outdoors as well as in, and somebody may want to replace the piece that's your heart's desire.

19. If you buy flowering plants for indoor decoration, look for long-lived, winter-hardy plants you can add to your garden later. In cold-winter areas, a pot of minidaffodils is perfect; a pot of paperwhites is a one-time splurge.

20. Keep a running tally of the money you spend, and you'll find it easier to say no to impulse buys.

21. Compare prices of large versus small bags of planting mix, manure, and other amendments. If big bags are a bargain, and you can haul and store them, you'll not only save money but also eliminate future trips to replenish your supply.

22. Need a lot of mulch or topsoil? Buy by the truckload instead of by the bag. You'll save lots of money—as well as the trouble of opening and disposing of all those plastic bags.

23. If you don't know where to start, consider a one-time consultation with a landscape designer to get a professional's opinion for the possibilities of your place.

24. Bricklike paving is almost as beautiful as the real thing and usually ends up costing less. Squares of paving that give a multibrick effect take much less time to install than individual bricks. There are fewer crevices for weeds to take hold. And they're less likely to frost-heave over winter than "real" bricks.

25. Buy the best-quality grass seed you can find. Make sure the seed label promises a germination rate of 85 percent or better and the package contains no more than 0.5 percent weeds. Pass over any lawn seed that doesn't promise "no noxious weeds." It's not a bargain!

Cost-Conscious Choices

Willing to try your hand at do-it-yourself projects, wait patiently for small plants to grow, and grow some plants from seeds and cuttings? Then you can have a five-star garden on a fast-food budget! Let your ingenuity guide you to making cost-effective choices along the way.

Get a Bargain on Basics

Before you put that first plant in the ground, think about the cost of basic garden making. Supplying water, amending soil, and laying paths can make a big dent in your budget if you don't plan ahead. Luckily, there are plenty of proven ways for frugal gardeners to stick to their goal.

Water, Water…Anywhere?

Watering adds to the expense of your garden. It's far more frugal to choose plants that can survive on local rainfall.

Aim for thrifty sprinkling. Most gardens need some watering, while plants are getting established, during droughts, or for better veggies. If your garden needs additional irrigation, install the system before you plant so you don't disturb already-landscaped areas. Invest money up front on automatic timers for your sprinkler systems. It's money well spent because you know you won't lose plants because you forgot to water, and you won't waste precious water by forgetting to turn off the sprinklers.

Low-water gardens can be luxurious. In regions of the country where rainfall is low and water bills are high, frugal gardeners devote less land to lawns and instead opt for areas of paving and drought-tolerant plants. Every year, new cultivars and hybrids are being introduced to the market. South Africa and Australia, two countries with climates similar to the arid Southwest, are rich resources for new introductions. Nowadays, a drought-tolerant garden in San Diego can be as full of diverse flowering plants as a water-rich garden in Seattle!

☛ FREE STUFF!

Mucho Mulch

An excellent—and free!—source of must-have mulch is a tree-trimming company. Most are more than happy to dump their load of shredded or chipped leaves, bark, or wood chips on your driveway for free because it saves them a trip to the landfill. These materials can't be beat for mulching and making paths, and any leftovers make fine compost.

Consider where you want the mulch dumped before you call the tree-trimming company. You may be looking at that pile for a while before you manage to move it all into the garden, so choose an out-of-the-way location if possible. The truck will need clear overhead space to lift its body for dumping and solid ground to support its heavy weight.

Saving on Paving

Creativity is the key to achieving the look you want with less expensive materials than you originally envisioned. If your heart is set on fieldstone, for instance, but your wallet can't afford a path of closely set stones, use a stepping-stone style—and a fraction of the rock.

Pamper your back. Remember to take it easy when working with paving materials. Use the strength of your legs, not your back, to lift heavy loads. Do the heavy work in small doses to avoid strain. An abused and aching back can end up costing you as much as hired help would have!

Go local to save money. Choose materials of local origin instead of those that must be trucked in. In one region, bluestone or limestone may be a luxury; in another, where they are locally quarried, they can be relatively inexpensive. Not only will shopping smart for local materials save you money, it will give your garden a correct sense of place. The beloved stone walls of New England were built from the abundance of rocks harvested out of the plowed fields. A similar garden wall looks great in the Northeast—but way out of place in the Southwest, where stones from the local arroyo are just as evocative and as beautiful in their own place.

Cutting the Cost of Plants

Probably your biggest garden budget item will be plants. Permanent plants—perennials, trees, and shrubs—can eat up a major chunk of your gardening dollars. But if you stick to one of the basic commandments of frugal gardening, you can have the plants you want at a price you can afford.

Start small. A shrub in a 1-gallon container or a seedling tree will cost considerably less than more mature ones. Although you won't get the immediate gratification of a fully filled-in space, you'll have the pleasure of watching the young plant grow. Keep in mind that smaller plants settle in more quickly than larger specimens and many catch up in size in one to two years. Perennial flowers cost much less as small plants and practically nothing when you start them from seed. Chapter 2, "Save Money on Plants," will give you lots of other great ideas for trimming costs.

COST CUTTERS
All-Brick Alternatives

Brick is beautiful, but paving brick that won't crumble when exposed to the elements requires deep pockets. Cut corners in a literal way by mixing other materials with brick.

▼ Trim a pathway by edging the brick center section with landscape timbers instead of more brick.

▼ Instead of an all-brick patio or walkway, intersperse squares of brick with sections of cheaper exposed-aggregate concrete.

▼ A poured concrete patio that's colored and molded to look like brick creates the same effect as actual brick at a fraction of the cost.

Planning for Planting

Strategic planning is the frugal gardener's secret weapon. A master plan for the garden lets you pinpoint which spaces need the most time and money at any given stage. A notebook or calendar that records successes and failures will help you repeat the first and avoid the latter. It will also help you remember the names of your garden plants. The names of those plants and cultivars may be as familiar to you as those of your dear friends when you first plant in spring, but by the winter they may be a distant memory— especially once marauding critters carry off your plant tags!

The Garden Year at a Glance

Imagine the fun of keeping a year-by-year account of your garden in words and pictures! Commercially published garden journals are attractive and inspiring, but a three-ring binder will serve you even better. The loose-leaf notebook gives you the flexibility to add and remove pages as you need and to move information around as you refine your record keeping.

Include graph paper for drawing garden plans, ruled paper for your notes, plain paper for gluing invoices, empty seed packets, and catalog descriptions of plants you've bought or hope to buy, and heavy paper or photo-album refills for displaying garden snapshots.

Map your gardens. If you've ever inadvertently dug into a clump of dormant spring bulbs, you'll appreciate the value of a garden map that shows where even the sleeping plants are. Get a copy of your house plot from your tax assessor's office, and use it to create a base map that shows your lot boundaries drawn to scale. Use graph paper to draw more detailed maps of specific beds with plant names and locations clearly marked.

Keep a paper trail of purchases. Save your invoices and receipts as well as seed packets and plant labels. If you ordered from a mail-order company, paste in the plant description printed in their catalog. This information leaves you well armed if you need to go back to the company with any complaints and serves as a helpful reminder if you want to order the same seeds again. Add notes through the season on how well the plants do in your garden to guide future purchases.

Sharpen your weather sense. A daily log of temperature highs and lows, frosts, hail, and other climate vagaries will give you an excellent sense of the weather in your area. Over the seasons, you'll notice patterns that can make a big difference in timing: If fall rains start in November, for example, you'll want to get new shrubs and trees in the ground to take advantage of the free watering.

Gauge the rain. Rain gauges cost only a couple of dollars and quickly become addictive. Checking the gauge—and recording the figure—after each rain will help you judge how much water your plants are getting.

Track your planting dates. Keep notes of when you plant and how fast seeds germinate and grow. Look at your weather

Collect your garden's history in a three-ring binder that you can refer to over and over again through the years to gain wisdom about plant choices, weather patterns, and your evolving garden. It can be just as much fun to look back as it is to look ahead.

info and your planting info, and you'll get a feel for the best time to plant your seeds in next season.

Attack pests on time. Note the date any pest or disease problem begins and the way you deal with it. You'll notice trends (perhaps the Japanese beetles in your neighborhood make their first strike during the first week of June) that will better prepare you to counterattack. Note how successful your offensive measures are for future reference. Jot down any

new control methods you hear of or read about.

Summarize your season. As you look over your year's notes and photographs, take a few minutes to record how your various gardening adventures turned out. What worked? What was a disaster? What died? What thrived? What should you try next year? By jotting all this information down while it's fresh in your mind, you'll create a great starting place for next season's planting.

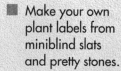

Frugal Gardener Checklist

■ Prioritize your master garden plan and implement it as your time and budget allows.

■ Plant young trees and shrubs first; they take longest to mature.

■ Take the time to amend the soil. The ideal garden soil is loam rich in organic matter that drains well but doesn't dry out too quickly. You should be able to squeeze it into a ball, and then crumble it easily.

■ Plan an adequate watering system for the garden. Include an automatic timer for your sprinklers.

■ Save your store-bought herb jars and refill them with your home-dried culinary herbs. If you fill a jar with the same herb, you won't even have to bother making labels. Date your herbs, however.

■ Invest in one or two special plants, such as a large specimen tree or shrub, that will be a dramatic focal point in your garden.

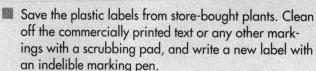

■ Make your own plant labels from miniblind slats and pretty stones.

■ Save the plastic labels from store-bought plants. Clean off the commercially printed text or any other markings with a scrubbing pad, and write a new label with an indelible marking pen.

■ Grow plants that give you a harvest that would be high priced or hard to find in the store: fancy lettuce mixes, luscious strawberries, saffron crocus.

■ Deadhead annuals or pick bouquets to encourage continued flower production.

Why spend money on plant labels when the makings can be yours for free? Cut old miniblind slats into 6-inch pieces and write on them with an inexpensive, indelible pen. Or go artistic with smooth stones and pen or paint.

CHAPTER TWO

$AVE MONEY ON PLANTS

L ET'S FACE IT. GARDENERS LOVE PLANTS. And frugal gardeners are no exception! But it's hard to stick to your frugal intentions when faced with a garden center full of lush, beautiful, and unusual plants, whether they're ornamentals, vegetables, shrubbery, or trees. So how do you go about saving money on plants when you really want to purchase at least one of everything you crave?

There are lots of ways to save. Start with a plan so you know what you need and have space for, and you'll be less likely to overspend. Choose the right plants for your climate and site to avoid the expense of replacing poor performers. And grow your own plants. Whether you start from seed, take root or leaf cuttings from existing plants, or organize a neighborhood plant swap, you can get just about all the plants you need to fill your beds for little or no money. Then when you're faced with that one-of-a-kind, gotta-have-it, perfect specimen plant, you'll be able to indulge yourself in a little guilt-free splurging.

43

How Many Do You Need?

It's hard to stay in frugal mode when you have a new garden to fill or an old one that needs livening up. A trip to the garden center can end with plants filling every inch of trunk space, floor, backseat, passenger seat—and between the seats! Keep your garden on budget by starting with a realistic look at what you need. Then make a list and stick to it. But don't fret if you occasionally yield to love-at-first-sight in the nursery—purchasing an occasional unplanned treasure is part of the fun of gardening.

The Difference between "Enough" and "Too Many"

Garden plants need elbow room. They need space to grow to their full size and to stretch their stems and branches without fighting their neighbors for breathing room. Planting more than you need is not only bad for the budget, it leads to more maintenance chores later.

Bare Is Better

A new garden is bound to have some bare spaces. It takes a while for plants to fill in and knit together. Stuffing every square inch of ground with plants right from the start may look great the first season, but by the following year, your plants will be seriously overcrowded. Instead of cramming everything in cheek-by-jowl, follow the spacing guidelines on the label or in the catalog for the plants you've picked.

Breathing Room Means Better Health

Not only will you waste money by over-planting, you'll be paying for your mistake in precious hours and afternoons, too, because your crammed plants will need lots of maintenance to trim them back or separate them later. Crowding stresses plants, which must fight for air, water, and nutrients. And stress makes them sitting ducks for attack from pests and diseases. When air moves freely around the plants and daily needs aren't a struggle, they're much better prepared to shrug off problems.

Shaving Numbers Saves Money

Considering the high price of perennials, not to mention even more expensive trees and shrubs, eliminating a plant or two here and there can add up to major savings in a hurry. Do you really need five azaleas for that corner of your front yard? Three may make a big enough splash of spring color.

Watch out for the hard sell. Even garden designers, who should know better, tend to overplant because they feel pressure from the owner to create an "instant garden." Also, if they work for a garden center or earn a commission from the purchased plants, they have an added incentive to sell more plants. All the more reason to use your common sense to figure out how many plants you really need, no matter who designs your garden.

John Paty of Washington, D.C., hired a renowned landscape firm to develop a plan for his 800-square-foot front garden. Because he was working on a budget, he paid for the plans and then bought and planted his own plants. In several cases he cut back on the recommended number of plants to save money. Instead of 32 'Goldsturm' rudbeckia plants (*Rudbeckia fulgida* var. *sullivantii* 'Goldsturm'), for instance, he planted just 20 because he knew that the plant grows quickly in an expanding clump. His savings were significant. The plan also called for ten cotoneasters. Three plants were ample, though they took longer to cover the area than the ten would have. His frugality saved him money as well as a lot of dividing and thinning within the first two years of planting.

Bigger Is Not Always Better

The bigger the pot, the higher the price! A shrub in a 2-gallon container generally costs more than twice as much as a plant in a 1-gallon pot because it takes the grower extra seasons of care, and the price increases significantly with each larger size.

But the payoff doesn't match the price. Larger plants tend to experience more transplant shock than younger specimens: It takes a longer time for their roots to grow enough to support vigorous new topgrowth. Some large plants will take several years to reestablish their root systems before they begin growing again! Meanwhile, many younger specimens will catch up to and even outgrow the larger plant. Start with smaller, younger trees and shrubs, and they'll look just as good as their bigger brothers within a few years. Young perennials catch up to their bigger, older brethren even more quickly—in many cases, within a single season.

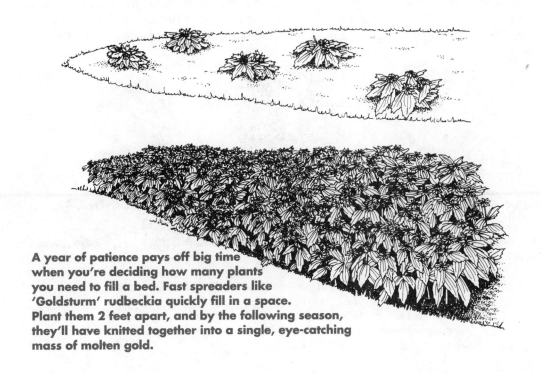

A year of patience pays off big time when you're deciding how many plants you need to fill a bed. Fast spreaders like 'Goldsturm' rudbeckia quickly fill in a space. Plant them 2 feet apart, and by the following season, they'll have knitted together into a single, eye-catching mass of molten gold.

Figuring Size the Smart Way

Before you purchase any plants, whether they're perennials, groundcovers, trees, or shrubs, check a reference book like the ones listed in "Recommended Reading" on page 269 to find out their spread, or width, at maturity. Then measure the space in the bed, and figure out how many plants you actually need.

Math 101 for Thrifty Gardeners

One simple equation combined with a little homework will save you money if you do the math before you head to the garden center. Once you've decided the plants you want to include, jot down their estimated mature spread so you can determine how many plants you'll need. Then make a rough sketch to double-check your plan.

Let's say you want to plant a row of beautiful heavenly bamboo shrubs (*Nandina domestica*) to create a solid backdrop of bright red berries and flaming leaves for your dwarf purple asters (*Aster novae-angliae* 'Purple Dome') in autumn. Your planting area is 9 feet long. You find out that the nandina you want has a mature spread of 3 feet; the asters, 18 inches. Here's how to work out the math:

1. To figure out how many nandinas to plant, divide 9 feet by 3 feet (the spread of the nandina). That shows you that you'll need three bushes to fill in the space.

2. You'll have to change feet to inches to calculate the number of asters: 9 feet × 12 inches = 108 inches. Divide 108 inches by 18 inches (the spread of the asters), and you'll see that you need to plant six asters.

3. If the numbers don't divide evenly, round down instead of rounding up to get the number of plants to buy. Plants don't read the books, and their mature spread is generally an estimate, not a hard and fast number—it varies according to the conditions, climate, and care they receive.

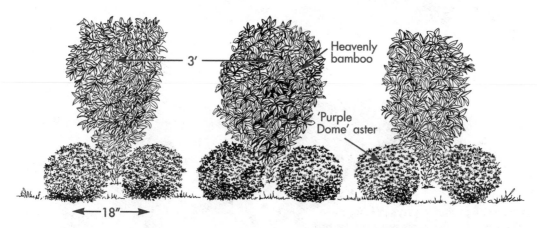

Easy equations help you figure out exactly how many plants you need, so you don't overbuy. Keep in mind that plant size varies somewhat depending on soil, climate, and care, and that most perennials, even the clump-forming types, gradually expand their girth with age.

A measuring tape is a great tool for frugal gardening. Shrubs are big investments, especially when you're planting a hedge instead a few isolated specimens. Buy and plant the minimum by measuring carefully as you plant.

Make a Tape Measure Your Ally

When it's time to plant, pull out your trusty tape measure to make sure of the correct spacing. Eyeballing or guessing at the planting space can mean a difference of a few inches between each plant. That doesn't sound like much, but multiplied by an entire bed or hedge, it can mean the price of another few plants to fill in the leftover space. If you're planting a 30-foot-long hedge, and the plants should be spaced 30 inches apart, carelessly lessening the spacing by only 2 to 3 inches between plants will shorten your hedge by a plant or two.

Measure from Center to Center

Measure spacing from the center of one plant (or planting hole) to the center of the next. For example, if you're planting a hedge of yews, which each have a 6-foot spread at maturity, measure from the trunk, not the outside tips of the branches.

To make this easier, invest in a plastic-coated, wind-up tape measure for outdoor use. In the garden, it is very easy to get dirt in a metal carpenter's retractable tape measure. Once that happens, the clogged works no longer retracts the tape. Notch a stake at the length you need to separate plants, then use the stake as your measuring tool.

Where to Buy Your Garden Plants

Thanks to the huge popularity of gardening, every year brings us more places to buy plants and supplies. More and more catalogs are being stuffed in our mailboxes, and garden centers and nurseries are springing up like mushrooms after a rain.

But not all garden centers and nurseries are created equal. Reasonable prices are a big consideration, but they're not the only objective frugal shoppers keep in mind. Good warranties are a must. Reliable advice from knowledgeable salespeople is another big plus. And healthy plants are the biggest cost saver of all. Plants that cost more up front may save you money in the long run because of their excellent quality.

Of course, the cheapest way to acquire plants is to grow them yourself from seed. For more about seed savings, see page 70 of this chapter.

What Will They Cost?

The price of a plant can vary dramatically, depending on where you buy it. In general, prices are lowest at discount store garden centers and garden superstores. You'll usually pay more at an independent nursery or through a catalog.

Before you plunk down cold hard cash, do some comparison shopping. Buying plants may seem like a small purchase because they cost little individually. But add up the total cost of furnishing a garden, and you'll see that comparing prices is as important when choosing plants as when buying a new sofa. Compare and become familiar with the prices at garden centers, discount stores, nurseries, and catalogs so you know when a plant is a good buy.

Check the Fine Print

Reputable plant sellers of any kind, retail or mail-order, guarantee their plants. Before you hand over money for plants, find out exactly what the terms of the warranty are. Get a copy in writing, and file it with the receipt for the plants.

❖ Will you get a refund? A replacement? A credit?

❖ Is there a time limit on the warranty?

❖ Will you have to supply the dead plant for proof?

❖ Are there exceptions to the offer?

❖ If you bought the plant through the mail, who pays shipping costs for the replacement?

The Glories of the Garden Center

The proliferation of garden centers and gardening superstore chains is good news for gardeners. Mass-market sellers can order in huge quantities at lower wholesale costs—and pass the savings on to you. Competition keeps prices lower, too. Big chains know that their customers are value-driven, so they tend to keep their prices on a par with each other. Garden center prices can be pleasantly low compared to the price tags at nurseries and in catalogs. Strolling the aisles of flowers, shrubs, and trees can turn up all kinds of delightful bargains, especially if you shop early in the season when selection is at its peak.

Arm Yourself with the Ads

Some national garden centers and discount stores offer a price-match policy: If a competing chain advertises the same item for less, they'll match the price. That's a great deal for you because you won't have to waste time shopping around for the lowest price tag. Get in the habit of reading the newspaper advertising supplements from various retailers, and take them with you when you shop. It's a good idea to keep each week's collection of ads in the car in case of impulse stops.

Speak up to save money. Before you start loading up your cart, find out exactly how the store's price-match policy works. Don't be shy about asking the store to match another retailer's price if that is their policy, but do make sure that what you're buying is the exact product advertised by the competitor. If you're lucky enough to have price-matching retailers in your area, your savings on name-brand tools, garden furniture, and other supplies can really add up.

Shop with Your Eyes Open

Shopping at big chains can save you significant money, but the savings at garden centers and discount stores are balanced by a couple of caveats: Selection is usually more limited than at nurseries or in catalogs, and plants are usually not cared for as carefully as at a mom-and-pop shop or smaller business with trained employees.

How can you buy wisely? Follow the guidelines in Chapter 1, "Get the Garden You Want—The Frugal Way," to make sure the plants you buy at garden centers are vigorous and healthy and will live a long, happy life in your garden.

Plan to do your own homework. Some chain stores have trained horticulturists on staff, but many clerks are less than knowledgeable. If you want one-on-one attention, it's best to patronize a local nursery, where the usually higher prices of the plants reflect the additional customer advice they offer.

Time your shopping for healthy plants. Plant care can be irregular at garden centers, and sitting around in a plastic pot under less-than-ideal conditions doesn't do any plant much good.

Get the healthiest plants by shopping early in the season or as soon as new shipments arrive from growers.

Think Seasonally, Buy Locally

Garden center or discount store plants are sometimes trucked in before their time to tempt folks like us into impulse purchases instigated by the sight of blooming flowers. Frugal gardeners remember that it's better for a plant's health to bloom at its own appointed time than to undergo the stresses of adapting to unseasonable weather when brought into bloom in a warmer climate. In early spring, when our hunger for flowers is at its peak, many garden centers oblige by trucking in pansies and other early bloomers. But because these plants haven't adjusted to the rigors of our local climate, they may languish when moved from the sheltered garden center to our own gardens.

---

2 for the Price of 1

A bargain is not always visible on the price tag! Sometimes a more expensive plant is the better buy. If you go shopping for perennials, you may find decent-sized plants for, say, $3 apiece. Before you buy, check the larger, more expensive specimens of the same plants—in many cases they're big enough to be sliced in half before planting, giving you two for the price of one. If the price tag on the bigger pot is less than twice the price of two smaller plants, you'll save by buying big.

Cultivate Your Local Nursery

Prices at local nurseries are usually higher than at mass-market garden centers, but the quality and selection of the plants are usually an improvement. The human factor is another plus of shopping at a local nursery instead of an impersonal chain store.

Get on a first-name basis. It's the personal touch that makes a local nursery so much fun to visit. Find your local favorite and shop there regularly, and it won't be long before people who love plants as much as you do will greet you by name. Many nurseries are willing to special-order plants that they don't have in stock.

Look for well-formed plants. Many nurseries grow their own, pampering their plants to get the most out of them. Trees and shrubs are pruned to best advantage, and evergreens are lush and dense.

Ask for advice about alternatives. Nurseries usually have staff with expertise who can answer your questions, make suggestions, and solve problems. If the plant on your most-wanted list isn't a good choice for your region, a nursery owner should be able to recommend an alternative that will thrive in your garden and create the look you want. (If you can't find anyone at the nursery who is willing or able to advise you, find another nursery!)

Be a Clever Catalog Customer

In the cold months of winter, looking at plant catalogs rich with color photographs of beautifully blooming, healthy plants is a deep pleasure but also a temp-

FREE STUFF!

No Charge for Good Advice

Once you've found a nursery that stocks top-quality plants and has at least one or two knowledgeable people on staff, you've hit the jackpot for free gardening advice. Timing is important, though: If the place is swamped with customers, don't expect much undivided attention. Saturday is a notoriously busy day at most nurseries; visiting on a weekday is a much better idea.

tation to spend money. Catalog prices are generally higher than those in garden centers and nurseries, especially once you add the cost of shipping and handling. But the selection is usually unbeatable. Many mail-order catalogs offer cultivars and native plants that are hard or impossible to find elsewhere.

Just as with every other plant outlet, not all catalogs are created equal. It's up to you to weed out the best from the plethora of offerings that will fill your mailbox once you're earmarked as a catalog customer.

An Education at Your Fingertips

Catalogs are a great basic education in plants. Read them often enough, and you'll start to absorb Latin names as well as become familiar with an astonishing array of perennials and other plants. The excellent color photographs, especially landscape shots, will help you visualize their potential in the garden.

Keep lists as you peruse your catalogs, or flag the pages of plants you fall in love with with small self-stick notes. If plant names aren't yet a second language with you, carry the catalogs along when you visit nurseries and garden centers to comparison-shop for similar plants.

Too Good to Be True?

Some catalogs show pictures that will make your mouth water but ship plants that turn out to be a disappointingly far cry from such perfection. Read the fine print carefully to find out what size and quality of plants the company supplies. Perennial seedlings will take a year of waiting before they bloom. "Field-run" perennials are dug just as they grow in the nursery row and may include the top dogs as well as the runts. Trees and shrubs may be one- or two-year-old seedlings instead of plants ready to take their place in your garden. Bulbs may be puny instead of fat top-graders. When in doubt, a call to customer service should reveal the truth.

Consider a Plant Collection

Many catalog companies have started marketing collections of plants, many sold at a small discount, that have the same cultural requirements and combine well to create an attractive garden.

Expand your specialty. In love with hostas? Can't get enough thyme? Lust after lavenders? Ready-made samplings that focus on one plant or another are an easy way to expand your passion for a plant while keeping costs low.

Eliminate confusion. Perennials for filling a small garden commonly form the basis for the collections, which can be a great comfort if the vast choice of plants

for any given garden situation leaves you overwhelmed. Sometimes a planting plan is part of the bargain.

Shave costs and satisfy needs. Collections can also be a great way to trim costs, if most of the plants in the collection are ones that you want. Depending on the discount, it may be cheaper to order two or more collections than to buy the same plants individually.

Use a critical eye. These professionally selected collections are helpful and reassuring, but be sure to look at any accompanying art with a critical eye. Photos of such collections usually tell the truth about what to expect, though they may be shot when the little garden is at its peak of color. Illustrations are trickier: Artistic license allows illustrators to show all plants blooming at once, when in fact their bloom is staggered over a period of months.

Buyer Beware

Beware of any catalog or mail-order advertisement that names the plant only by a common name. You may not get what you expect. Common names vary in different parts of the country, and sometimes growers make up their own names for plants in an inspired marketing effort. If you aren't familiar with the plant, don't fall for a pretty name! Reputable mail-order companies include both the accepted common name and the botanical (Latin) name of each of the plants in their catalogs.

 **20 SMART SHOPPING TIPS**

1. Decide which plants will be the backbone of your garden, and buy those before you indulge in extras.

2. Invest in trees and shrubs ASAP. They take years longer than perennials to reach their potential.

3. Keep impulse buying to a minimum. Spontaneous plant purchases demolish the budget and may not fit into your overall garden scheme.

4. To find reliable plant sellers, ask neighbors with gardens you admire where they bought their plants.

5. Before you order from a catalog for the first time, ask gardening friends if they've had experience with the company and if they'd order from it again.

6. Get a guarantee—in writing.

7. Save receipts. If problems arise, you'll be prepared. If the plants are a delight, you'll know where to get more.

8. Save on delivery charges by shopping with a friend who has a pickup truck or other high-capacity vehicle.

9. Transport plants carefully. Tuck in branches and stems tenderly to avoid snapping them. Tie branches if they're traveling in an open truck.

10. If you're buying in quantity, ask about discounts.

11. Buying at nurseries and garden centers instead of from mail-order catalogs lets you choose the pick of the crop.

12. Bone up on the preferences of plants you want. Hardiness zones don't tell the whole story; humidity, soil, and other factors can mean the difference between success and failure, too.

13. Buy flowering plants in bud, not in full bloom, and you'll get to enjoy the flush of flowers much longer.

14. Check the plant's roots for general good health.

15. Inspect the trunks of trees for knicks, cuts, and skinned patches that can cause later problems.

16. If you have a large project, such as covering a bank with creeping thyme, where you need more than 50 plants, call the nursery in fall to order the plants for spring. Because they will be growing the plants especially for you and have the guaranteed sale months in advance, they may be willing to sell them to you at a lower price.

You spend time selecting the best-formed plants at the nursery, so be careful not to damage them when you put them in the car. Carefully tuck in any protruding branches, and make sure the containers are secure before driving off.

17. Buy groundcovers in flats instead of individual pots. You'll pay less money per plant.

18. If you have a lot of space to cover, invest in perennials that multiply quickly by spreading roots or self-sowing.

19. Trim hedge costs by mixing inexpensive shrubs with pricier plants—privet with azaleas, for instance.

20. Can't use a whole flat of flowers? Split it with a friend or neighbor and you'll both save money.

Penny-Wise Plant Choices

For long-term, low-cost, and high gardening satisfaction, look for easy-care, robust plants. Plants that grow vigorously with little or no pampering are the number-one choice for frugal gardeners. They free your time—always a valuable commodity! Plants that resist pests and diseases also pay off because they aren't constantly languishing on the critical condition list, requiring special sprays or other care.

Plants that divide easily, grow fast, or produce lots of easy-sprouting seeds are perfect for penny-wise gardens. If you've got a big space to fill and a small budget, go for plants such as daylilies, sedum, and rudbeckia that grow and spread rapidly and thrive when they're divided. Self-sowing annuals and perennials make sense—and cents!

Don't overlook groundcovers, either. They provide a wide choice of foliage and flower shape and color and, as their name implies, cover ground rapidly.

Natives Need No Pampering

Plants that are naturally suited to your climate are good penny-wise choices. Native plants are particularly well adapted to their local conditions—after all, they've evolved with ways to survive and thrive through whatever extremes your region can throw at them.

Southwestern plants laugh at continued drought; southern plants luxuriate in humidity that would leave foreigners gasping; and northern natives are prepared for cold spells that would be fatal for lesser plants. Prairie natives are unfazed by temperature extremes and windswept sites that would wipe out many other plants. Instead of struggling to make your garden hospitable to plants that come from other areas, you can sit back and relax when you plant undemanding natives.

Hardiness Is Half the Story

Those zone numbers you see on labels and in catalogs and reference books are a good guideline when it comes to choosing plants that will thrive in your region, but they're only half the story. USDA Plant Hardiness Zones (see page 280) are based solely on minimum winter temperatures. And cold, unfortunately, isn't the only thing that can kill a plant or cramp its style. Summer heat or humidity, soil type, seasonal rainfall patterns, and even snow cover or lack thereof can all affect a plant's ability to flourish. When it's time to select your plants, check the zone number first. Then consult a good reference book to find out whether your garden fills the bill in other ways, too.

FRUGAL GARDENER'S GUIDE

The Top 10 Natives by Region

Choose these regional American treasures for your garden and you'll be rewarded with naturally well-suited plants that thrive with no special treatment—a boon for timesaving, penny-pinching gardeners!

NORTHEAST AND MID-ATLANTIC	MIDWEST	SOUTH	SOUTHWEST	NORTHWEST
PERENNIALS				
Blue cohosh (*Caulophyllum thalictroides*)	Butterflyweed (*Asclepias tuberosa*)	Amsonia (*Amsonia tabernaemontana*)	Autumn sage (*Salvia greggii*)	Dogtooth violet, fawn lily (*Erythronium albidum, E. oregonum, E. revolutum*)
Bluets (*Houstonia caerulea*)	Eastern shooting star (*Dodecatheon media*)	Boltonia (*Boltonia asteroides*)	Blanket flower (*Gaillardia × grandiflora*)	Douglas iris (*Iris douglasiana*)
Canada lily (*Lilium canadense*)	Obedient plant (*Physostegia virginiana*)	Red flag iris (*Iris fulva*)	Chocolate flower (*Berlandiera lyrata*)	Fringecups (*Tellima grandiflora*)
Cardinal flower (*Lobelia cardinalis*)	Perennial sunflowers (*Helianthus* spp.)	Red mallow (*Hibiscus coccinea*)	Firecracker penstemon (*Penstemon eatonii*)	Goat's beard (*Aruncus sylvester*)
Columbine (*Aquilegia canadensis*)	Prairie coneflower (*Ratibida pinnata*)	Rose mallow (*Hibiscus moscheutos*)	Gloriosa daisy (*Rudbeckia hirta*)	Golden iris (*Iris innominata*)
Green-and-gold (*Chrysogonum virginianum*)	Purple coneflower (*Echinacea purpurea*)	Southern blue flag (*Iris virginica*)	Mexican hat (*Ratibida columnifera*)	Inside-out flower (*Vancouveria planipetala*)
Heartleaf aster (*Aster cordifolius*)	Rough blazing star (*Liatris aspera*)	Stiff-leaf aster (*Aster linearifolius*)	Nodding onion (*Allium cernuum*)	Lupine (*Lupinus polyphyllus*)
New England aster (*Aster novae-angliae*)	Sky blue aster (*Aster azureus*)	White false indigo (*Baptisia alba*)	Plains zinnia (*Zinnia grandiflora*)	Thrift (*Armeria maritima*)
Stokes' aster (*Stokesia laevis*)	Stiff goldenrod (*Solidago rigida*)	Wild ginger (*Asarum canadense*)	Winecup (*Callirhoe involucrata*)	Western columbine (*Aquilegia formosa*)
Wild geranium (*Geranium maculatum*)	Turtlehead (*Chelone glabra*)	Zigzag iris (*Iris brevicaulis*)	Yellow columbine (*Aquilegia chrysantha*)	White evening primrose (*Oenothera caespitosa*)

(continued)

FRUGAL GARDENER'S GUIDE

The Top 10 Natives by Region—Continued

NORTHEAST AND MID-ATLANTIC	MIDWEST	SOUTH	SOUTHWEST	NORTHWEST
SHRUBS				
Bayberry (*Myrica pensylvanica*)	American cranberrybush (*Viburnum trilobum*)	Arrowwood viburnum (*Viburnum dentatum*)	Apache plume (*Fallugia paradoxa*)	Manzanita (*Arctostaphylos* spp.)
Beach plum (*Prunus maritima*)	Aronia (*Aronia arbutifolia,* especially 'Brilliantissima')	Fragrant sumac (*Rhus aromatica*)	Brittlebush (*Encelia farinosa*)	Ocean spray (*Holodiscus discolor*)
Mountain laurel (*Kalmia latifolia*)	Blackhaw (*Viburnum prunifolium*)	Oak leaf hydrangea (*Hydrangea quercifolia*)	Chollas (*Opuntia* spp.)	Oregon grape holly (*Mahonia aquifolium*)
New Jersey tea (*Ceanothus americanus*)	Bottlebrush buckeye (*Aesculus parviflora*)	Piedmont azalea (*Rhododendron canescens*)	Chuperosa (*Justicia californica*)	Red flowering currant (*Ribes sanguineum*)
Pagoda dogwood (*Cornus alternifolia*)	Prairie rose (*Rosa setigera*)	Piedmont rhododendron (*Rhododendron minus*)	Fairy duster (*Calliandra eriophylla*)	Rhododendrons (*Rhododendron* spp.)
Pinkshell azalea (*Rhododendron vaseyi*)	Serviceberry (*Amelanchier alnifolia*)	Plumleaf azalea (*Rhododendron prunifolium*)	Indigo bush (*Amorpha fruticosa*)	Salal (*Gaultheria shallon*)
Red-osier dogwood (*Cornus sericea*)	Shrubby cinquefoil (*Potentilla fruticosa*)	Possum haw (*Viburnum nudum*)	Mountain marigold (*Tagetes lemonii*)	Serviceberry (*Amalanchier alnifolia*)
Swamp azalea (*Rhododendron viscosum*)	Smooth sumac (*Rhus glabra*)	Saw palmetto (*Serenoa repens*)	Ocotillo (*Fouquieria splendens*)	Silk-tassel bush (*Garrya elliptica*)
Sweet fern (*Comptonia peregrina*)	Summersweet (*Clethra alnifolia*)	Silky camellia (*Stewartia malacodendron*)	Red hesperaloe (*Hesperaloe parviflora*)	Wax myrtle (*Myrica californica*)
Winterberry (*Ilex verticillata*)	Winterberry (*Ilex verticillata*)	Wax myrtle (*Myrica cerifera*)	Threeleaf sumac (*Rhus trilobata*)	Western azalea (*Rhododendron occidentalis*)

FRUGAL GARDENER'S GUIDE				
The Top 10 Natives by Region—Continued				
NORTHEAST AND MID-ATLANTIC	MIDWEST	SOUTH	SOUTHWEST	NORTHWEST
TREES				
American holly (*Ilex opaca*)	Ashe magnolia (*Magnolia ashei*)	Bull bay magnolia (*Magnolia grandiflora*)	Alligator juniper (*Juniperus deppeana*)	Bigleaf maple (*Acer macrophyllum*)
Canoe birch (*Betula papyrifera*)	Bald cypress (*Taxodium distichum*)	Carolina silverbell (*Halesia carolina*)	Blue palo verde (*Cercidium floridum*)	Douglas fir (*Pseudotsuga menziesii*)
Eastern dogwood (*Cornus florida*)	Canoe birch (*Betulus papyrifera*)	Franklin tree (*Franklinia altamaha*)	Desert olive (*Forestiera neo-mexicana*)	Gambel's oak (*Quercus gambelli*)
Eastern redbud (*Cercis canadensis*)	Cucumber tree (*Magnolia acuminata*)	Fringe tree (*Chionanthus virginicus*)	Desert willow (*Chilopsis linearis*)	Madrone (*Arbutus menziesii*)
Hickories (*Carya* spp.)	Dogwood (*Cornus florida*)	Live oak (*Quercus virginiana*)	Honey mesquite (*Prosopis glandulosa*)	Pacific dogwood (*Cornus nuttallii*)
Scarlet oak (*Quercus coccinea*)	Eastern red cedar (*Juniperus virginiana*)	Longleaf pine (*Pinus palustris*)	Ironwood (*Olneya tesota*)	Rocky Mountain juniper (*Juniperus scopulorum*)
Serviceberry (*Amelanchier laevis*)	Eastern redbud (*Cercis canadensis*)	Red buckeye (*Aesculus pavia*)	Mescal bean (*Sophora secundiflora*)	Vine maple (*Acer circinatum*)
Sugar maple (*Acer saccharum*)	Serviceberry (*Amelanchier alnifolia* cvs.)	River birch (*Betula nigra*)	Quaking aspen (*Populus tremuloides*)	Western hemlock (*Tsuga heterophylla*)
White oak (*Quercus alba*)	Witch hazel (*Hamamelis virginiana*)	Sabal palm (*Sabal palmetto*)	Texas ebony (*Pithecellobium flexicaule*)	Western red cedar (*Thuja plicata*)
Witch hazel (*Hamamelis virginiana*)	Yellowwood (*Cladrastris kenytukeya*)	Yellowwood (*Cladrastris kentukeya*)	Valley cottonwood (*Populus fremontii*)	Western redbud (*Cercis occidentalis*)

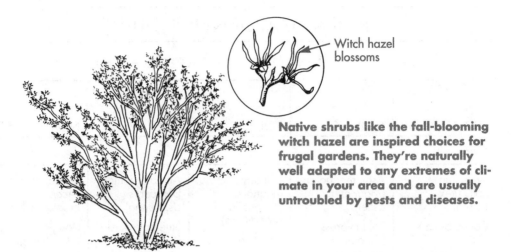

Witch hazel blossoms

Native shrubs like the fall-blooming witch hazel are inspired choices for frugal gardens. They're naturally well adapted to any extremes of climate in your area and are usually untroubled by pests and diseases.

Bareroot Basics: Saving with Bareroot Stock

A large part of the cost of any containerized plant is the soil and the pot it's growing in. Not only do the soil and pot cost the grower money (and time), they greatly increase shipping costs. Take a gallon-size plant complete with container and soil, multiply it by hundreds for a nursery shipment, and you have a lot of costly weight and bulk to transport.

Bareroot plants are less expensive than those sold in containers, and the selection is usually better because bareroot plants take less room at the nursery.

Shop Early for Bargains in Bareroot

Bareroot plants are available in late winter to early spring, when the plants are dormant. For best buys, visit as soon as the stock arrives so you can bring home the pick of the crop and get it in the ground before the roots suffer damage.

Visit a nursery or garden center during the bareroot season and you'll find plenty of shade trees, fruit trees and bushes, shrubs, perennials such as hostas, daylilies, and dahlias, and perennial edibles such as asparagus, strawberries, and rhubarb. Catalogs also ship bareroot plants early in the season, and some ship perennials bareroot through late spring.

Bad Roots Are No Bargain

The roots of bareroot plants are easy to check for signs of health. Roots should be plump, not moldy, shriveled, or dried. If you've ordered the plant through the mail or if the roots were covered with peat or other materials when you purchased them, let the provider know if the roots show any sign of problems.

A Good Soak Means a Fast Start

Those exposed roots are vulnerable, so you'll want to plant bareroot stock as soon as possible. Soak the roots of trees, shrubs, and fruit plants in a bucket of water for a few hours before you plant. Position the plant in its hole at the original soil level, usually visible as a stain on the stem.

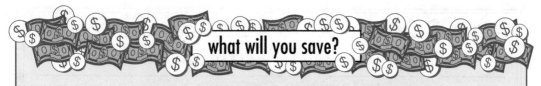

what will you save?

Buy Bareroot for Big Savings

In their bareroot state, trees, shrubs, and perennials cost a fraction of what you pay later in the season for the same plants sold in containers. How big a fraction? Generally from about a third of the price of a containerized plant to perhaps as much as one-half to two-thirds of the price. For example, you can buy two or three hostas bareroot, packaged with sawdust or peat moss in plastic bags, for the same price or less than you would pay later in the season for one hosta growing in a container.

The savings on trees and shrubs are enormous as well. A package of three bareroot forsythia bushes can cost as little as $6 at discount stores, while a single young forsythia in a plastic pot can run $10. Three for $6, or three for $30—frugal gardeners spot the bargain right away.

Tender Perennials Live Forever—Even in Cold Climates!

You'll never have to spend money again on impatiens, fuchsias, zonal and scented geraniums, wax begonias, and other tender perennials if you carry them over inside during cold winters. Although many gardeners think of these plants as annuals, they're actually perennials that come from Mexico and other parts of the world where winter freezes are rare or nonexistent. In warm regions such as Southern California, the plants keep growing—outside—12 months of the year.

In colder climates, keep your tender plants alive over the winter either by potting up and bringing the plants indoors before the first frost or by rooting cuttings to keep indoors until the following spring.

Cut Down on Indoor Care

Cuttings of tender perennials root easily at any time of the year, a trait that you can take advantage of to shorten the indoor stays of your plants. Wait until fall, but be sure to act before the first frost! Delaying the process means you have to nurture the plants indoors for less time than if you took cuttings in summer.

A Windowsill's Worth Will Fill the Garden Next Year

Be realistic about how much space you have for storing rooted cuttings. You can start a lot of cuttings in very little space, but once the roots have begun to grow in earnest, each plant will need more soil to grow.

Limit yourself to one windowsill worth of space for each type of tender perennial, and you'll have plenty of plants by early spring to start a new collection to fill your gardens again—from cuttings, natch!

Carry Over Tender Perennials Indoors

These "annuals" are actually tender perennials that will live forever if you protect them from freezing cold. A handful of cuttings will give you enough plants to start a whole new crop next spring.

Ageratum (*Ageratum houstonianum*)
Browallia (*Browallia speciosa*)
Coleus (*Coleus* × *hybridus*)
Fuchsias (*Fuchsia* spp. and cvs.)
Heliotrope (*Heliotropium arborescens*)
Impatiens (*Impatiens walleriana*)

Lantanas (*Lantana* spp. and cvs.)
Thunbergias (*Thunbergia* spp.)
Wandering Jew (*Tradescantia fluminensis*)
Wax begonia (*Begonia semperflorens*)
Zonal and scented geraniums
   (*Pelargonium* spp. and cvs.)

Groundcovers That Get the Green Light

When you need to hide bare soil fast, look for fast-growing groundcovers, which multiply faster than a sixth-grader learning the times tables. A single rooted sprig of *Mazus reptans*, a rapidly growing groundcover for partial shade to sun in USDA Plant Hardiness Zones 5 to 8, will spread to cover 12 inches in one season. A sturdy plant, it outcompetes grass and thrives in poor soil as well as good. In spring, the evergreen plant covers itself in a mass of purple, orchid-like flowers.

Keep in mind that it can be difficult to put the brakes on fast-spreading plants. If you don't want them to infiltrate other areas, install a barrier of plastic or metal edging before you plant to keep them in their place.

A windowsill holds enough small pots of cutting-grown tender perennials to let you fill your garden for free next spring. As a bonus, you get to enjoy their bloom all winter!

Speedy Spreaders Cover Ground Fast

It doesn't take an Einstein to recognize the financial savings you'll get from planting groundcovers that spread quickly. Fewer plants means the cost to plant an area is much lower. But the payoff isn't only in dollars and cents: Your bare spots will be covered more quickly, giving your garden that all-important aesthetic appeal, plus you'll save hours of time and labor you would have spent weeding and mulching if you waited for slower-growing groundcovers to fill in the area.

Ajuga, bugleweed (*Ajuga reptans*)
Chamomile (*Chamaemelum nobile*)
Creeping phlox (*Phlox stolonifera*)
Creeping thyme (*Thymus praecox*)
Crown vetch (*Coronilla varia*)
Forget-me-not (*Myosotis scorpioides*)
Horseshoe vetch (*Hippocrepis comosa*)
Houseleek (*Sempervivum tectorum*)
Ivy (*Hedera helix* cvs.)
Lamium, or dead nettle (*Lamium maculatum*)
Lily-of-the-valley (*Convallaria majalis*)
Mazus (*Mazus reptans*)
Mexican snowball (*Echeveria elegans*)
Pachysandra (*Pachysandra terminalis*)
Prostrate rosemary (*Rosmarinus officinalis* 'Prostratus')

Prostrate speedwell (*Veronica prostrata*)
Rock cresses (*Arabis* spp.)
Rock soapwort (*Saponaria ocymoides*)
Siberian tea (*Bergenia crassifolia*)
Snow-in-summer (*Cerastium tomentosum*)
Sweet woodruff (*Galium odoratum*)
Trailing gazania (*Gazania rigens leucolaena*)
Vinca, periwinkle (*Vinca minor, V. major*)
Virginia creeper (*Parthenocissus quinquefolia*)
Wild gingers (*Asarum* spp.)
Wintergreen (*Gaultheria procumbens*)
Wooly yarrow (*Achillea tomentosa*)
Yellow stonecrop (*Sedum reflexum*)

Save-Your-Wallet Shrubs

Shrubs can be a budget breaker, especially if you're tempted by big plants at big prices. One way to trim costs is to choose small-sized specimens of fast growers. Leyland cypress (× *Cupressocyparis leylandii*), for example, is a columnar conifer that grows 3 to 5 feet a year. Within two years, a scrawny, 1-gallon plant 2 feet tall will be a substantial 8-foot-tall shrub. Good reference books, such as those listed in "Recommended Reading" on page 269, will tell you how fast shrubs grow.

Mix and Match for Fast Hedges

Fast-growing shrubs are fabulous for giving a quick fill, while slower-growing shrubs such as yew, boxwood, and holly are taking their time. Quick-growing shrubs such as viburnums,

Fast-Spreading Shrubs

If you want a fast-growing hedge, a specimen plant, or a shrub border that matures quickly, choose from the shrubs in this list.

American elderberry (*Sambucus canadensis*)
Creeping cotoneaster (*Cotoneaster adpressus*)
Creeping mahonia (*Mahonia repens*)
Fragrant sumac (*Rhus aromatica* 'GroLow')
Japanese kerria (*Kerria japonica* 'Pleniflora')
Red-osier dogwood (*Cornus sericea*, also known as *C. stolonifera*)
Rugosa rose (*Rosa rugosa*)
St.-John's-wort (*Hypericum calycinum*)
Summersweet (*Clethra alnifolia*)
Sweet fern (*Comptonia peregrina*)
Ural false spirea (*Sorbaria sorbifolia*)
Winter jasmine (*Jasminum nudiflorum*)

forsythia, weigela, and the glossy-leaved euonymus 'Manhattan' (*Euonymus kiautschovicus* 'Manhattan') are great for fast hedge effects. As your slow-growing shrubs begin to mature in hedges or gardens, you can transplant the quick-growing ones to another spot that needs livening up. That way they won't be wasted!

Use Spreading Shrubs to Cover Difficult Areas

Hate lugging the lawn mower up that steep bank? Wipe out your mowing woes by planting difficult areas with fast-spreading shrubs that spread into close-knit colonies. They'll fill in quick and thick, making drudgery a thing of the past.

There are several new rose introductions that are especially effective for growing on slopes as groundcovers, such as 'Magic Meidiland', which has a low, creeping habit with clusters of medium pink, semidouble flowers. Fragrant possibilities include 'Baby Blanket' (pink; delicate sweet scent), 'Garden Blanket' (lavender pink; fruity scent), 'Sun Runner' (yellow; citrus scent), and 'Magic Carpet' (lavender pink; spicy scent).

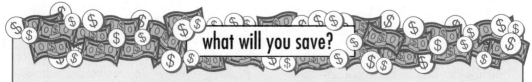

what will you save?

Mix 'n Match Shrubs to Save

Fast-growing shrubs like privet and forsythia usually cost much less to buy. That's because they're easier to propagate and quicker to reach a salable size than slower-growing plants like hollies and rhododendrons, which may range from about $15 to $25 each or more. If you substitute just three or four cheaper shrubs, at about $5 to $10 each, in your garden plan, you'll save a bundle.

Make More of Your Plants

Start with plants that propagate easily, and you can increase your inventory without spending another penny. With a few simple tricks of the trade under your belt, you'll be literally making the most of your garden in no time.

Math Trick for Frugal Gardeners: Multiply by Dividing

The easiest way to propagate perennials is by dividing a healthy growing clump into two or more plants. A few minutes' work with a shovel or trowel, and you'll have an armload of new plants to add to the garden. Dividing perennials is good for them, too. They respond with a new burst of vigor and better flowers.

The number of new plants you get from the original plant will depend on the size of the clump, the type of plant, and the size of the divisions. If you want hefty new plants that look full grown the following season, chop accordingly. If you're willing to wait for them to fill in, any size division that has roots attached will work. A single clump of daylilies can yield 10 or more new plants; a mat of creeping thyme may give you 100 rooted pieces; a clump of tall garden phlox, perhaps 6.

Roots Are the Clue to Easy Division

Any perennial with multiple stems arising from fibrous roots is a prime candidate for going under the knife (or spade). A clump of yarrow is perfect for this kind of surgery because each piece will have several growing stems with attached roots. Trying to "divide" a single-stemmed delphinium or gaura plant, on the other hand, is asking for trouble.

Plants with spreading rhizomes, like bearded iris, are good for dividing, too. But perennials with fat, fleshy taproots, like oriental poppies and butterfly weed, are best propagated by methods other than division—those thick roots are much harder to reestablish than a handful of fine, fast-growing fibrous roots, where there are plenty of extra roots to take up the slack if a few are damaged.

How do you know what kind of roots your perennial has? A little underground investigating will uncover the truth. Just brush away some soil with your hand to find out.

When to Divide

It's easiest to divide plants when you don't have a lot of foliage and branches to contend with. Not only is it easier on you, it's easier on the plant, too, because the reduced roots won't have to support a plant in full growth.

Spring and fall are best. Spring and fall temperatures are cool enough not to stress the plants after they're transplanted, but warm enough to encourage new roots to develop quickly. However, if your ground freezes quickly in fall, don't divide plants then because, chances are, the plant won't have enough time to establish a good root system for winter survival.

Summer division is OK. You can divide plants in summer, too, but be forewarned: No matter how much you water them or

Get 50 Perennials from a Single Garden Center Plant

A good-size clump of chives represents a wealth of new plants. You can separate each rooted bulblet from the mother plant and have 50 or more single-stemmed plants. Do the job in spring, and by midsummer each individual with be a small clump. Chives also self-sow, and if you transplant each seedling so none die from overcrowding, you could end up with thousands of plants from one.

Mums are just as generous about multiplying. Buy a hardy mum plant in spring and snip all the stems into 4-inch cuttings. They'll root quickly in moist soil, making multitudes of new mum plants.

shade them, they'll wilt from the shock and take some time to recover. Make your divisions on a cloudy day or in the early morning or evening when the heat is less intense. About an hour before you plan to dig, water the plant slowly and deeply. Try to keep as much original soil around the roots as possible, and replant the divisions immediately. The division may die back considerably. As long as the roots are still alive, you needn't worry. Look for signs of growth once the weather cools in autumn.

No-Fail Plant Division

Some gardeners like to dig up the parent plant and perform surgery while it's out of the ground. Other people like to slice while the plant is still rooted in soil, levering out the divisions as they're cut free from the parent. The first approach takes less muscle power and saves your back; it requires a sharp spade and a lot of force to cut

Drive a sharp spade into the clump of perennials you want to divide, splitting it in half. Continue until the plant is sliced into sections.

Slice beneath each section to free it from the soil. Replant as soon as possible.

through the roots of bigger, deep-rooted perennials, such as daylilies. The second technique is a good one for shallow-rooted plants like creeping thyme that don't take a lot of heavy labor, and it's also good for summer division because the parent plant will suffer less shock to its system.

If the plant is out of the soil, cut or pull the root mass into smaller pieces. A sturdy chef's knife or cleaver is a handy tool, but don't use your pride-and-joy cutlery and do keep the sharpening stone nearby— this is blade-dulling work. If the plant is still in the soil, insert a sharp spade into the center of the root mass and slice off a section of the plant.

Don't Stop Dividing

Depending on its size and the type of plant, one "mother" plant can be divided into 2, 3, or even 50 new plants. Allow one or two years for the new divisions to grow, and then they too can be used as mother plants, each divisible into two or more plants. The savings are exponential, doubling and redoubling at a tremendous rate.

Daylily duplication pays off. A single daylily, for instance, which may have cost you $5 initially, may yield 4 divisions at the beginning of its second season. With that first slicing up of your plant, you're already ahead $15. Another one to two years in the ground, and those 4 divisions, plus the parent, become 12, for a savings of $55. One more round of division turns your 12 plants into 36. At $5 each, your daylily holdings are now worth $180. The best part is, they're all yours for free!

Swap divisions for new plants. Some perennials need to be divided, even if you don't really want more. Instead of accumulating dozens of daisies, swap for some bearded iris from a friend.

Cut Costs with Cuttings

Something for nothing—it's the frugal gardener's favorite way of making more! An amazing number of plants, including herbs, annuals, perennials, trees, and shrubs will grow roots from a piece of branch or stem removed from the original plant.

Rooting cuttings can be as simple as sticking the stem in soil. It's a valuable method of propagation for shrubs and other plants that don't produce viable seed or are difficult to grow from seed.

Experiment with the Easiest

Many plants are remarkably easy to root, and the personal satisfaction and cost savings are significant. If your soil is decent—not rock hard or bone-dry— prunings from rose plants that are stuck directly into the ground with no extra thought or care will root, as will quince, forsythia, willow, and spirea. Ivies, geraniums, and even houseplants like jade plant are just as simple.

Great Success with "Greenies"

"Green" cuttings from herbaceous plants like perennials, annuals, and herbs and softwood cuttings from the new growth on woody plants are gratifyingly easy to start. Take these cuttings in spring or early summer when the stems or branches are green and flexible, before the new growth hardens.

Rooting Aids

Enhance your chances for success by using the right rooting medium. Most cuttings root best in a well-drained, soilless potting mixture that contains a 50-50 blend of any two of these ingredients: sand, peat moss, vermiculite, and perlite. Rooting hormones that speed up the rooting process can improve your odds, especially for softwood cuttings. The mixtures come in varying strengths; the label will list the plants recommended for the formula.

Some cuttings, including ivies, willows, rambler roses, oleander, poplars, and houseplants such as African violets and wandering Jew, root well in nothing more than a glass of water. Let the roots grow without disturbance: Don't change the water (just top off as needed)!

What You'll Need
for Taking and Growing Cuttings

A stack of plastic or clay pots or a flat, some planting medium, and recycled plastic bags from produce are all you need for simple cuttings. Keep the rooting medium evenly moist, and keep your cuttings warm (75° to 80°F is ideal). Provide light, but no direct sun. You can create your own miniature greenhouse to maintain heat and moisture by putting a sheet of plastic over the pot or flat planted with cuttings.

How to Take a Cutting

Follow these simple steps for foolproof cuttings every time. The job is easy and the rewards are enormous.

Step 1. Take 3- to 5-inch cuttings of perennials and 6- to 12-inch cuttings for shrubs. Remove the bottom two leaves and pinch off the top pair. Also, remove any flowers. Don't be discouraged if your new cutting wilts the first day or two; it will revive.

Step 2. Poke a hole for the cutting in the rooting medium with a pencil or chopstick, and insert the cut end to a depth of 1 to 2 inches, depending on the length of the cutting. Gently tamp down the soil.

Step 3. Water well, and keep the cutting moist and humidified, either with frequent waterings and mistings or by covering with a plastic bag left loose to allow some airflow. Keep out of direct sun.

Step 4. To test for roots, give the cutting a very gentle tug. If you feel resistance, then the roots are growing.

Perennials That Root Easily from Cuttings

Try these fast-rooting perennials first. As you become more confident taking cuttings, you can try many other perennials and see how they do. A good perennial encyclopedia will tell you which other perennials you can propagate from cuttings.

Artemisias (*Artemisia* spp.)
Bleeding heart (*Dicentra spectabilis*)
Candytuft (*Iberis sempervirens*)
Catmints (*Nepeta* spp.)
Chrysanthemum (*Dendranthema* cvs.)
Dahlias (*Dahlia* cvs.)
Dianthus (*Dianthus* spp.)
Garden phlox (*Phlox paniculata*)
Loosestrifes (*Lythrum* spp.)
Purple rock cress (*Aubrieta deltoidea*)
Rock cresses (*Arabis* spp.)
Snow-in-summer (*Cerastium tomentosum*)
Soapwort (*Saponaria officinalis*)
Threadleaf coreopsis (*Coreopsis verticillata*)
Turtleheads (*Chelone* spp.)
Veronicas (*Veronica* spp.)
Vinca, periwinkle (*Vinca minor, V. major*)

Get Plenty of Perennials from Cuttings

It's fun to experiment with cuttings of your favorite perennials. A snip here, a snip there, and before you know it, your garden will be overflowing with a plenitude of these usually pricey plants.

Cuttings take longer to grow to full size than plant divisions, but you can get many more plants this way—a dozen cuttings from a single clump of dianthus is just getting started. As is usually the case with frugal gardening, a bit of patience pays off!

Shrubs, Trees, and Vines
That Root Easily from Cuttings

Enjoy free trees, shrubs, and vines when you propagate them yourself from cuttings. It's a frugal way to save big bucks, since these woody plants seldom come cheap.

Shrubs

Barberries (*Berberis* spp.)
Brooms (*Cytisus* spp.)
Butterfly bush (*Buddleia davidii*)
Euonymus 'Manhattan' (*Euonymus* spp.)
Flowering maple (*Abutilon* spp.)
Forsythias (*Forsythia* spp.)
Fuchsias (*Fuchsia* spp.)
Heaths (*Erica* spp.)
Honeysuckles (*Lonicera* spp.)
Hydrangeas (*Hydrangea* spp.)
Hypericums (*Hypericum* spp.)
Mock oranges (*Philadelphus* spp.)
Potentillas (*Potentilla* spp.)
Pyracanthas (*Pyracantha* spp.)
Roses (*Rosa* spp.)
Rose-of-Sharon (*Hibiscus syriacus*)
Spireas (*Spirea* spp.)
Trumpet creeper (*Campsis radicans*)
Viburnums (*Viburnum* spp.)
Weigelas (*Weigela* spp.)

Trees

Sweet gum (*Liquidambar styraciflua*)
Birches (*Betula* spp.)
Catalpas (*Catalpa* spp.)
Colesium maple (*Acer cappadocicum*)
Flowering cherries (*Prunus* spp.)
Ginkgo (*Ginkgo biloba*)
Goldenrain tree (*Koelreuteria paniculata*)
Smoke tree (*Cotinus coggygria*)
Willows (*Salix* spp.)

Vines

Bittersweet (*Clastrus* spp.)
Boston ivy (*Parthenocissus tricuspidata*)
Bottlebrushes (*Callistemon* spp.)
Honeysuckles (*Lonicera* spp.)
Virginia creeper (*Parthenocissus quinquefolia*)
Wisterias (*Wisteria* spp.)

Woody Cuttings Reward Patience

Softwood cuttings from your shrubs, trees, and vines are simple—a snip with the pruners, a thrust into moist soil, and you're done. You can forget all about your cuttings for a year or two, except to water them as you would other garden plants, and they'll keep growing until they're big enough to move into permanent homes.

Bury Your Shrubs to Make Babies

Burying your shrubs alive sounds like drastic treatment, but it's really a labor-saving way to make lots of plants from one parent in just a year. Known as "dropping," this is a great technique for small, bushy shrubs. Try it with heathers, heaths, dwarf rhododendrons, and andromeda. Here's how:

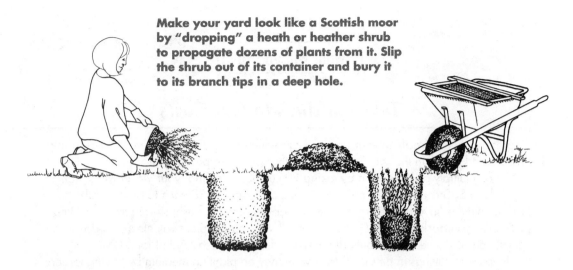

Make your yard look like a Scottish moor by "dropping" a heath or heather shrub to propagate dozens of plants from it. Slip the shrub out of its container and bury it to its branch tips in a deep hole.

1. Start with a store-bought plant in early spring. Dig a hole deep enough to cover all but the top tips of the branches, which should protrude 1 inch or so above the soil level.

2. Slip the plant out of its container and put it in the hole. Fill in the hole with rich, light, sifted soil.

3. The following spring, unearth the plant by levering under the parent's roots with a spade. Using a gentle mist hose setting, wash away the soil around the branches. You'll see roots on each of the branches.

4. Prune off the branches from the mother plant at the base of the stem, and plant each newly rooted stem immediately in pots or directly into the ground. Replant the mother plant, which should recover in a year or two.

The following year, unearth your wee shrub, hose it off gently, and sever the rooted branches from the parent for replanting.

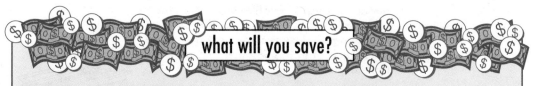

Take Cuttings to Cut Costs

Starting cuttings directly in your garden costs you nothing except the time it takes to snip a stem and stick it in the soil. So any plants that result are pure profit!

If you multiply a single mum by taking 20 cuttings in spring, your wallet will be fatter by at least $60 come fall (20 new plants would cost about $3 each to buy). Shrubs take longer, but the payoffs are bigger: A two-year-old butterfly bush, started from a cutting, would set you back about $10 at a nursery. If your parent plant volunteered a dozen cuttings, you can have a great butterfly bush border for free, instead of for $120!

If you root cuttings in pots or flats, save money on planting medium by buying larger-sized bags of soil-mix ingredients. If you have a willow tree, soak willow twigs in water to make a natural rooting hormone for your cuttings. Willow water is the frugal alternative to expensive rooting compound.

Superlative Savings from Seed

I doubt if there's a gardener among us who hasn't yielded to the temptations of store-bought plants. Sometimes there's just no resisting! But that doesn't mean you can't grow your own to fill at least part of your gardens. The more you grow yourself, the more you'll save. And once you discover how easy it is, you'll be a true convert to the fun and savings of doing it yourself. It takes more time and trouble to grow plants from seed rather than to buy started plants, but the rewards are both financially and personally satisfying. Looking at a garden plant you once knew as a seed gives you a real sense of the everyday miracle of growing things.

Grow Your Own to Save Big Bucks

Growing plants from seed will save you more money than any other frugal trick. A packet of seeds costs about the same as a four-pack of young annuals or veggies at the garden center. With a minimal investment in time, you can have a flowerbedful instead of just four.

Most annuals and vegetables are simple to grow from seed started right in the garden. Perennials and herbs take a little longer to sprout and grow, but they're generally easy enough for even novices to start successfully.

Get More Choices— Grow Plants from Seed

Seed catalogs offer a world of choices compared to the paltry few varieties you'll find at garden center plant tables. Tons of tomato cultivars and a pantry full of hot pepper varieties are just the beginning. This is your opportunity to sample veggies and do your own evaluations of growing habits, disease resistance, and length of time to harvest. Set foot into the world of flowers grown from seed, and you can indulge in all kinds of exotic beauties.

Plants That Sow Themselves: Free Plants for Life!

Frugal gardeners rejoice in self-sowing annuals and perennials because they multiply themselves with no added help. They reproduce by dropping ripe seeds into any bare space around themselves.

Handling Hybrids

Hybrid self-sowing plants produce offspring that may look like they came from a completely different branch of the family tree than its parents. Petunias, pansies, and special cultivars of 'Sensation'-type cosmos, like 'Seashell' with its delightful rolled petals, revert to their wilder-looking origins when they sprout from self-sown seeds. But you'll still have a garden full of beautiful bloom, so just enjoy the surprises.

Thin for Bigger, Bushier Plants

Many self-sowing plants reproduce so prolifically that the self-sown seedlings will choke each other out. If you want to keep the self-seeding process going year after year, be ruthless about thinning out overcrowded plants. Give each seedling space to grow and you'll be rewarded with stronger, better formed plants. You can always pot up the extras for plant sales or friends.

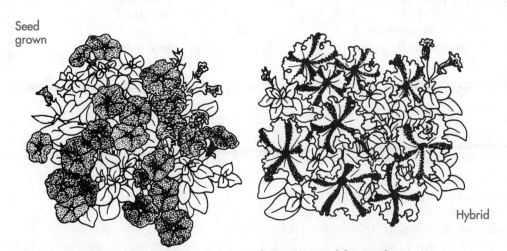

Seed grown

Hybrid

Garden-center petunias revert to their ancestral form when you allow them to self-sow. The graceful plants have smaller, simpler flowers in lovely shades of pink, lavender, and white, plus a delicious fragrance that's commonly lacking in their hybrid parent.

Flowers That Sow Themselves

Self-sowing plants are a real boon in the garden. You get all the flowers you can use without spending any money and without putting forth any effort! They're worth their weight in gold, or at least in store-bought seed packets. Considering that a 20-foot border can easily consume $50 to $200 worth of garden center six-packs of flowers, especially annuals, your savings with self-sowers will make you congratulate yourself for your good sense. Thin the seedlings to the desired thickness, move them around wherever you need them, and use extras to swap with friends for still more free plants.

Annuals

Asters (*Aster* spp.)
Bachelor's button (*Centaurea cyanus*)
Calendula (*Calendula officinalis*)
California poppy (*Eschscholzia californica*)
Chinese forget-me-not (*Cynoglossum amabile*)
Cleome, spiderflower (*Cleome hasslerana*)
Cosmos (*Cosmos bipinnatus, C. sulphureus*)
Dill (*Anethum graveolens*)
Garden balsam (*Impatiens balsamina*)
Larkspur (*Consolida ambigua*)
Love-in-a-mist (*Nigella damascena*)
Mignonette (*Reseda odorata*)
Moss rose (*Portulaca grandiflora*)
Poppies (*Papaver rhoeas, P. somniferum*)
Sunflower (*Helianthus annus*)
Sweet alyssum (*Lobularia maritima*)

Perennials and Biennials

Columbines (*Aquilegia* spp.)
Foxgloves (*Digitalis* spp.)
Hollyhock (*Alcea rosea*)
Lupines (*Lupinus* spp.)
Rudbeckias, black-eyed Susans (*Rudbeckia* spp.)

Saving Your Own Seed

A few minutes' time in the garden will yield hundreds of seeds for planting next season. Plants are super-generous with their seed bounty, so why not take advantage of this to save big next year? If you don't plan to use all the seed yourself, a labeled envelope or two of homegrown seeds makes a great little gift. And saved seeds give you trading power with other gardeners, who may have just the seeds you want in their own collections.

Select for Strong Plants

Save the seeds from your best plants so that future generations are good quality, too. Pick the plants that exhibit the qualities you most want to encourage—maybe

FREE STUFF!

Seed Shakedown

Free seeds are available almost anywhere that plants are growing. Marigold patches outside your favorite restaurant, bachelor's buttons in the field, your neighbor's heirloom columbines—all are great potential candidates for free seed. Always ask gardening friends, neighbors, business owners, or landowners for permission to collect when the time is ripe. Be sure to stress that you'll take only an unobtrusive sample, not strip the plants wholesale.

Avoid stripping every seed from the plants—a quick shake into an envelope will give you plenty, and leave others to sow themselves for next time around.

If you want plants that breed true, look for open-pollinated cultivars (listed in catalogs as "OP") or "heritage" varieties in specialty seed catalogs like those listed in "Resources for Frugal Gardeners" on page 263. Or collect seed from self-sowing plants that have settled into a self-selected steadiness. Keep in mind, though, that the progeny of hybrids can be a delightful surprise!

Labor-Saving Harvesting

Common sense and your own ingenuity are your allies when it comes to developing seed-harvesting methods that work best for you. Consider the structure of the plant and the seedhead when you plan your strategy.

Corral seeds that scatter. In the case of some plants, such as dill, onions, and lettuce, the seeds will drop and scatter as

there's a shell-pink cosmos in the batch that you prefer over its purpler cousins or a corn poppy that's bushier than its brothers. In the case of vegetables, opt for the ones that tasted best and showed the fewest signs of disease or insect damage. Those strong, positive characteristics will be passed along in the genetic makeup of the seeds.

The Hazards of Hybrids

Many cultivars of veggies and flowers are hybrids—carefully bred crosses of two selected parents. In your own garden, seeds you collect from hybrid plants aren't likely to yield offspring that matches the parent.

A stack of little brown lunch bags are an indispensable tool for seed collecting. Slip them over the heads of plants before the seeds drop, tie tightly with twine, and the plant will do the work of dropping the seeds into the bag for you.

soon as they are ripe. Tie small paper bags over the ripening seedheads before the seeds loosen and fall, and you'll catch a bounty.

Get pods to give up their plenty. When you see pods or seed capsules of plants like larkspur and cleome plumping up and beginning to turn from green to tan, snip the stems of pods and let them finish drying in a shallow box or on newspaper until the seeds rattle loosely in the pod or the pod splits open when you touch it. Break open and shake out the pods over a bowl to collect the seeds.

Save the seeds from soft fruits and veggies. To save seeds from wet fruits such as tomatoes and melons, pick the fruit when it is a little overripe. Scoop out the seeds, place them in a glass bowl (so that acid and other compounds from metal or glazes don't react with the fruit juices), and let them sit for one to two days. Then place the seeds in a sieve and wash off the juice and any excess pulp with running water. Dry the seeds on a paper towel. Once dry, the seeds will probably stick firmly to the towel. Roll or fold the towel with the seeds still on, and store it in a resealable plastic bag. When it's time to plant, tear up the towel and plant each seed with its bit of towel, or lay the entire towel, seed side up, on your planting medium and cover with a thin layer of seed-starting mixture. The paper towel will soon disintegrate.

Successful Storage Means Longer Life

Seeds don't last forever, though some come darn close! Radishes, for instance, may lose viability in as little as three years, while bean seeds may sprout a century after storing. Seed life isn't only in the genes, though—the length of time a seed stays useful depends on the way it's stored. Dry and cool are the keys.

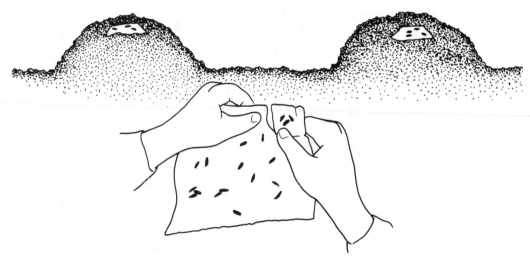

Dry seeds from wet, pulpy fruits and vegetables on paper towels after washing in a sieve or colander. Leave the seeds "glued" to the paper towel when dry, and roll it up for storage until planting time next year—then tear off a piece at a time and plant, paper towel and all.

Dry seed before storing. Dry your collected seeds thoroughly for about a week after harvesting, either outside out of direct sunlight if the relative humidity is low, or indoors. Ideal temperature for drying is between 75° and 100°F—an old-fashioned attic could be ideal! Try putting the seeds under an incandescent lightbulb to reduce the humidity in the surrounding air and to increase the temperature slightly. Do not dry any seeds in the oven; temperatures above 100°F may damage them. Once they are thoroughly dry, store the seeds in a cool place in an airtight container.

Avoid heat and moisture. The two elements that rob a seed of its freshness are heat and damp. According to Dr. J. F. Harrington, seed physiologist emeritus at the University of California, Davis, the life span of a seed can be doubled for every 1 percent drop in seed moisture. A 10°F drop in storage temperature has the same effect. Stored with 14 percent moisture content at 90°F, a batch of onion seeds were all dead in a week. Another batch was dried to 6 percent moisture and stored in a sealed container. After 20 years in storage, these onion seeds germinated.

Airtight containers are the key. Small top-flap envelopes are handy for storing seeds because you can keep them separate and labeled easily, but they are not moisture-proof. If you want to store your seeds in envelopes, put the envelopes into a sealed container such as a resealable plastic bag. Mason jars with new lids and plastic or metal jars or cans with tight-fitting gasketed lids are also good containers for saving seed. Plastic film canisters with their tight-fitting lids work well for storage, too.

'Great Northern' Beans 9/8/98

Condensation inside your seed-storing resealable bags or containers spells trouble. Dump out the seeds and spread them to dry in a warm, low-humidity place to remove the moisture, then repack.

Last step—label! Forget about trusting your memory. Make planting time next year a breeze by labeling your collected seeds with the name of the plant and its cultivar names, if you know it ('Brandywine' tomato, for instance). Also include the date, so you can use up your oldest seed first.

Make Room in the Fridge

Storage temperature is not as crucial to extending a seed's life as thorough drying and a tightly sealed storage container, but it will help extend the shelf life of your seeds. Keep them below 75°F. A cooler spot, such as a dry cellar or the refrigerator, is even better. You can even freeze your seed if you want to keep it a long time. Be aware, however, that frozen seed is fragile; it can become brittle and break easily even with normal handling. Keep your frozen seed in rigid containers—a plastic storage bowl will hold a lot of little envelopes—so it doesn't get damaged as you move items in and out of the freezer, and handle the seed with care when you remove it from storage.

Count Sprouts before Planting

If you are planting older seed and have some doubt about its viability, run a quick germination check before you plant to determine how thickly you should sow. Sprinkle seeds onto several layers of moistened paper towels or newspapers. Roll them up, and keep the paper moist. Keep the rolled-up seed in a warm place. Check every few days to see how many of the seeds have sprouted. If germination is lower than "almost every seed sprouts," plant seeds more thickly when you sow beds or indoor starter pots. If no seed sprouts, or hardly any, it may be worth buying a fresh pack of seeds from the store.

Flowers for Free

Ah, the glories of a garden filled with flowers that didn't cost one red cent! It warms a frugal gardener's heart. Here are some easy growers that will repay your seed-collecting efforts with a summer full of bloom.

Annuals

Ageratums (*Ageratum* spp.)
Asters (*Aster* spp.)
Calendula (*Calendula officinalis*)
California poppies (*Eschscholtzia californica*)
Cleome (*Cleome hasslerana*)
Cosmos (*Cosmos* spp.)
Impatiens (*Impatiens walleriana*)
Larkspurs (*Consolida* cvs.)
Lobelias (*Lobelia* spp.)
Marigolds (*Tagetes* spp.)
Moonflower (*Ipomoea alba*)
Morning glories (*Ipomoea* spp.)
Nasturtium (*Tropaeolum majus*)
Nigellas, love-in-a-mists (*Nigella* spp.)
Petunias (*Petunia* spp.)
Snapdragons (*Antirrhinum* spp.)
Sunflowers (*Helianthus* spp.)
Zinnias (*Zinnia* spp.)

Perennials and Biennials

Asters (*Aster* spp.)
Butterfly weed (*Asclepias tuberosa*)
Columbines (*Aquilegia* spp.)
Coreopsis (*Coreopsis* spp.)
Foxgloves (*Digitalis* spp.)
Hollyhock (*Alcea rosea*)
Honesty (*Lunaria annua*)
Purple coneflower (*Echinacea purpurea*)
Rudbeckias (*Rudbeckia* spp.)
Salvias (*Salvia* spp.)
Sunflowers (*Helianthus* spp.)
Sweet pea (*Lathyrus odoratus*)
Sweet rocket (*Hesperis matronalis*)

FRUGAL GARDENER'S GUIDE

How Long Seed Lasts

You don't have to throw out all your seed packets every year and start fresh. Frugal gardeners save money by using those packets as long as they're good. Here's a guide to how long veggie seeds generally remain viable. Remember, the older the packet, the more thickly you should sow the seed to compensate for decreased viability.

VEGETABLE SEED	USE WITHIN	VEGETABLE SEED	USE WITHIN
Asparagus	3 years	Kohlrabi	3 years
Bean	3 years	Leek	2 years
Beet	4 years	Lettuce	6 years
Broccoli	3 years	Muskmelon	5 years
Brussels sprouts	4 years	Mustard	4 years
Cabbage	4 years	Okra	2 years
Carrot	3 years	Onion	1 year
Cauliflower	4 years	Parsley	1 year
Celeriac	3 years	Parsnip	1 year
Celery	3 years	Pea	3 years
Chervil	3 years	Pepper	2 years
Chicory	4 years	Pumpkin	4 years
Chinese cabbage	3 years	Radish	5 years
Ciboule	2 years	Rutabaga	4 years
Collard	5 years	Salsify	1 year
Corn	2 years	Sorrel	4 years
Cucumber	5 years	Spinach	3 years
Dandelion	2 years	Squash	4 years
Eggplant	4 years	Swiss chard	4 years
Endive	5 years	Tomato	4 years
Fennel	4 years	Turnip	4 years
Garden cress	5 years	Watercress	5 years
Kale	4 years	Watermelon	4 years

FRUGAL GARDENER'S GUIDE

Seed Savings

Saving seed costs you nothing but a little time. If you planted store-bought seed packets for just five common flowers and one vegetable, you'd spend at least $8 (and as much as $15) on seed alone. If you planted store-bought plants, the difference is staggering: $40 to $93 for plants, depending on what bargains you got, compared to a nice round zero dollars, zero cents, for saved seeds. A glance at the chart shows you how fast the savings from saving your own seed can add up.

PLANT	NUMBER PLANTED FROM SAVED SEED	PRICE PER STORE-BOUGHT SEED PACKET	SAVINGS OVER SEED PACKET PRICES	PRICE PER STORE-BOUGHT PLANT	SAVINGS OVER PLANT PRICES
Marigolds	20	$1–$2	$1–$2	50¢–$1	$10–$20
Purple coneflower	6	$2–$3	$2–$3	$2–$5	$12–$30
Sunflowers	10	$1–$2	$1–$2	—	—
Hollyhock	6	$1–$3	$1–$3	$2–$5	$12–$30
Calendula	10	$1–$2	$1–$2	50¢–$1	$5–$10
Cherry tomatoes	3	$2–$3	$2–$3	50¢–$1	$1.50–$3
TOTAL SAVINGS	—	—	$8–$15	—	$40.50–$93

Sow Seeds Outdoors for Maximum Ease

What could be easier than sprinkling seed directly onto soil? Take advantage of plants that thrive when sown directly into the garden, and you'll save yourself the time and effort it would take to nurture seedlings indoors or under cover—as well as the cost of the added equipment you would need.

Take the Temperature of Your Garden

If you plan to grow a lot of seeds outdoors, invest in a soil thermometer. Rushing the season is something we all try to do, but it can be risky when planting seeds. If your seeds need warm soil to germinate and you plant them too early in the season, you risk losing them. Because soil temperature does not fluctuate as rapidly as air temperature, you cannot determine the

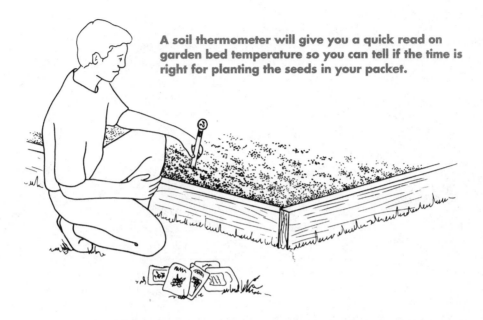

A soil thermometer will give you a quick read on garden bed temperature so you can tell if the time is right for planting the seeds in your packet.

warmth in the soil by the air temperature. Soil temperatures can vary throughout the garden because of microclimates. If you are sowing outdoors early in the spring, check the soil temperature of each bed.

Better Beds Mean Better Growth

Before you plant seeds outdoors, prepare a welcoming home for your new plants-to-be. Dig in organic amendments such as compost to make the soil loose and moisture retentive. Rake the soil with a short-tined tool to break up any clods and remove any rocks that surface. Avoid walking on the bed so your footsteps don't compact your carefully prepared soil. When seeds have soil of good tilth and fertility in which to spread their roots, they'll reward you with fast, vigorous growth.

Water Works Magic

Moisture is what makes seeds sprout, so keep your seedbed sprayed. Once the seeds are planted, sprinkle the bed with enough water to thoroughly moisten the soil around each seed, but not so much that the water dislodges the seed. A slow, gentle spray is most effective.

Once seeds are planted and watered, they will die if they are allowed to dry out before they germinate. Unless Mother Nature sends rain to do the job for you, you'll need to water them daily to keep the seed moist and growing. In very hot, dry weather you may have to water twice a day, in the morning and afternoon. You can cut back on the watering as the seedlings develop more extensive root systems.

Spray wands that deliver a fine mist are inexpensive (about $10 at discount stores) and earn their keep in a hurry, thanks to their ease of use. They allow you to water efficiently by delivering a generous dose of water without washing seeds out of the soil.

Perennials from Seed

Starting perennials from seed can be as simple as growing annuals, if you start with easy growers. "Anything from the Composite family—daisies, rudbeckias, coreopsis—will germinate," says Betty Mackey, a garden writer who works and gardens in Wayne, Pennsylvania. "Yarrow and asters are easy enough. The hardy hibiscus, such as 'Lord Baltimore' and 'Disco Belle', are simple from seed. Plant them as you would plant corn. They really come up, and they're showy, hardy perennials." She also suggests growing hollyhocks, columbine, and foxglove from seed.

Perennials take a little longer to germinate than fast-sprouting annuals, and they're slower to acquire size, so many gardeners like to start them in pots or flats, where they're protected from competition with weeds until they reach transplantable size.

Start an Indoor Greenhouse for Pennies

In cold climates, you can get a jump on the season by getting seedlings well established by the time the soil is warm enough to plant them outdoors.

Vegetables to Sow Outdoors

Quick growth and a fast crop are what you'll get from these veggies, which are all simple to start from seed sown directly in your garden patch.

Beans, bush
Beans, pole
Beets
Carrots
Collards
Corn
Cucumber (except where the season lasts less than 90 days)
Endive
Kale
Kohlrabi
Mustard greens

Parsnips
Peas
Potatoes
Radishes
Spinach
Swiss chard
Squash, summer (except where the season lasts less than 90 days)
Squash, winter (except where the season lasts less than 90 days)
Turnips

This advance planning is especially important for warm-season vegetable and herb crops such as tomatoes, melons, peppers, basil, and cilantro. Starting perennial seeds indoors lets you give them a controlled environment and special care to help guarantee their success in your garden.

Thrifty Seed-Starting Containers

Purchased pots pay off in convenience, but if you're looking to cut costs, take a lesson from recyclers and look around to see what containers you can reinvent as seed starters. Yogurt cups, cottage cheese containers, take-out containers from fast-food restaurants, grocery store salad bars, or cell packs you've saved from the nursery last year

all work great and cost absolutely nothing. Paper cupcake liners make excellent inexpensive miniature pots, and the best part is you can plant them directly into the ground, since the thin paper will deteriorate quickly.

Do you have that in a size 8? Lyn Belisle of San Antonio, Texas, sows seeds in a cardboard shoebox lined with aluminum foil with the shiny side up. For drainage, she pokes holes through the bottom of the box and foil. Then she fills the box halfway with soil and plants her seeds. The foil in the top half of the box magnifies the heat and light, speeding up germination and improving early growth. This system is particularly useful for heat-loving plants such as basil, tomatoes, and peppers.

COST CUTTERS

Best Buy: Fluorescent Shop Lights

Incandescent lights can get too hot and don't generate the ultraviolet light required by plants, and "grow lights" can be pricey. The frugal gardener turns to fluorescents!

Shop lights cost only $5 to $10 a fixture, bulbs included. Hang the lights from chains so you can move them up as your plants grow. Position the lights about 12 inches from the top of the plants.

Plant Trays Save Time and Effort

Seed-starting trays with plastic lids make it easy to sow an indoor garden. Look for them at garden centers and in catalogs. If you allow about 1½ square inches per seedling, each 10 × 20-inch tray will hold 98 plants.

Make Your Own Medium

Your garden soil may be top-notch, but turn to a soilless mix when you're ready to start seeds. No matter how good your soil looks, it can harbor organisms that put seedlings at risk. Bagged seed-starting mixes are easy to find, but you can pinch pennies by making your own.

1. Combine equal parts of milled peat moss and horticultural grade (fine) vermiculite. Wear a disposable face mask to avoid breathing in the fine particles.

2. Add hot water to the medium until it is moist enough to stick together, but not dripping wet. (The hot water keeps seeds warm.)

3. Fill your flats or containers to within about ¼ inch from the top, and then plant your seeds, following the directions on the packet for depth and spacing.

It's the Heat—And the Humidity!

Seeds germinate best in a warm, humid environment. To maintain humidity, cover your containers with clear plastic to create a minigreenhouse. To avoid letting seeds dry out, use yogurt cups with clear plastic lids, or any handy container that will hold moisture and keep those seeds fresh. Or a clear plastic bag or kitchen plastic wrap will do the trick. Air out your tabletop greenhouse if it fogs up inside by briefly opening the plastic, then resealing it before the soil can dry.

Recycle the plastic cup—and lid!—from your lunchtime yogurt into a perfectly sized seed-starting pot. Punch a few drainage holes in the bottom before filling with soil mix. Use the lid to maintain humidity after sowing; when seeds sprout, open the cup to let in fresh air.

Turn Home Appliances into Heaters

Most seeds need warm soil—ideally no less than 65°F—in order to sprout. If the interior of your home tends to be cooler than this, especially at night, look for another heat source. You can buy a heating pad for plants, but why bother when you have warm spots you can put to use for free? The top of the refrigerator, water heater, or clothes dryer will add that cozy touch your seeds crave.

Plan Ahead to Prevent Problems

Once your plants are up and growing, they need light and air to keep them healthy. Plan ahead so you can shop around for good prices on growth-boosting lights.

Fresh air at the first sign of green. Fresh air costs nothing, but to supply it at the right time means you'll need to keep a close eye on your indoor garden. Once the seeds germinate, remove the plastic covering to allow air to circulate; otherwise, you are likely to lose your entire collection of babies to a complex of fungi known as damping-off.

The more light, the better. At this point, your seedlings need a lot of light—at least 12 hours a day. Otherwise, they are liable to get thin and leggy. If you have a good sunny window, you can use that, but make sure to rotate your plants about every four days so they get even exposure to light. If you don't have a south-facing sunporch or

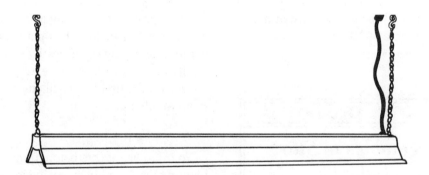

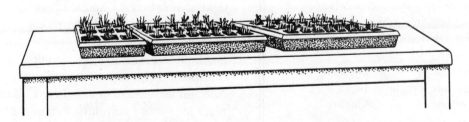

Inexpensive "shop light" fluorescent fixtures supply much-needed light to growing seedlings in an indoor garden. Fasten the lights to chains held by hooks so they're easy to raise one gradual step at a time as the plants grow.

windows to supply abundant natural light, give your plants the light they need with fluorescent bulbs or grow lights in shop-light fixtures.

Regular food and water. To keep the soil moist without damaging the fragile seedlings, mist plants daily. Or set your seed tray on top of several layers of wet newspaper, which will act as a capillary mat with water being absorbed through the drainage holes in the bottom of the container. Once every two weeks, feed your seedlings with a weak mixture of water-soluble organic fertilizer.

Compost tea can be a lifesaver for seedlings, too, since it can prevent the dreaded fungal disease damping-off from getting a foothold. Spray the tea on your plants and the soil weekly, and you may never see a seedling topple over from the base.

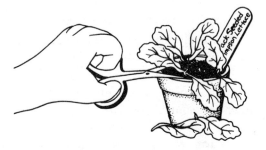

Special seedling snippers—a.k.a. manicure scissors—are a frugal gardener's friend when it's time to remove extra plants from overplanted containers. Let the sturdiest seedlings stay, and weed out the puny ones.

Maneuverable Tools from the Medicine Chest

Too many plants in a pot? Give your seedlings breathing room by snipping off extras at ground level. Manicure scissors will let you wiggle into the tight spots without damaging other nearby seedlings. Or, if you want to repot the extras, lift them with the tip of a pencil and move them to other containers.

Welcome to the Real World

Your last act of care before transplanting your seedlings outside is to prepare them for the transition from their protected environment to the brighter light, strong breezes, and temperature shifts of the outdoors. This process is known as hardening off.

About two weeks before you plan to transplant them, take your seedlings outside and leave them in a sheltered, shaded place for about four hours. Repeat the process daily, increasing the time by 30 minutes each day and gradually increasing the light exposure (unless they're plants for shade!).

Vegetables to Start Indoors

Get a jump on the season by having transplants ready to go when planting time is nigh. These veggies are easy to start indoors.

Broccoli	Eggplant
Brussels sprouts	Leeks
Cabbage	Onions
Cauliflower	Peppers
Celeriac	Tomatoes
Celery	

Annuals to Start Indoors

Some annuals take longer than others to reach blooming size, so it makes sense to give them a head start indoors.

Ageratum (*Ageratum houstonianum*)
Bells of Ireland (*Moluccella laevis*)
Brachycome (*Brachycome iberidifolia*)
Browallia (*Browallia speciosa*)
Carnation (*Dianthus caryophyllus*)
Chinese forget-me-not (*Cynoglossum amabile*)
Chrysanthemum, painted daisy (*Chrysan-themum carinatum*)
Dusty miller (*Centaurea cineraria*)
Zonal geraniums (*Pelargonium* × *hortorum*)
Heliotrope (*Heliotropium arborescens*)
Impatiens (*Impatiens wallerana*)
Lobelia (*Lobelia erinus*)

Mimulus (*Mimulus hybridus*)
Nemesia (*Nemesia strumosa*)
Nicotiana (*Nicotiana alata*)
Nierembergia (*Nierembergia hippomanica*)
Petunias (*Petunia* cvs.)
Portulaca (*Portulaca grandiflora*)
Salvias (*Salvia* spp.)
Snapdragon (*Antirrhinum majus*)
Statice (*Limonium sinuatum*)
Stock (*Matthiola incana*)
Wallflowers (*Cheiranthus* spp.)

Budget-Wise Bulbs

Spring-blooming bulbs, the glory of the early season garden, are something not even the most frugal gardener wants to do without. As usual, there are tricks to trim costs!

Boost Bulb Power by Planting in Groups

A dozen daffodils sprinkled through the garden one by one announce "I can't afford more than this!" to the world. In-stead of parceling out your precious bulbs, do just the opposite: Make a statement by planting them in one, two, or three generous clumps of at least five bulbs each for large bulbs like tulips and daffodils and eight or more for small bulbs like grape hyacinths and crocus. Clumped together, they'll draw more attention and look better, too—as if you had intended them to be centerpieces. Fill in with groundcovers or other foliage plants such as hostas so the soil won't be bare, or add a bark-chip mulch.

If your budget for bulbs is tight, make the most of what you can afford by planting in groups to maximize impact. A single, eye-catching clump of five to eight daffodils is worth its weight in gold in the spring landscape, so position it carefully beside a rock or tree to add even more impact.

Join Forces for Best Prices

Pare costs of spring-blooming bulbs by buying in large quantities for lowest prices. If you can't use that many bulbs yourself, join with bulb-loving friends or family to order bulbs at wholesale prices from suppliers like those listed in "Resources for Frugal Gardeners" on page 263. The price per bulb when you buy by the hundred can be half of what you'd pay when you buy only a half dozen to a dozen at a time! Pool your buying power and buy as large a quantity as you can. Then have a bulb-distributing party, with each buyer supplying their own bags and making their own labels as bulbs are divvied up.

Choose Bulbs That Multiply

Many bulbs multiply naturally, slowly producing offsets or even sowing themselves to make more flowers. Although you won't see drastic changes in the number of blooms from one year to the next, the process will make a big difference over the course of several years or a lifetime. Take advantage of this tendency, and save money on your bulb bill over the years.

Daffodils, crocuses, snowdrops, and many other spring bloomers form ever-widening clumps to savor or divide. In fact, they'll benefit from occasional dividing. For more choices, see "Bulbs That Add Up" on the opposite page.

Bulbs That Add Up

Brent Heath, co-owner of Brent and Becky's Bulbs in Gloucester, Virginia, recommends the following varieties (plus many more not listed here) to multiply and spread over the years, adding to the bounty of your display as time passes.

Crocus chrysanthus
Crocuses (*Crocus* spp.)
Daffodils: 'Honeybird', 'Carlton', 'Flower Record', 'Ice Follies', 'Pink Pride'
Daffodils, double: 'Cheerfulness', 'Erlicheer', 'Flower Drift'
Daffodils, miniature: 'Baby Moon', 'Minnow', 'Mite', 'Tete a Tete'
Giant spring crocus (*Crocus vernus*)
Glory-of-the-snows (*Chionodoxa* spp.)

Grape hyacinths (*Muscari* spp.)
Star-of-Bethlehems (*Ornithogalum* spp.)
Snowdrop (*Galanthus nivalis*)
Snowflakes (*Leucojum* spp.)
Spanish bluebells (*Hyacinthoides hispanica*, formerly *Scilla campanulata*; *Endymion hispanicus*)
Spring star flowers (*Ipheion* spp.)
Windflower (*Anemone blanda*)
Winter aconites (*Eranthis* spp.)

Bulb Care for Years of Beauty

Even the tidiest of us frugal gardeners tolerate fading bulb foliage because we know it means more flowers next year. During the time the foliage is yellowing and gradually dying back, nutrients from the leaves are returning to the bulb to be stored for the following year. So whatever you do, don't cut it back.

Get Rid of the Rubber Bands!

Avoid constricting your bulb investment by tying up fading foliage into little packets held by rubber bands. That procedure has the same result as cutting off the leaves because they can't get the air and light they need. Instead, interplant your bulbs with hostas, daylilies (one per five daffodil bulbs), Russian sage (*Perovskia atriplicifolia*), baby's breath (*Gypsophila paniculata*), yarrow (*Achillea* spp.), and other perennials that emerge in late spring. As the perennials leaf out, they will distract attention from or completely hide the fading leaves and add another season of interest to your garden.

A Hearty Meal at Just the Right Time

Boost the productivity of your bulbs by fertilizing them in the fall when their roots start growing. Choose an organic fertilizer especially formulated for bulbs or a slow-release organic fertilizer.

No Animals Allowed!

Daffodils won't be bothered by nibbling animals because they contain toxins that make them unpalatable or even poisonous to hungry rodents (the name *narcissus* comes from the same root as narcotic). But many other bulbs are a feast to voles, moles, mice, and squirrels. Try throwing a handful of sharp gravel into the planting hole with each bulb. The burrowing animals won't want to scratch their noses.

Squirrels seem to be partial to crocuses. Given a chance, they will consume hundreds of bulbs in one season, decimating an entire collection. Avoid the problem by choosing varieties that are less tasty to them. According to Brent Heath (see "Bulbs That Add Up" on page 87), *Crocus tommasinianus* and *C. t.* 'Barr's Purple' are both squirrel resistant.

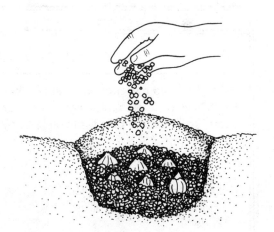

A handful of sharp gravel at planting time will help discourage foraging varmints from feasting on your finest bulbs.

Plant Tulips That Return Reliably

Most of the modern hybrid tulips give only one or two good years of bloom. Frugal gardeners bypass the new but fleeting varieties and depend on more reliable tulips that come back in strength for three to five years, or more. Foster tulips, such as 'Red Emperor', are old reliables.

Many Darwin tulips and lily-flowered tulips also return year after year. Species or botanical tulips are the best repeat performers in all but the most southern climate zones. Look for *Tulipa fosteriana, T. greigii, T. kaufmanniana, T. pulchella , T. bakeri, T. batalinii, T. praestans*, and *T. turkestanica*. In mild climates where the bulbs won't get a winter chill, try *T. clusiana* 'Candy Stick' or 'Lady Tulip' with 12-inch stems topped by red- and white-striped blossoms.

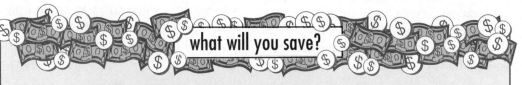

what will you save?

Bulbs by the Dozen Bring Big Savings

Buying bulbs in bulk can yield dramatic savings. Instead of a dozen daffodil bulbs for $6, the going rate at many nurseries and garden centers, you may get 100 daffs for as little as $30. That's 30¢ a bulb instead of 50¢ each—a savings that really adds up when you plant bulbs by the dozen!

Plant Swaps, Exchanges, and Sales

One of the biggest joys of frugal gardening is giving away plants and seeds from your garden and receiving plants from other gardeners. Getting new plants is always fun, especially when you can trade some of your own for them. And you'll remember special people and places when you see those plants growing in your garden.

Share the Bounty

Ross Melcher, a retired army colonel and school teacher in Redlands, California, had hundreds of bearded iris. One of his pleasures was to take friends through the garden in spring when the plants put on their spectacular display of floral color. The Melchers loved to share. Visitors were encouraged to note down the flowers they liked best (each plant was labeled with its cultivar name). In the fall, when it was time to divide the iris, Ross would give his friends divisions that they had requested the previous spring.

Plants that divide readily, especially those that multiply quickly, are ideal candidates for sharing with friends.

Pass Along Plants and Seeds

Gardeners count their wealth in many ways besides dollars. Seed collecting and sharing is a special way to share your garden with others, especially if your friends and family live out of town.

Alicia Klaffky, an artist living in Kensington, Maryland, has a beautiful stand of cleome, also known as spider-flower, an annual that typically blooms in white, pink, deep rose, and purple. Alice's collection is all purple. When their seeds ripen, she collects them to share with her friends, who simply have to scatter the seeds over a fertile bed where they want cleome to grow the following spring. The self-sowing plants continue the planting year after year.

Passing out cuttings or divisions from your prized perennials are other ways to share a bit of your garden with friends and relations. See the list of perennials that root well from cuttings on page 67.

It's a Party!

Plant swaps and parties are a fun way to share plants with friends. Have a spring gathering where everyone brings a plant and takes a plant. Plants from your garden also make wonderful hostess gifts that will be remembered much longer than a plate of brownies.

Plant samples are great for house-warming gifts, too. They're especially welcome when someone has just moved into a newly built house where landscaping is minimal. Either pot up some perennial divisions and wrap the pot in pretty foil, or cut a bouquet of annuals and attach a packet of seeds that you saved so that the new homeowners can plant them for their own bounty of beautiful flowers.

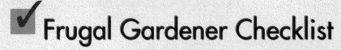

✔ Frugal Gardener Checklist

■ Save money with math by figuring the minimum number of plants you need—before you shop!

■ Substitute some less expensive shrubs for the higher-priced specialties.

■ Get comfortable with cuttings—they're easier to start than you think!

■ Invest in one or two special, hard-to-find plants, and then create more of them by rooting cuttings or dividing the original plant.

■ Start perennials and biennials from seed every year to have a continual fresh supply of new and different plants.

■ Visit your nursery or garden center in late winter or early spring to get the best selection and freshest stock of minimally priced bareroot trees, shrubs, fruit plants, and perennials.

■ Buy perennials that are big enough to be divided immediately.

■ Save money on "annuals" by overwintering tender perennials indoors.

■ Near the end of the growing season, save seed from your favorite flowering annuals, and sow it the following spring.

■ Plant bulb varieties that multiply and spread each successive year.

Snip 12-inch pieces from your butterfly bushes (*Buddleia davidii*) while growth is young and flexible. Stick them in moist soil to root, and you'll have a whole hedge of flutterby magnets in just one or two years. While you're at it, why not add a row of 'Moonbeam' coreopsis (*Coreopsis verticillata* 'Moonbeam') in front, started from 4-inch cuttings?

CHAPTER THREE

THE FRUGAL GARDENER'S TOOLS

TOOLS LEVERAGE YOUR LABOR, making it possible for you to achieve the results you want in less time and with less effort. Save money on tools by being a wise shopper, but avoid making the mistake of buying cheap, low-quality tools—making do with a poorly made tool that's frustrating to use is no bargain. Tools that make the job easier will pay for themselves again and again. And they won't break in the middle of a job.

Good-quality tools are expensive, so you'll want them to last as long as possible. Look after your tools to keep them in good shape, keeping blades sharp, wood handles oiled, and moving parts in good working order. See "Keep Your Tools Working Longer" on page 114 for more detail.

Avoid impulse purchases. Wait until you have a real need for a specialized tool before you go out and buy it. If you need an expensive tool such as a shredder or rotary tiller only rarely, it may be thriftier to rent it.

91

Tooling Up the Frugal Way

For frugal gardeners, tools present two temptations: to save money by purchasing cheap tools is well nigh irresistible. And, on the opposite end of the spectrum, it's hard for even frugal gardeners to resist the use of power tools. But a cheap tool is no bargain if it bends, breaks, or dulls after a few uses. And to buy a power tool if you don't really need it is a waste of your hard-earned money.

Try It On for Size

Before you buy a tool, make sure it fits. Handle it to make sure it's a good size for you. Check your grip on the handle and imagine yourself using it for an hour or longer. Is the handle smooth and easy to grasp? Hand tools like trowels sometimes have ridges on their handles for a better grip, but they can become annoying with prolonged use. Think about the weight of the tool, too, and heft it a few times as you would in the garden to make sure it's neither too heavy nor too light. If you're short in stature or have small hands, you may find that tools scaled for children are more comfortable than full-size tools.

Muscle Power Saves Money

If your garden is small, hand tools are a better choice than gas- or electric-powered equipment. They cost less to buy and maintain, and they take a fraction of the storage space. You'll save time, too, because small jobs are usually quicker to do by hand than machine. You can cultivate a small veggie patch with a hoe in just about the time it would take to haul out a tiller, check the gas and oil, and start it up.

Tools for 3 Essential Garden Jobs

A few basic tools are all you need to adequately perform the three essential jobs in your garden: planting, pruning, and general maintenance. Armed with these basics, you can begin.

Over time, especially if you garden a lot, you'll probably want to add to your basic collection. Follow the frugal ap-proach and hold off on spending money on more tools until you know whether you will really use them.

Watch out for tempting toys. The garden world is full of gadgets and gizmos designed to do specialized jobs in the garden—or simply to garner a slice of the multimillion-dollar garden industry. Some items touted as valuable tools may be merely expensive toys or useless contraptions, offering no improvement at all on the tools you already own. Other newfangled or unfamiliar tools, though, can be real time-savers when it comes to gardening. Before you buy, think about how you'll use the tool and how often. Then you can decide whether it's a smart addition to your collection.

Tools for Planting

The basic tools for planting are a trowel for down-on-your-knees hand-planting and a shovel for digging holes and moving plants. If you have heavy, dense, or rocky soil, you'll also want to add a pick or mattock; the narrow, heavy-duty blades of these tools make it easier to break through hard clods and pry out stones.

The Best Trowel Money Can Buy

Durability and comfort are the top two criteria for any tool, and they're especially important when you're choosing tools that you'll be using intensively. Poorly made trowels, constructed of thin metal with a flimsy handle joint, bend at the tip and at the joint between the blade and the handle. Once that happens, the tool is virtually useless. Even if you manage to bend the blade back into shape, the fatigued metal will quickly bend again the next time it is put to work.

Bare-Bones Basics

If you're just beginning your gardening life, start your tool collection by investing in the no-frills minimum—five tools that will allow you to plant your garden, keep it tidy, and move soil amendments and mulch around with ease. These tools are all you need for your basic collection:

- **Short-handled trowel:** for setting small plants in place, transplanting seedlings, loosening soil in small areas, and filling containers.

- **Shovel or spade:** for digging planting holes and transplanting perennials, herbs, and shrubs.

- **Leaf rake:** for keeping beds and lawn tidy.

- **Hoe:** for slicing off weeds, chopping soil into finer particles, making planting furrows and shallow holes.

- **Garden fork:** for moving mulch and leaves and turning compost.

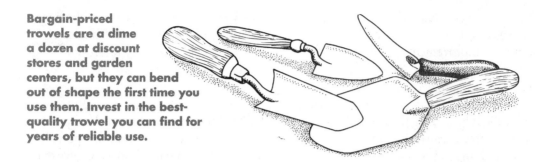

Bargain-priced trowels are a dime a dozen at discount stores and garden centers, but they can bend out of shape the first time you use them. Invest in the best-quality trowel you can find for years of reliable use.

Top quality for a ten spot. Terrific trowels can be yours for about $10—an investment that will last for decades of everyday gardening. The most durable trowels are made of a single piece of strong metal, usually cast aluminum or stainless steel. The handle is formed from the same piece of metal. It may be bare metal or have a plastic or vinyl handle applied over the metal shank.

How does it feel? You'll spend many hours digging and planting with a trowel, so before you buy, grab the handle firmly and make thrusting motions to make sure the trowel feels comfortable in your hand. If your grip or arm strength is limited, look for trowels with specially curved handles that increase leverage by their design instead of with your muscle power. Be alert, too, for protruding bumps on the handle that could cause blisters. The handle of a hand tool should feel comfy as soon as you grip it.

Getting the Shaft

A frugal gardener is a wise gardener—always thinking how to pinch pennies and make work easier. Replacing the handles of shovels or other garden tools is a chore we'd rather live without, so stave it off by selecting a shaft with as much consideration as you select a blade.

- Wood handles are the standard in garden tools. They're tough and hold up for years unless you abuse them by using your shovel as a crowbar.

- Metal handles are sturdy but generally heavier than wood, and they can be mighty chilly to get a grip on when it's cold outside.

- Plastic-covered metal or wood handles are another option. They're strong, but they are colder than wood alone. Since early spring and fall are prime digging times, you may want to hold out for plain old wood if you live in a cold climate.

Digging for the Right Spade...
or Shovel

Whether you use a shovel or a spade, one of these digging tools is essential in every garden. Although you'll find dozens of shovel and spade sizes and blade shapes in catalogs and at garden centers, many gardeners get by with a single, all-purpose basic shovel with a rounded point and a long handle. You'll use it for digging holes, moving soil, shoveling compost, and performing other everyday garden activities. Look for a shovel blade with a turned-over edge along the top so that you can step on it more comfortably.

Keep nonstick coatings in the kitchen. Most shovel blades are made of carbon steel, which stays fairly rust-free with frequent use and an occasional oiling. Some manufacturers offer nonstick blades, coated with a synthetic covering that makes soil slide right off. Because soil slides off a noncoated shovel easily anyway and because the coating wears away with the abrasion of frequent use (just like that frying pan on your stove), it's best to stick to a basic blade and keep the nonstick coatings in the kitchen.

Size matters. Handling a shovel with ease as you sling soil and move compost is all a matter of finding the right balance. If you're shorter than 5 feet, 6 inches, try out a short-handled shovel; it may be a better fit. Garden centers typically stock just two lengths of shovel handles—long and short—but catalogs and tool specialists stock various heights. If the standard long-handled shovel is too much for you to, well, handle, you can buy a shorter version or downsize your own as described at right.

The Frugal Gardener's Workshop:
Downsize for a Perfect Fit

A TOOL HANDLE that's the perfect length for your reach is a joy to use in the garden. A few tool dealers sell tools with a range of handle lengths other than the standard long and short, but such custom sizes can be costly. Save dollars by downsizing standard-issue, long-handled tools to fit.

Materials and Tools

Shovel or other long-handled tool

Saw

Wood file

Sandpaper, coarse and fine grit

Linseed oil

Directions

1. Mark the excess length to be removed.

2. Clamp the handle in a vise and saw off the tip at the mark.

3. Use the file to round the head of the handle.

4. Sand with coarse-grit sandpaper, then with fine-grit paper, until the handle is smooth.

5. Use an old rag to wipe down your customized handle with linseed oil. The oil will seal the wood so it can't get wet, swell, and crack with use.

Spades for Special Needs

Adding a short-handled, square-bladed spade to your repertoire will make it easier to dig flat-sided ditches and cut neat edges to beds or along walkways. You may also find a short-handled spade more convenient for moving loose soil.

In times gone by, when royalty had gardens that common folk could only lust after, a snitch in time was sometimes the name of the game. Armed with a narrow-bladed "poacher's spade," plant thieves could lift a treasured specimen without disturbing its herbaceous neighbors. This tool is just as valuable today for moving plants into and out of crowded beds without wreaking havoc on nearby plants.

A narrow poacher's spade slips easily between plants in a dense border, letting you zero in on perennials for transplanting without harming the roots or branches of neighboring plants.

Hack with a Mattock

It's easy to snap the handle of a shovel or spade when you're working in heavy or rocky soil, if you give in to the temptation to lever out a stubborn stone. Raised beds are a practical way to get around these problem soils, but if you're planting shrubs or trees, you'll most likely be digging in unimproved areas, where the soil may be hard-packed or rocky. Instead of using your shovel for this work, switch to a pick or mattock to make digging planting holes less of a chore. These narrow-headed chopping tools have blades as strong as a chisel. Use them to hack through hard-as-a-rock soil and to chop chunks of soil into smaller pieces, which you can then mix with compost, aged manure, or other soil amendments to improve growing conditions. In rocky soil, these tools slide between the stones as you dig instead of getting stopped in their tracks by obstructions the way a wide-bladed spade or shovel would. You can also use their hefty heads to pry reluctant rocks out of the soil. Keep a shovel or spade handy so that you can scoop out loose soil as you dig the hole.

Tools for Pruning

Pruning keeps plants healthy and vigorous—words that are dear to a thrifty gardener's heart. No time or money spent replacing plants, fewer pest and disease problems, and better bloom are just a few benefits of good pruning.

A top-quality pair of hand pruners goes a long way when it comes to most garden pruning duties. A quick squeeze of the blades takes care of just about all lightweight pruning. You'll be able to snip off

If your soil grows a great crop of rocks, save your shovel's neck by using a narrow-bladed, heavy-duty pick or mattock to chop out a hole and pry out stubborn stones as you dig. Keep your shovel at hand, though, for fast removal of loosened soil and stones from the hole.

spent flowers, cut back dead plants, keep roses tidy, thin out flowering shrubs, prune grapes for the new season, and slice through branches about as thick as your finger. For heavier jobs, add a pair of long-handled pruners (loppers) and a handsaw for removing thicker branches. Complete your pruning kit with hedge shears if you like the formal look.

Divide That Price Tag
by 20 Years' Use

Buy the best hand pruners, loppers, and shears you can afford. Forty dollars may seem extravagant for a pair of hand pruners, but you'll pat yourself on the

back for your good investment every time you use the smooth-working, easy-operating tool. You'll use hand pruners more than any other pruning tool; a quality pair can last for decades. A $40 pair of pruners that lasts 20 years winds up costing only $2 a year; a $10 pair of discount-store pruners will dull and loosen after only one or two years.

Go for comfort. Loppers and shears may have wood or Fiberglas handles. Both are durable, but Fiberglas is lighter, an important factor since you'll often be using these tools with your arms raised. Wood handles take more maintenance, too, to keep them smooth and splinter-free.

Fix it yourself. Top-of-the-line manufacturers, such as Felco, sell replacement parts for their pruners, so if a spring breaks or a blade is damaged beyond repair, you can fix it yourself for a fraction of the cost of a new pair.

Garish Is Good

Elegant dark green handles may look good on a pair of pruners, but you can bet they'll have a much shorter useful life. That's not because their quality is low, but because that pretty hunter green becomes invisible as soon as you set the tool down against some greenery. Even the best of us will doubtless set our pruners down and walk off when we're distracted by kids, the phone, or delivery people. Those lovely green handles disappear in a flash when they're forgotten in the garden. By

the time you find them, it'll probably be winter, and the blades will be rusted beyond reclamation. Bright orange, on the other hand, is such an unnatural color that it sticks out like a spotlight in any season, making it easy to find a pair of misplaced pruners.

Shear Time-Savers

Frugal gardeners are always looking for ways to shave time off maintenance chores. Here's where refining your tool collection comes in handy. If you have more than a few stems to snip off in the garden, you may want to add a pair of garden shears to your repertoire. The advantage of shears over loppers or other pruners is that the blades are longer, so you can slice through many stems with a single stroke. Use shears to neaten lawn edges, snip off straggler weeds around tree trunks, and keep shrubs in line.

To shear or not to shear. There's no law that says you have to shear your yews into flat-topped boxes or round your boxwood into perfect spheres. Letting your shrubs and hedges grow to their natural form is the most frugal approach—then you spend no time clipping bushes into shape and need no shearing tools at all.

Keep your hand pruners in easy grabbing range with a belt holster so you can do a little pruning every time you stroll your garden. You'll find the chore requires just a fast snip here and there instead of a whole afternoon dedicated to the job.

Pruner Practicalities

- Hand pruners may use an anvil action, with the blade striking a plate, or a scissors action, with the blades slicing past one another to make the cut. Both work well, so choose whichever you prefer.

- Avoid pruners with a serrated blade. Smooth-edged blades are easier to sharpen and produce cleaner cuts than those with a bread-knife edge.

- Make sure the handles on hand pruners are comfortable for your grip. Well-stocked garden centers, catalogs, and other suppliers offer sizes to fit the diminutive grasp as well as medium- and large-sized versions. You can also find pruners for left-handed users.

- When you buy your pruners, spend a few more dollars for a whetstone, an abrasive block for sharpening pruner blades (and other tools). Just slide it over the blade edges to keep them ready for action.

- A leather holster for hand pruners is a practical accessory: It keeps them in easy reach at your hip for on-the-spot maintenance every time you stroll your garden.

But if you like a more formal look, you'll need hedge shears to keep your hedge or specimen shrubs in shape.

Match shears to the job. Shears that you hold in one hand and operate by squeezing the handles are lightweights, great for neatening grassy edges around rock walls or other places where a tidy crew cut is necessary. They can't handle anything tougher than grass or very soft-stemmed weeds, though.

For trimming shrubs or perennials, turn to standard shears, which have sturdy blades and handles. Most shears have a notch in one blade so that you can corral a thick, tough stem and snip it off easily. You can buy standard garden shears in lightweight to heavy-duty models, depending on the task at hand. If you're

slicing off green stems that formed this year, such as the new growth on a privet hedge, lightweight models will do the trick. Thicker, woody stems from an established shrub need more power.

Know your limits. Hedge shears come in three varieties: hand powered, gas powered, or electric powered. If pinching pennies is your only motivation, hand clippers are the way to go: They're cheap to buy and cost nothing to operate. Unless you count the ache in your muscles, the price of liniment, and the extra time they take, that is.

Before you buy hedge shears, be realistic. If you have just a few shrubs that need shearing, choose hand shears rather than gas- or electric-powered ones. It takes just a little labor to keep two or

Not Just for Hedges

Garden shears come in handy when it's time to pinch back perennials and other flowers—a task that encourages the plant to branch and grow dense and bushy with a bonus of more flowers. Instead of using your thumb and finger to snip off the tips of the stems of your mums, fall asters, phlox, and other flowers, make quick work of the job by giving the plant a once-over with shears.

three flowering or evergreen shrubs clipped into formalized shapes. On the other hand, if you have long or tall formal hedges, using hand shears will quickly make your arms ache. In that case, it may be wiser to invest in an gas- or electric-powered hedge trimmer.

Call in the Big Guns

Electric trimmers are effective on lighter-weight shrubs that are within reach of an outlet. Gas trimmers allow you to trim far away from any electrical source and can cut through thicker wood, but they are more expensive to buy. If you need a gas-powered hedge trimmer but only need to use them once or twice a year, consider renting. If you decide that buying your own is more cost-effective, follow the guidelines for purchasing power tools on page 108.

Shopping for Saws

If you plan to remove bigger branches than your pruners and loppers can handle, a saw is the next item on your pruning tools list. Forget that image of Paul Bunyan you have in mind—short, lightweight garden saws cut quickly with a minimum of effort.

All-purpose does the trick. Unless your yard is in dire need of major cleanup, a single all-purpose pruning saw should do the trick. This small handsaw has a blade 12 to 18 inches long, which is attached to a comfortable curved wooden handle that you grasp like a pistol grip. The Grecian saw is a variation on the general pruning saw: It has a blade curved downward like a crescent moon and teeth that cut on the pull stroke. Both are great for general sawing, and they fit easily into confined spaces where branches are growing close together. Attached to a long pole, the Grecian saw does a fine job cutting off higher branches that are out of reach.

Know when to fold 'em. Folding saws are weaker than nonfolding types because the attachment at the hinged handle makes them susceptible to bending under pressure. However, if you have a large property, you may find that a folding saw is more convenient to carry around than a pair of heavy loppers, which makes it easy to keep up with maintenance on your regular garden strolls.

Paul Bunyan alert. When a thick branch needs removal, turn to the bow saw, which has a rugged, toothed straight blade attached to either end of a large curved handle. You'll need some elbow grease to do the job, but the saw cuts surprisingly quickly. Unless you live in Tornado Alley where after-storm cleanup is a regular routine, you'll rarely need this heavy-duty saw. Besides, chances are your neighbor has one hanging in the garage—ask!

Add 5 feet to the length of your arms. "Limbing up" a shade tree to allow more light into the yard is a task you may not think you can do yourself because the tree limbs you want to remove are out of reach. Before you call in an arborist or attempt to balance on an unsafe ladder, shop around for a pole saw, which adds several feet to your reach. If you only need to remove a few limbs, chances are you can do it yourself. The money you'll save will easily outweigh the price of the tool.

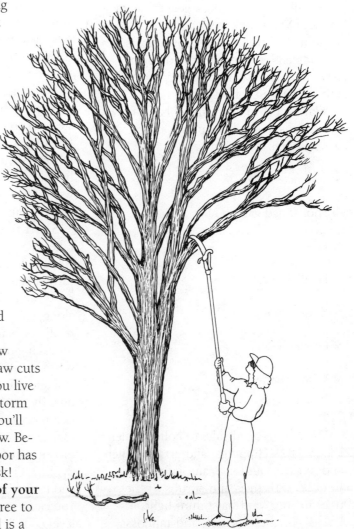

That branch may be over your head, but it's not necessarily out of reach if a pole saw is part of your tool collection. This handy device makes tree maintenance a cinch—no unstable ladder, no arm strain, no ragged bark tears from stretching to reach. It's safer for you and healthier for your trees.

Tools for Garden Maintenance

When it comes to garden maintenance, saving time is just as big a goal as saving money. Who wants to spend hours weeding, cultivating beds, spreading soil amendments and fertilizer, and edging beds when you could be planting or admiring the fruits of your labors?

Make some room in the toolshed for these items that will keep your maintenance chores simple and easy:

❖ Leaf rake

❖ Short-tined garden rake

❖ Hoe

❖ Hand weeder

❖ Edging tool

❖ Ground cloth

❖ Wheelbarrow

Rake in the Savings

Use a long-tined rake to collect fallen leaves, grass clippings, and errant mulch and to clean out twigs and fallen fruit from beneath trees and shrubs. If the trees in your yard have thin, light leaves—birches, locusts, and mimosas, for instance—you're in luck! You'll be able to get by in leaf-raking season with the cheapest rake of all: bamboo. Lightweight, inexpensive bamboo rakes look flimsy, but they're surprisingly durable if you don't ask more from them than they're made for. If all you need is minimal leaf cleanup on a smooth lawn, you'll get more than your money's worth out of a bamboo rake.

If your trees are oaks, maples, or others with heavy leaves and lots of them, you'll need to spring for a metal- or poly-tined leaf rake instead of a bamboo rake. As with other tools that see heavy-duty wear and tear, a metal leaf rake needs to be well made to hold up under the rigors of its job. Shop for a high-quality rake instead of going for the lowest price tag. Look for a sturdy, secure connection where the head of the rake joins the handle. A rubber grip on the long handle will add to your comfort level by preventing blisters.

Short tines are optional. A garden rake with short metal tines makes fast work of leveling and smoothing newly turned beds. It collects clods of soil, rocks, and weed clumps as you pull it along, so the bare soil is fine-textured and ready for planting. This tool is also good for raking out leaves and twigs from beneath shrubs because its short tines are stiff and inflexible. One of the more infrequently used garden tools, a garden rake is subjected to less abuse than other basic tools, so pinch pennies by buying a medium-grade brand instead of the top of the line. Or go the total cheapskate route and forgo the short-tined rake altogether. You can use a hoe turned on its side to level your beds and a leaf rake for garden cleanup.

The Hoe: A Tool of Many Talents

Frugal gardeners love their hoes, and for good reason. A hoe can do the jobs of several garden tools in one. You can use it to loosen and break up soil, of course, but you can also use it to smooth out beds, slice off weeds, make planting furrows, and even to pull out leafy debris beneath shrubs.

Form follows function. What kind of hoe you choose is a matter of personal taste as well as use. A triangular-bladed hoe lets you get right to the point when hacking out weeds. The tip penetrates the soil easily, and the wider back of the blade lets you lift the weed out, roots and all, with one upward thrust. Flat-bladed hoes are excellent for lightly scraping the soil surface to slice seedling weeds off at ground level. Both types are great for loosening soil and chopping up clods.

There are legions of hoes to choose from: stirrup, swan-neck, Warren, onion, and on and on. Try to borrow your friends' and use them before making your selection.

Weeders Pull Their Weight

Handheld weeding tools include various basic triangular-blade designs, plus a bewildering array of neck angles, blade shapes, and other diversities. All have their place, and eventually you may want to accumulate a selection of several kinds, depending on the weeding problems you encounter most often. As with hand trowels, be sure to spend a little extra and buy a better-quality weeder that will serve you well for years, without the annoyances of a bent blade or loose or uncomfortable handle.

❖ For removing young weed seedlings, a sharp-bladed Cape Cod weeder is ideal. The longer, skinny neck supporting the blade lets you wiggle it into tight quarters to slice off weeds beneath perennials or among the eggplant, for instance.

The Multipurpose Hoe

Frugal gardeners get plenty of use out of a hoe, using it as an all-purpose tool. Here are a few ways to get the most out of this indispensable basic tool:

■ Held at an angle, a hoe blade is a handy row maker, scribing out a narrow, shallow furrow for seed planting.

■ Laid on its side and dragged over the soil, a hoe blade can smooth out new beds and rake off stones and other obstructions, much like a garden rake.

■ Spread mulch in tight quarters with the aid of a hoe, pushing and pulling wood chips or other materials around the plants.

■ Use a sideways or upright hoe blade to spread soil amendments over a newly dug bed. Then you can follow through by using the hoe as a chopper to work the amendments into the soil.

❖ Many gardeners are learning to embrace—figuratively, of course—the Japanese gardening knife. This heavy-duty precision tool features a sharp serrated blade that excels at giving that Samurai slice to pesky weeds, right at root level.

❖ A dandelion digger is another indispensable hand-weeding tool. Reducing the power of the lever to its simplest, this inexpensive tool lets you pry out taprooted perennial weeds (including dandelions, but also dock, sorrel, burdock, and many others) with just a flick of the wrist.

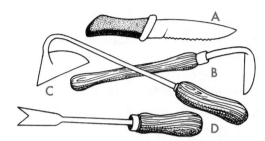

The Japanese gardening knife (A) delivers a killing thrust to chickweed, plantains, and ragweed, severing them below the soil. If multitudes of small weed seedlings plague your gardens, turn to the Cape Cod weeder (B) or Dutch weeder (C) to cut them off at soil level. For firmly entrenched tap-rooted weeds like dandelion, it's the well-named dandelion digger (D) to the rescue.

Create an Illusion of Tidiness

A neat, sharply defined edge along your beds instantly makes them look tidy and well tended, even if you haven't pulled a single weed in weeks. Edging may sound like tedious work if you've never done it before, but it actually goes quickly. This easy, satisfying job takes only a little time but pays off in big labor

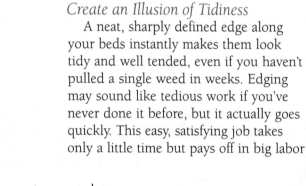

To prevent creeping weeds and grass from invading your beds, use an edging tool to slice vertically around the perimeter of the bed. Then cut in at a 45-degree angle from outside the cut edge, and remove the wedges of soil from around the bed. The shallow, angled trench of open space that results is a no-man's-land that will stop most weed roots in their tracks.

Make a Handy Ground Cloth

A bedsheet is the basis of a handy garden helper you'll use over and over to collect leaves and weeds or move mulch and other materials. If your linen closet has no ready candidate, check your local thrift shop for a double-size, polyester or poly/cotton-blend sheet (more durable than all-cotton fabric). Sew woven handles at the corners as shown below for easier handling. Bundle the cloth and lift it into a wheelbarrow when you're ready to transport the material, or simply slide it along the ground behind you. When you've finished using the sheet for the day, shake it out and fold it neatly until next time.

Step 1. Sew 12-inch strips of polyester or poly blend webbing, about 1½ inches wide, to the four corners of the sheet, to make loops for handles.

Step 2. Spread out the cloth nearby while you weed a bed. When you're sitting on the ground to work, it's a lot easier to toss weeds onto a large, ground-level sheet than to try to fling them into a smaller, higher wheelbarrow.

Step 3. When you're finished weeding, use the loops to collect the cloth into a four-cornered bundle. Lift into a wheelbarrow or garden cart for easy transport or, if you're hauling lightweight material, sling the bundle over your shoulder like Santa Claus.

savings. Not only does an edged bed look better, it will save you weeding chores. Invasive grasses and weeds are reluctant to leap the gap cut by an edging tool. A once-a-month once-over is usually all you need to invest to keep beds in shape.

Use the long-handled edging tool, with a blade shaped like a half moon, to cut a trench along the edge of the bed, as shown on page 104.

A Handy Helper That Costs Nothing

One of the most ingenious and cheapest labor-saving garden "tools" is a ground cloth. An old sheet or shower curtain liner will do the trick, or you can buy a ready-made cloth at garden centers or camping stores. Spread the cloth next to you when you're weeding, and toss the weeds onto the cloth as you work. When you're finished, bundle up the corners, load the cloth into the wheelbarrow, and carry it to your compost pile. You can also make good use of a ground cloth when raking leaves, collecting grass clippings, or moving lightweight mulch.

Back-Saving Wheelbarrow

No garden tool shed would be complete without a wheelbarrow. This handy hauler can save you countless steps—as well as painful backaches—by making it easier to move loads of mulch, topsoil, compost, and plants around your property.

When shopping for a wheelbarrow, you can choose between metal or polyethylene. Keep in mind that metal will eventually rust from wear and moisture, so your best bet is to invest in a more durable poly model. They're lightweight, and depending on what size you buy, you can haul up to 200 pounds or more of materials.

Tools for Lawn Maintenance

A lawn is a fact of life for most of us, so you may as well make the most of it. Just regularly mowing the grass—before it "needs it"—will do wonders at making your whole yard look better. A lawn mower is the one indispensable tool you'll need. If you have a lot of nooks and crannies where a mower can't reach, you can turn to your hand shears or invest in a trimmer to make the finishing job go much faster. A fertilizer spreader makes applying compost or other organic fertilizers a swift and easy job.

Looking at Lawn Mowers

Hand-powered, or reel, lawn mowers are perfect for small lawns. A good-quality one won't come cheap, but it will be a joy to use. It will be easy to push, and without the distraction of noise and gas fumes, you can enjoy the whirring sound of the blades and the sweet smell of cut grass as you work. As an added bonus, a reel mower takes up less storage space than a power mower.

Electric mowers don't pollute the air with dirty exhaust, but keeping track of the cord while you mow can be frustrating. Gas-powered mowers are the most popular choice for most homeowners because of their practicality and ease of use, but they do contribute to air pollution, not to mention noise pollution.

Buy Used to Save Big

Mowers are often plentiful in the "for sale" classified ads of local newspapers. Folks graduate to newer, more deluxe models, or they trade in a walk-behind mower for a riding mower. Tinkering with mower engines is a time-honored tradition, and many backyard mechanics rehabilitate these long-lived machines to make a few dollars at resale.

With new mowers selling for $200 and up, buying used can save you big. A selling price of $50 to $100 is fairly typical. If you're shopping for a used riding mower, the savings can be even greater—a few hundred dollars for a mower that might cost $1,000 or more new.

Start it cold. When you call to schedule a time to see a used mower, tell the owner that you want to start it cold. Touch the engine to make sure you can't detect any lingering warmth. Mowers are notorious for being easier to start when they're warm.

Give it a good workout. Put the mower through its paces at the seller's house to make sure all parts are in working order. The engine should run cleanly, with no stuttering and no smoking. Controls should respond promptly. Remove and replace the bagger if it has one to make sure the connections are in good shape. Inspect the bag for holes. Look closely at the grass blades cut by the mower after you try it out. If the cut edges look chewed and ragged, the blades will need sharpening—not a fatal flaw, but a reason to dicker the price downward by $10 to $20.

Save on Mower Repair

If you don't know how to repair your mower yourself, check your local newspaper for "handyman" ads or ask around your neighborhood for mechanically inclined fix-it folks. The price for repairs is usually much more reasonable than it would be at a dealer or through a large commercial shop.

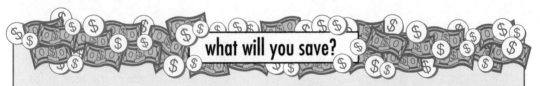

what will you save?

The Right Tool Can Save Your Back—And Your Billfold

The right tool really makes a difference. The savings in labor, backaches, sore muscles, and general frustration is difficult to put a price on. Consider the cost of a single visit to the massage therapist or chiropractor, and you'll see that investing in tools pays off fast.

James Walsh, who gardens in Vienna, Virginia, remembers the time he saw a woman struggling to collect free wood-chip mulch at a community recycling center with a shovel. It was clear she would soon give up and probably go out and buy bagged mulch. Wanting to help, James lent her an extra fork he had in the car. She was thrilled to discover how much easier the job was with the proper tool. After they were finished, James collected his fork and went home to unload. A few hours later, he came back for another load. The woman was also back again, this time collecting mulch with a shiny new pitchfork.

Spreader Shopping

If you fertilize your lawn with aged manure, compost, or bagged organic fertilizers, you'll need a spreader to apply your materials. Rotary spreaders provide more even distribution than drop spreaders, avoiding those green-patch blues where your lawn is marked at every spot where a heavier dose of fertilizer was dumped. Check moving sales for good buys on spreaders.

The Temptations of Trimmers

Powered by gas or electricity, trimmers accomplish the finishing touches of your lawn maintenance in a fraction of the time that it would take with hand tools. Unfortunately, they also create noise and air pollution. Before you buy a trimmer, consider whether you can eliminate the trouble spots in other ways. Perhaps you could lay a mowing strip so that the mower can get right to the edge of beds. Or spread wood chips or other mulch around trees or along fences.

Before you purchase a new or used trimmer, assess the type of jobs you'll need it to do. A lightweight model with a narrow-gauge string is adequate for edging beds, but you'll need a heavier-duty string trimmer to whack away coarse weeds.

Bargain Buys on Used Power Tools

You can save hundreds of dollars on expensive power equipment if you buy secondhand. Before you snatch up that bargain, however, find out why the item is for sale. If the owner is moving to a

---

☛ COST CUTTERS

Search for Secondhand

As with mowers, trimmers can be a bargain when you buy them used. Check the classified ads in your local newspaper, watch bulletin boards at the supermarket or library, and scour garage sale listings: You may find a trimmer at a giveaway price.

Be sure you try it out before you buy, however. A used trimmer isn't a bargain if you have to make expensive repairs to it. If you're unfamiliar with trimmers, have the owner show you how to operate it and how to refill the string or replace the blade when necessary.

---

smaller property where the tool won't be needed or upgrading to a newer model, the odds are that the machine is in good working order. Whatever the reason for the sale, always ask for a demonstration. Start and use the machine yourself if possible. Shy away from any power tool that is difficult to start, runs roughly, or gives any other indication that there may be a mechanical problem. Unless you are handy with repairs, a used machine with multiple maintenance problems that require new parts may end up costing you more than new equipment in the long run. If you do decide to buy, ask the owner for the instruction manual and any service records.

Reincarnate Your Old Screwdrivers and Soup Spoons

Reuse, recycle, and let your imagination run wild to come up with new uses for familiar objects. Here are a few ideas to get your creative juices bubbling:

◼ If your screwdriver has a broken tip, don't throw it away; just give it a new job description. An old screwdriver is great for levering out deep-rooted weeds such as dandelions. Phillips screwdrivers and flat-headed screwdrivers work equally well.

◼ Check your recycling bin for thin polystyrene foam packing sheets or small-size bubble wrap, and attach it to the handle of your tools with duct tape for a cushy grip.

◼ Check the thrift shop or your kitchen drawer for a worn but sturdy paring knife. Make sure it has a handle that fits over an extension of the metal blade (the "tang") and is riveted into place. Use it to slice off weeds with fleshy roots, such as dock, below ground level.

◼ An old tire iron makes a good pry bar for removing rocks.

◼ Run an old dinner knife between bricks or cracks in paving to remove shallow-rooted weeds with one swift stroke.

◼ When your bamboo rake starts looking seriously gap-toothed because of broken tines, save the best section, cut away the rest, and voila! You'll have a custom rake to use in tight quarters between perennials.

◼ Old kitchen spoons and forks are excellent implements for working in the tight spaces of a rock garden or container planting. They're also ideal for transplanting seedlings.

◼ Give an old garden hose a second life as a support for a hanging basket from a tree. Slip a piece of hose over the length of wire that will be in contact with the tree to protect the branch from being cut by the wire hanger.

Dinnerware becomes a garden tool when you think creatively. A knife makes a great patio weeder.

 **25 SMART SHOPPING TIPS**

1. View tools as an investment. If you spend more up front to get a tool that is well made, it will last longer and do the job better.

2. If the price tags of good tools make you hesitate, just compare the cost of that shovel, say, to the price of the shrub you'll be planting with it. Suddenly the tool will seem like a bargain—and that's just one shrub.

3. Get to know your neighbors. They can be a great source for tools you only use occasionally. Always return the tool, cleaned, as soon as you're finished with it, and be prepared to return the favor.

4. Look for used tools at moving sales, which are usually advertised in the garage sale section of the classified ads. Many people would rather sell cheap than lug them along.

5. Send for mail-order catalogs from companies that specialize in or carry a large assortment of tools, such as those listed in "Resources for Frugal Gardeners" on page 263. It's an education to see the wide variety available, and prices may be lower than at retail stores even when you add in shipping costs.

6. Wooden handles have one advantage: If one breaks, you can replace it. That's not true of metal and plastic.

7. Handles made of ash or hickory are stronger and more durable than those made of other woods. Hickory is stronger but also heavier than ash, so it's ideal for short-handled tools such as hammers and axes.

8. Inspect the wood of the handle, looking for knots, which weaken the structure. Ideally the grain of the wood should run the length of the handle, rather than spread out in rings.

9. Look for tools with carbon steel or stainless steel heads. Rust-proof stainless steel is more expensive than carbon steel, and soil tends to slide off the surface easily. Carbon steel will not rust if you clean and dry it after each use. Special protective coatings will wear off with time, minimizing their value.

10. Spend the extra money for tools that have the business end and the neck forged from one piece of metal rather than spliced together. Single forged tools are stronger and will last longer, making them a better buy.

11. Shop around before you buy. Visit several hardware stores and garden centers, and talk to the salespeople about the different tools they carry. Ask about the quality of each brand and about the advantages of different designs. Most stores carry only a few brands, so you'll learn about more brands by visiting more stores and being able to do a comprehensive price-to-quality evaluation.

12. Handle a tool before you buy it to find a comfortable fit. The weight, balance, length of the handle, shape of the blade, and many other factors will affect how comfortable the tool will be for you to use.

13. Pantomime doing the job for several minutes to get a sense of how comfortable a tool is to hold and manipulate. Make sure the handle fits comfortably into your own hand.

14. Choose tools with replaceable parts so that you can repair them when they're broken, rather than having to replace them at much higher cost.

15. Read the fine print on warranties for power tools such as trimmers. Be sure there is a convenient service center nearby for those inevitable repairs.

16. Learn the fine art of bargaining when you're considering used tools. Most sellers will knock at least a few dollars off the advertised price. Key question: "Would you take a little less for this?"

17. If you have a neighbor with whom you're friendly or a nearby family member, consider buying more expensive, occasional-use tools together and sharing ownership.

18. The length of a shovel handle affects the leverage and thus the ease with which it's used. Most people are comfortable with a handle that reaches to their shoulder.

19. If you're left-handed, shop mail-order catalogs for pruners made to fit your perspective.

20. Modern hand tools are getting easier to operate. If your hand strength is too limited for your favorite old pair of pruners or grass shears, replace them with a new pair that's easier to use.

21. Household auctions are another great source of used tools. Shovels, garden rakes, and wheelbarrows can be had for a fraction of their cost new. Go early to scope out the bargains and handle the tools before you buy.

22. Can't find a classified ad for the tools you're looking for? Post your own "wanted" notice on bulletin boards at the local laundromat, library, supermarket, or coffee shop.

23. If your budget won't allow the high-priced tools you need, compromise with cheapies that will last a year or two until the purse strings loosen. Even a $6 shovel has plenty of usefulness in it; treat it gently and it may surprise you with its long life.

24. Snapped necks are the number-one cause of tool demise. Keep your shovel and your trowel intact by resisting the all-too-common urge to use them as pry bars for stubborn roots or rocks.

25. Be a good hinter: Let your friends and family know you'd appreciate garden tools for special occasion gifts.

Smart Storage Saves Time and Tools

Spend the time to organize your tool storage space so that each item has its own place. You'll save time looking for misplaced tools, you won't accidentally buy a tool you've forgotten you already own, and you'll be less tempted to leave tools outside where they'll be subject to the stresses of sun and rain.

Hang your tools on a wall to eliminate clutter. Run a 2 × 4 along the wall at a height that will accommodate long handles, and then hammer in nails or pegs in pairs to hold the heads of long-handled tools. Or drill a hole in the handle of each tool, and use the hole to hang each handle on a headless nail. Perforated hardboard with removable metal hooks is excellent for hanging smaller tools. Draw an outline of each tool on the wall or board. That way you'll know what belongs where, and you'll be able to tell at a glance if anything's missing.

Start a Lifelong Tool Collection

A toolshed filled with favorite hoes, spades, and diggers gives a frugal gardener almost as much pleasure as Midas's storehouse of gold. Tools are so essential to gardening that they quickly become like friends—the simple, trusty dandelion digger you reach for at the first sign of lawn invaders, the hoe you've had so long its handle is worn smooth and shiny from your grip, the shovel that planted the young shade trees that now shelter your toolshed—they're so reliable that they are a pleasure to use.

Of course, once you have the basics, you'll start to look around for other tools to add to your never-ending collection. You'd be amazed by what's out there! But even if you never become a collector,

you'll still want to keep your tools in good shape so they last for many long years of useful life.

Eliminate Effort with Special Tools

Specialized tools, such as a narrow-bladed poacher's spade, pruning saw, and dethatching rake for lawn maintenance, are great to add to the toolshed when your budget permits. Learn what's available, and then decide whether owning such a tool would make your gardening life easier.

Educate yourself with catalogs. Several companies specialize in garden tools. Perusing mail-order catalogs, such as the ones offered by the companies listed in "Resources for Frugal Gardeners" on page 263, will give you a good education in specialized tool uses.

Save Your Tool's Life

Avoid asking your tools to do more than they're made for. Instead of hacking through stout branches with your undersized hand pruners, for instance, use a pair of long-handled loppers to slice off bigger branches neatly and quickly.

Pass on the Rejects

Most of us have at least a few tools that spend more time in the toolshed than in the garden. Maybe they're too heavy or too awkwardly balanced or too flimsy for real work. We let them clutter up our valuable storage space in the vain hope that someday they'll transform into tools that are just right. If you're harboring rejects in your toolshed, be ruthless. Weed them out and send them to the thrift shop, or stick a price tag on them at your next garage sale.

A Yearly Dab'll Do You

An application of linseed oil protects and preserves the wooden handles of your tools just as it does your fine furniture. Wooden handles are vulnerable to the effects of weather. Unless you keep them oiled, they'll dry out and grow rough and unpleasant to touch. Very dried out wood becomes brittle and splits and breaks easily. Amazingly, you can protect your wooden handles with just a single yearly treatment, preferably when you put them away for the season. Oiled handles stay smooth, not splintery, and are a pleasure to grip. Here's how to use linseed oil:

1. Clean off any clinging mud or dirt from the wood handles of your tools. Make sure they're completely dry before you proceed to the next step.

2. Set a can of linseed oil in a pot of boiling water for a few minutes, until the oil is very warm. Warm oil penetrates wood better than cold oil.

Make Your Tools Last Forever

Thrifty gardeners treat their tools right so they last a long time. They won't last forever, of course, but for years, maybe decades. Garden tools are made to withstand the elements and some abuse, but if you give them a little TLC, they'll last longer, look better, and be a greater pleasure to use.

Wipe wood handles with warm linseed oil to keep them smooth and snag-free.

3. Dip a soft cloth in the oil and wipe the wooden handles of all your garden tools. Apply the oil liberally and allow it to soak in, then wipe off the excess with a clean, dry cloth.

4. Store your tools in their usual place.

Rust? No Problem, Unless You Can't Cut It

Every time you push your spade into the soil or plunge your trowel into the earth, you wear off the rust that may have formed on the metal tool since its last use. Rust just isn't much of a problem, other than cosmetic, for well-used garden tools. If a shovel or spade rusts away before it wears out, it is either very cheap or you haven't used it for many, many years. A strong spray from the hose after use will keep your spades, shovels, and trowels clean. If

you prefer a rust-free look, you can either wipe down your tools with an oily rag or thrust them into a bucket filled with oily sand. Fill a 5-gallon bucket about two-thirds full with coarse sand, pour in half a quart of linseed oil, and mix well to distribute the oil. The sand's abrasive action will rub off rust particles, and the oil will prevent new rust from forming. Wipe off oil and sand before storing.

Tools with cutting blades and moving parts—pruners, loppers, and shears—are another story. Rusty blades are dull and don't cut well. Rusty springs don't move like they should, and rusty hinges may get stuck entirely. To prolong the life of your pruning tools, wipe the blades with an oily rag and lubricate the moving joints and springs at the end of the growing season with 3-in-1 or another all-purpose lubricating oil.

what will you save?

Keep Your Tools Working Longer

Tool maintenance pays off in benefits to you that go beyond money. You need to be able to rely on your tools—when there are plants waiting for holes to be dug, that shovel had better be ready. Treat your tools right, avoiding abuse and giving them a bit of occasional maintenance, and they'll be ready when you are. Oiling wooden handles and lubricating moving parts makes using the tools a pleasure instead of frustrating and maybe even painful. Splinters are no fun, and they can even knock you out of commission in the garden for a day or two.

Take care of your tools and you'll save on replacement costs, too. Even better, you'll enjoy the satisfaction of seeing your tools all cleaned and neatly put away at the end of the gardening year and the pleasure of getting them out fresh and ready for work the following spring.

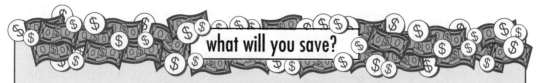

what will you save?

Buy Tools by the Box

Depending on the bargain you drive, you can probably buy four or five—or even an entire collection—of used hand tools for the price of one new tool. Giveaway prices are the rule at most garage sales—generally only $1 for a shovel or hoe. Trowels and other hand diggers and weeders can sometimes be found for as little as 25¢! That's what makes garage-sale shopping so addictive—the thrill of the hunt. On the other hand, if you'd rather spend your Saturday mornings in the garden instead of driving around on the garage-sale circuit, you'll save a lot of valuable time by spending more money and buying your tools new.

Help Your Hose
Find the Fountain of Youth

Subject to heat, pressure, freezing, and frustrated tugs, a hose's life is not an easy one. Without a little preventive action, you may be dismayed to discover that your nice new hose is in sad shape when you pull it out next year. Replacing hoses can run into money, especially if you use two or three of them. Make them last by relieving the stress of their existence. Keep in mind that anything that causes undue pressure on the hose can shorten its life.

Watch that nozzle. Hose nozzles with a shut-off valve that stops the flow of water are a gardener's delight but a hose's worst nightmare. When a hose is filled almost to bursting with water for long periods of time, the continuous pressure weakens the internal structure of the hose, leading to leaks and making the hose more prone to kinks as its walls lose their rigidity. If you use a hose nozzle with a shut-off valve, be sure to turn off the water at

the spigot and open the valve at the end of the hose whenever the hose will be lying idle for more than a few minutes. Never let your hose endure so much pressure that it looks like a snake that's just eaten a big meal.

It's not all it's cracked up to be. Always drain your hoses before winter. If you move a hose in which water has frozen, it can crack.

Keep it cozy. Snow and ice are no-nos for hoses, so if you live in a cold-winter area, always store your hoses in a sheltered place for the winter months. When you get out the hose for the first time the following season, carry it outside carefully and allow it to warm up in the sun before you unroll it. Jerking or otherwise playing rough with a cold or frozen hose can cause it to crack.

Lawn Mower Life-Savers

Electric- and gas-powered rotary lawn mowers need maintenance once a year. Empty out any leftover gas, then clean off the machine on top and bottom, removing vegetation, dirt, and grease. If you're mechanically minded or willing to learn, you can do the rest of the maintenance job yourself: Change the oil, check the spark plugs, clean the oil filter, and clean and sharpen or replace the blade. Your owner's manual will give you detailed and specific direction on how to perform these tasks for your specific model.

Avoid the rush. If you're not ready to tackle mower maintenance on your own, you'll need to take your mower into the shop for service. Most lawn mower shops have a surge of business in spring, when everyone suddenly thinks about mowing lawns again and realizes their mower needs attention. Avoid the rush and the long wait for service by scheduling an appointment for your mower during the winter months.

Stalking for Shovels

Garage and estate sales offer terrific opportunities to buy used tools at bargain prices. You'll need to be fast,

though, because tools are some of the hottest items in the garage sale market. Aggressive "garagers" who stalk the sales even before the published opening time commonly snap these up. Auctions can be another good source of used tools. Check the listings in your local newspapers, especially for house and estate auctions, where everything goes. Once again, it pays to "shop" early. It's easier to examine and try out the merchandise at an aution site if you prowl the grounds before the bidding starts.

Of course, if you need a tool immediately, you won't have the luxury of shopping at garage sales or auctions for used tools. Hardware stores, discount chains, home-supply stores, garden centers, and other retail outlets vary widely in the quality and prices of the tools they sell, so be sure to shop for quality as well as price. Many manufacturers rate their products according to quality, offering a low-priced entry-level version, a midlevel version, and a high-end product that will last for years. Compare both prices and quality to make sure you get the best bargain.

Long-Term Commitment Not Needed

Trying to decide whether to buy a rotary tiller, a posthole digger, or some other tool that you know you'll only use a few times? Take the pressure off (and relieve your wallet) with a visit to your local rental center—it's a real education. You'll be surprised at all the different types of tools and equip-

ment that are available. You can rent just about any piece of gardening equipment, from a pole saw to a heavy-duty rotary tiller or leaf shredder.

Add it up. If you expect to perform a task only once or twice a year, renting will probably be more cost-effective than buying. A rotary tiller, for example, may retail for $800; renting the same machine may run about $40 a day. You can rent the machine for about 20 years before the rental fee exceeds the purchase price—and you'll never need to store it, maintain it, or repair it during those two decades!

Split with a neighbor. Shave rental costs by sharing the machine with a neighbor: You use the rotary tiller in the morning, and he uses it in the afternoon. Sharing the rental also gives you another set of helping hands to heft heavy equipment in and out of your vehicle.

Sharp Wits Sharpen Their Own Blades

Sharp blades cut fast and smooth, making maintenance easier and faster. To keep your pruners, loppers, and shears working at their peak potential, you'll need a few simple accessories and some practice. Although you can pay to have this service done, it's usually quicker to do the job yourself rather than spending the time to drive to the shop, drop off the tool, and pick it up.

Sharpen the beveled edge. Before you set to work sharpening, look closely at the blades and notice how they are beveled, or sharpened on a slant at the edge. The beveled blade is what makes the cutting edge. In the case of clippers and shears, the beveled edge will be on the outside of the blade. Curved-blade pruning shears and clippers have only one beveled blade.

Sharpening these tools means restoring the beveled edge. No matter how your blades are made, sharpen only the beveled surface. If you begin

what will you save?

Repairs Add Up—In Savings

Living in a society with a throw-away mentality, we tend to forget how much money we can save by repairing broken tools. For a few dollars and a little time, you can extend the life of a tool for many years by mending it. The money you save on replacing the item adds up quickly. Tools kept in good repair also pay off in lessening daily frustrations: no more splinters, no more pinching your tender skin, no more babying along your limping shovel, no more hacking off branches with dull blades backed by brute strength. Tools that work like they're supposed to are a pleasure to use, which means you'll use them more often and your garden will look better.

smoothing off burrs and nicks on the unbeveled or square edges, you'll create gaps that will ruin the tool's cutting action.

Blade Sharpening for Beginners

All you need to keep your tools at their sharpest is a vise to clamp the tool in and an abrasive block called a whetstone. Whetstones are cheap and long-lasting and are available at any hardware, home-supply, or discount store. Got your supplies? Let's sharpen!

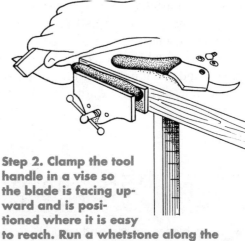

Step 2. Clamp the tool handle in a vise so the blade is facing upward and is positioned where it is easy to reach. Run a whetstone along the beveled edge, making every stroke from the hinged end of the blade to the tip. At the end of each pass, lift the whetstone and repeat the procedure until the blade is sharp. For best results, try to follow the angle of the original bevel. The steeper the angle you put on the blade, the sharper—and weaker—it will be. You want a balance between a sharp and strong edge.

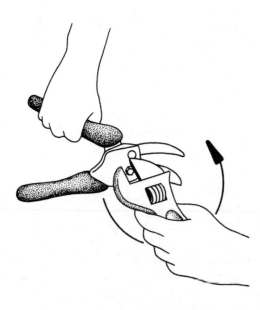

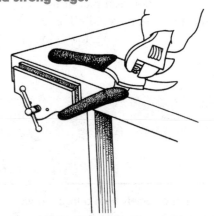

Step 1. Find the head of the bolt that fastens the blades together, and look for directional arrows. Remove the bolt, turning it in the direction of the arrow, and take the clippers apart. Some clippers are permanently joined together. If you can't take yours apart, clamp them in a vise with the blades held firmly open.

Step 3. When the blade is sharp, remove it from the vise and repeat the procedure for the second blade (but only if it's beveled). Replace the connecting bolt when you're all through, and try out your sharpened clippers in the garden. You'll be amazed at the difference.

Sharpen That Sod Cutter

Half-moon edging tools and straight-bladed spades, used to cut through sod and to create straight edges in the soil, benefit from periodic sharpening so that they slice easily through grass and roots.

Either clamp the spade in a vise so it is horizontal to the ground, or lay it on the ground with the blade facing away from you. With a smooth, contin-uous motion, run a bastard mill file across the blade from one edge to the other, following the same angle as the original edge of the blade. Lift the file at the end of each sweep so you always move it in the same direction. Repeat the motion, beginning at the same spot, until you have reproduced the original angle of the spade's tip. When the first side is sharp, turn the spade over and repeat on the other side.

When to Call In the Professionals

Be sure to consider your own skills and strengths before attacking a task that is new to you. The determination to tackle jobs that are potentially dangerous or that require more strength or experience than you have is a false economy. Cutting down a large tree, for instance, requires special skill and equipment and is best left to a profes-sional. Rotary tilling and aerating equipment are heavy and awkward, requiring a strong back to maneuver them over the ground.

If the task before you is more than you can handle, call professionals for estimates. Ask neighbors and friends for recommendations. Get at least three estimates to com-pare prices, and ask for references that you can call.

Quick Fixes

There was a time when mothers darned socks to extend use. Nowadays when our toes peek through, we simply buy new socks. Reknitting socks may be beyond our patience, but making simple repairs on our favorite garden tools is worth the time.

There are a number of easy repairs you can make that will give new life to old tools. It's simple to repair a hose, mend a cracked handle, or replace a broken one.

Replace Hose Connectors

In the normal course of events in the garden, the screw connectors on the ends of your hose are likely to get crushed (driving over them with the car is just one way this can happen). Repair kits and re-placement parts are widely available and inexpensive, and it takes just minutes to cut off the damaged end and replace it.

Some connectors are designed to clamp around the end of the hose with prongs, as shown on the opposite page; another style attaches to the hose with a band. Both kinds work well. If you have a good-quality hose, opt for brass couplers; they'll last longer than plastic ones.

Measure before you shop. Before you head for the hardware store, use a tape measure to determine the diameter of your hose. It's frustrating to try to pick out connectors when you aren't sure if your hose is ¾ inch or ⅝ inch in diameter.

How to Handle a Handle Repair

A cracked handle can give you splinters, pinch your hand, or worse yet, snap under pressure when you use it. Keep an eye on your tools for signs of cracks, and when you spot one, take action right away.

Quick Fix for Small Cracks

You can delay replacing a slightly cracked handle with a quick repair. Bind the handle by wrapping it in two layers of plastic electrical tape, extending the wrapping at least 6 inches beyond either side of the crack. That should keep the crack from continuing to grow and will protect your hand from possible splinters. Be aware, however, that the handle will never be as strong as it was before the flaw occurred.

Big Cracks Can Be Riveting

Tape alone won't help a big crack. This repair calls for stronger stuff: glue and rivets. Here's how to repair a seriously cracked handle:

1. Spread the crack wide enough to cover the two wood surfaces with wood glue or household white glue. Clamp together to dry.

2. Drill a hole that's sized to fit a rivet through the handle in the center of the crack. Depending on the length of the split, you may need to use more than one rivet.

3. Insert the rivet, and hammer the protruding ends into flattened domes. Make the tops of the rivet smooth, leaving no rough edges.

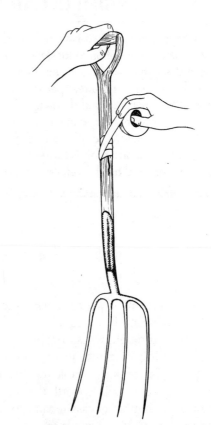

Smooth electrical tape makes a good short-term solution for a slightly cracked wooden handle.

2 for the Price of 1

A short hose is so handy it's surprising that hose makers haven't picked up on the idea yet. With a minihose there's no need to wrestle with a cumbersome coil of heavy hose when you only need a short length to reach nearby plantings or wash the dog. Make your own handy "half-pint" by recycling your long hose when it springs a leak. Cut the long hose in two at the spot where it leaks, removing the bad section, and attach new couplings, thus making one long hose into two shorter ones.

Step 1. Use a sharp knife to make a clean cut on either side of the leaking section of hose. Discard the leaky part.

Step 2. Soak the cut end of the hose in hot water for a few minutes to soften it so it's easier to work with.

Step 3. Attach the new connector following the package instructions. For clamp-on connectors like the one shown here, slip the connector over the cut end of the hose and squeeze the prongs tightly with pliers to hold it in place.

5 Easy Steps to Replacing a Handle

Broken handles, especially on shovels, are a fact of gardening life, thanks to the daily hard work these tools are called upon to do. When your handle snaps or cracks so badly it needs major repairs, it's time to replace it or buy a new tool. Frugal gardeners, of course, prefer the fix-it route. After all, the cost of a replacement handle is a fraction of what it costs to buy a whole new tool.

If you have a vise, it's easy to replace a handle. For a small investment in time and trouble, you save the price of a new tool and gain the satisfaction of salvaging an old favorite. Follow these steps, and your shovel, rake, or other tool will soon be good as new.

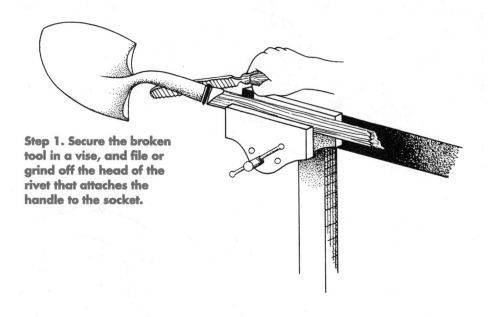

Step 1. Secure the broken tool in a vise, and file or grind off the head of the rivet that attaches the handle to the socket.

Step 2. Once the rivet is removed, use a hammer and nail or a nail set to force the pin out. Pull the damaged handle out of its socket. Once you've removed the old handle, you've accomplished the most difficult part of the task.

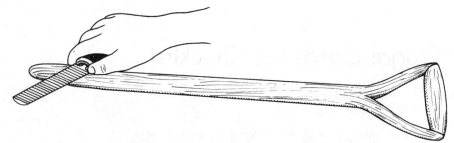

Step 3. Try out the new handle in the socket. If it's a tight squeeze, try coating the socket with oil or soap to allow the handle to slide in more easily. If the handle is just too big, file it with a wood rasp so it fits comfortably in the socket, and then slide it into place. Tap the end of the handle with a hammer or mallet to ensure it's pushed in as far as it will go.

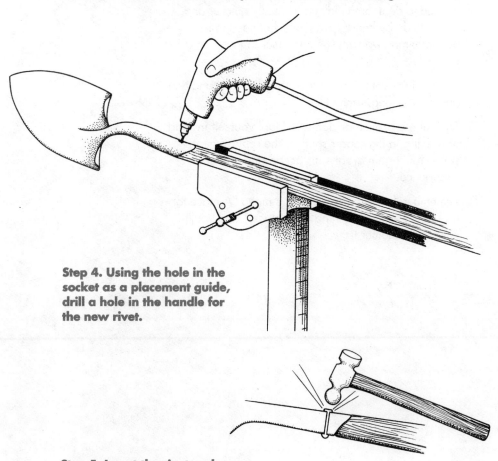

Step 4. Using the hole in the socket as a placement guide, drill a hole in the handle for the new rivet.

Step 5. Insert the rivet and secure the end by flattening it with a ball-peen hammer.

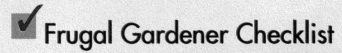

Frugal Gardener Checklist

- Before you buy a new tool, think if you already have one that will do the job as well.

- Instead of limiting your choices to what's in the nearby store, educate yourself with specialty catalogs and choose the tools that are right for you. Well-designed tools are a pleasure to work with, and your garden will benefit.

- Evaluate the size of the job before you buy the tool needed to do it. Small jobs are usually quicker and easier to do by hand. Large jobs that need to be done regularly may warrant spending extra money on a power tool.

- Oil and lube your tools so they stay in good condition and have a long, useful life.

- Try fixing a broken or damaged tool yourself instead of running to the repair shop or the replacement store. You'll gain great satisfaction and valuable experience.

- Remember the organized person's motto "A place for everything, and everything in its place," and you'll never lose another trowel.

CHAPTER FOUR

SAVE MONEY WITH SOIL AMENDMENTS

YOU CAN SPEND ALL THE MONEY you like on beautiful plants, but those plants will languish unless they have a nourishing environment in which to grow. Healthy, fertile soil is the literal foundation of your garden, so it makes sense to put your efforts into improving it. The key to healthy soil is a liberal use of organic amendments that improve soil texture, making it hospitable to plant roots and adding nutrients that plants can easily take up. Organic amendments include gardening standbys like compost, mulch, and aged manure. And don't forget to add seasonal supplements such as grass clippings and shredded leaves. You can leave them on top as mulch that will break down or dig them into the beds. Either way, they all help build great soil for a better garden.

125

Feed the Soil

You may not be able to see it, but your soil is very much alive. It teems with living organisms, from earthworms to bacteria, that spend their lives feasting on any bits of organic material they can find. When the soil is richly supplied with organic amendments, the living community within the soil is happy and well fed, and the soil is the better for it. These denizens of the soil turn that material into food for your plants. Frugal gardeners adopt the motto "Feed the soil, not the plant" as the thrifty way to a rewarding garden. Instead of constantly pouring money into chemical fertilizers to stimulate a rush of growth or bloom, spend time adding organic matter like manure and compost to your existing soil for a continued payoff with a low—or no—initial investment. Organic matter literally feeds the soil.

Organic: The "Cents-ible" Way to Go

Organic soil amendments, such as manure and compost, are the sensible and "cents-ible" approach to improving your soil and garden fertility. They increase soil fertility over the long term. Unlike chemicals, which are available to plant roots immediately, organic amendments depend on the microorganisms in the soil to break them down into a plant-usable form. Their effect is less immediately intense, but

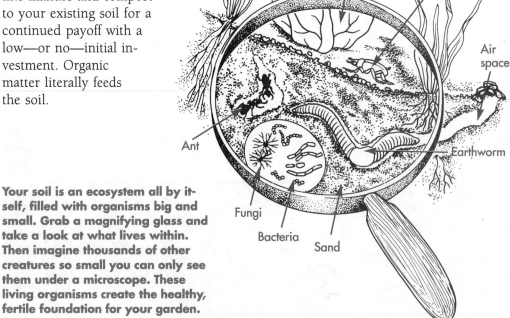

Humus (organic matter)

Beetle

Air space

Ant

Earthworm

Fungi

Bacteria

Sand

Your soil is an ecosystem all by itself, filled with organisms big and small. Grab a magnifying glass and take a look at what lives within. Then imagine thousands of other creatures so small you can only see them under a microscope. These living organisms create the healthy, fertile foundation for your garden.

they're sustained for a much longer time. You can't overdose your plants or burn them the way you can with chemicals.

You can't go wrong with organic matter. No matter what kind of soil you start with, adding organic soil amendments will only make it better. It's a no-lose deal!

Mix It Up

An ideal soil is a mixture of about 45 percent minerals balanced between clay and sand, 25 percent each of air and water, and about 5 percent organic matter.

But no matter what kind of soil you start with, organic matter will improve its texture, adding spaces for air and water to penetrate and making soil "fluffier" so that plant roots can move through it freely.

Success story. Nancy Schibanoff, a gardener in Del Mar, California, copes with heavy clay in some parts of her coastal garden and sand in others. "In the beginning, when I couldn't get anything to grow, I'd buy anything I heard was invasive," she said, explaining that she hoped invasive plants would be vigorous enough to thrive in her tough conditions. "Since then, I've learned that

Big Benefits from Organic Matter

Organic matter is a boon to frugal gardens. No other soil additives will give you so many benefits all rolled into one. Here's what you can expect when you add organic matter to your soil:

- Improved tilth, righting the balance between air, water, and nutrients.

- Better water retention, which means less watering, especially in sandy soil, because the organic matter slows the flow of water through the soil.

- Faster drainage in clay soil because the organic amendments lighten the composition, allowing water to flow through the soil properly.

- Better fertility because organic matter acts like a slow-release fertilizer, releasing nutrients into the soil as it decomposes.

- A thriving soil organism community because earthworms, insects, beneficial nematodes, bacteria, and fungi feed on plant material, turning it into the rich, brown, crumbly material known as humus.

- Great growing conditions because humus, which can absorb as much as 90 percent of its weight in water, creates the ideal growing medium for so many plants: moist, well-drained soil.

Avoiding the Feel-Good Fix

Chemical fertilizers quickly boost the fertility of the soil—but only temporarily. Apply chemical fertilizers to plants in clay soil, and your plants will respond with a burst of quick growth. Don't be fooled by this quick fix: As soon as your plants use up the fertilizer, their improved growth is over because the soil is unchanged.

Because chemical fertilizers do nothing to improve the "tilth," or general texture, of the soil, your plants will still be growing in heavy, dense clay that's hard for roots to penetrate and that lacks the air spaces that allow easy root growth and transfer of nutrients. To keep your garden flourishing, you'll have to keep applying a new dose of expensive chemical encouragement at regular intervals. And even that won't solve problems rooted in poor drainage or impenetrable soil structure.

Over time, extensive use of chemical fertilizers actually reduces the soil's viability because their concentration may kill off the essential microorganisms that make soil healthy. Toxic levels of chemical salts can build up. They may also leach into natural water sources, causing pollution.

the most important thing about gardening is what you put under a plant." Nancy made major efforts to improve her soil, adding bushels of organic matter. She also amends each planting hole whenever she adds new plants. Her favorite soil amendment is a rich compost made from worm castings, which she purchases from a local producer in Fallbrook, California. Now her garden grows luxuriantly.

Take a Hint from Rumpelstiltskin

Like Rumpelstiltskin spinning gold out of straw in the old fairy tale, you too can make valuables out of castoffs. Once you start looking for sources of organic matter, you'll gain a whole new perspective. No longer will raking fall leaves mean a weekend of labor with no payoff other than leaf-filled bags lined up along the curb. Instead, those leaves now become the raw materials needed to make garden gold.

What's "Organic Matter"?

Organic matter is simply stuff that once was alive. In the case of gardening, we'll limit it to plants. Though Native Americans taught Europeans what a dead fish could do for corn, incorporating animal remains is just too tricky for most backyard gardeners.

Organics are all around. Newspaper, cardboard, manure, straw, fall leaves, seaweed, coffee grounds, potato peelings, garden weeds, compost: All come from living, growing plants. And all can contribute to the garden alchemy of creating healthy, fertile soil. Once you start looking for organic material, you'll find it everywhere.

Freebies Welcome

"You get what you pay for" just doesn't hold true when it comes to soil amendments. Organic amendments are dear to a penny-pincher's heart because they cost much less and do a much better job of improving soil than higher-priced chemical additives. Better yet, many organic soil amendments are free for the taking.

If you're *really* lucky, your city may have a recycling center that composts municipal yard waste and chips branches for mulch. Proving that sometimes the best things in life really are free, these treasures are usually free to city residents.

Ask and Ye Shall Receive

Keep your eyes open and practice some creative thinking, and you'll find plenty of organic material that can be yours for the asking. Put up a note on your local post office, library, supermarket, or other bulletin board asking for materials, and you're likely to find even more sources. Here's a starter list of potential freebies:

❖ coffee grounds from coffee shops

❖ bagged leaves and grass clippings, but ask to make sure the yard wasn't treated with pesticides or herbicides, which could harm your garden plants

❖ decomposed manure from stables or farms

❖ vegetable peelings from restaurants

❖ past-their-prime fruits and veggies from supermarkets

❖ rained-on straw or hay from farms

❖ municipal compost piles

❖ municipal leaf-collection piles

Composting: Turn Garden Wastes into Garden Gold

Introduced 2,000 years ago by Marcus Cato, a Roman statesman looking to build soil fertility throughout the Roman Empire, composting is the main method for turning kitchen scraps, yard waste, your daily newspaper, and all kinds of other organic materials into one of the very best soil amendments. Nature's process of decomposition, the alchemy that occurs between microorganisms and raw materials during composting, is all it takes to transform garden waste into garden gold.

Finished compost, which is dark and crumbly with a delicious earthy fragrance, makes an excellent soil amendment, as well as an ideal mulch and a perfect top-dressing for fertilizing lawns. You just can't have too much of this good thing!

Be a Good Citizen

Not only is composting a sound horticultural practice, creating rich soil amendments from recycled garden trimmings, fallen leaves, and kitchen scraps, it is also environmentally valuable. Garden waste represents a huge percent of the bulk materials pouring into landfills. So pat yourself on the back for being a good citizen as you laugh all the way to the compost pile.

Keep It Simple

The art of composting is one of those gardening techniques that you'll get better at with experience. Don't worry about

Ashes to ashes, dust to dust, potato peelings to potatoes: The compost you make from organic matter, like the potato peelings being emptied onto this compost pile, becomes part of a satisfying circle when you use it to nourish the next generation of spuds.

following exact directions: All you have to do to create basic compost is to pile organic materials and let them rot. Just keep in mind that the necessary components of a compost pile are carbon-rich materials, nitrogen-rich materials, a bit of garden soil, and all-important air and water.

Pleased to Meet You, Ms. Green, Mr. Brown

"Wet" or "green" materials like weeds, fresh grass clippings, food scraps, and fresh manure are high in nitrogen. They decompose quickly because of their chemical makeup and their high water content. This speedy decomposition produces some

stinky side effects, namely ammonia and urea, which are produced during the process. Luckily, you can balance these fast acters with slow burners: the "dry" or "brown" carbon-rich materials, including dead leaves, straw, dry grass clippings, and newspapers. A mix of green and brown will achieve excellent, moderately fast results, with no smelly side effects.

Mix 1 to 4. Aim for a balanced recipe of roughly 1 part "green" materials to 4 parts "brown." Translated into the reality of a compost pile, that means you should alternate each 4-inch layer of, say, straw or dry leaves with a 1-inch layer of grass clippings or weed pullings.

Trust your nose. If your pile exudes an unpleasant ammonia smell, there's too much green material or not enough air. Fluff it with a fork or turn the pile, and mix in a generous dose of straw, newspaper, or other carbon-rich brown matter.

Let Your Bacteria Breathe

The microorganisms that cook your compost work best when there's air available to them. Just like feeding a fire with the air from a bellows, you can raise the temperature of your pile (an indication that bacteria are working hard) by incorporating air into the mix. Since nobody has invented a compost bellows yet, you'll have to do the work yourself by turning the pile.

Fluff with a fork. Loosen the pile every two weeks or so by turning over chunks with a pitchfork to let in air. Aeration is especially important in the

Keep a bag of shredded leaves or a bale of straw near at hand so you can bury kitchen scraps like eggshells or fruit that can lure raccoons, wasps, and other pests. A couple of inches of straw or leaves will keep your scraps where they belong—decomposing in your pile.

Fantastic Free Compostables

Composting is particularly gratifying to frugal gardeners because it costs nothing. When you see the rich, dark organic matter you shovel out of your finished pile, you won't believe it came from such humble beginnings. Any raw material of plant origin is fair game for the pile. Avoid animal products (other than eggshells), oils, and greases—they'll attract mice and other pests. The greater the variety of materials you put into your compost heap, the more nutritious the finished product will be. Add your own discoveries to the basics on this list:

- coffee grounds with the filter paper
- fall leaves
- grass clippings
- hay
- manure
- newspaper, shredded or torn into thin strips
- past-their-prime flower bouquets
- sawdust
- straw
- tea leaves, with bag
- vegetable or fruit kitchen scraps
- weeds, without mature seeds

summer. That's because a primary ingredient of your summer pile is likely to be fresh green weeds and grass clippings, which tend to clump together into one soggy mass, even if you add them to your pile in a thin layer.

Plastic ice cream tubs with handles and tight-fitting lids are great containers for collecting kitchen scraps and not only because they're freebies. The handle makes them easy to carry to the compost pile, the lid prevents odors from escaping, and the plastic makes them sturdy enough to reuse for weeks. Keep one in the sink or on the counter for easy access.

Soil Speeds It Up

Add a scattering of garden soil every few layers to "salt" the pile with bacteria and fungi to aid in decomposition. Garden soil is teeming with these handy helpers. You can also buy packaged compost starters, but unless your soil is seriously out of whack from pesticides or other chemical applications, the natural assortment of soil creatures will work just fine, saving you money in the process.

Spray Away

The faster you make compost, the sooner you can use it to improve your soil and feed your plants the nutrients it contains. A moist compost pile rots faster than a dry one, so give that pile a spritz with the hose to keep it cooking when rainfall is scarce. It also speeds things up if you lightly water layers of "brown" carbon-rich material like leaves or hay as you add them. Avoid getting too enthusiastic with that hose: A light sprinkling is

all that's needed because the green layers contain their own natural moisture. Unless deluges are the rule in your area, or at least during those seasons when they're not, make the top of the pile slightly convex to collect rainwater.

Small Bits Are Easier to Chew

Smaller particles break down faster than larger ones because more surfaces are available for microorganisms to work on. If you have a shredder, you can use it to chop your materials into bits before composting them. If you don't have one, try to find someone who will let you borrow theirs. Or chip in with compost-keeping neighbors and pool your money to rent a shredder periodically.

Fall cleanup is prime shredder time. Reserve a rental shredder for fall so it'll be ready and waiting to devour garden debris and raked leaves.

Storms leave a bounty. Branches and limbs decompose slowly in a compost pile unless you chip them first. If summer storms leave your yard or neighborhood strewn with downed debris, rent a chipper and downsize leafy branches into compostable crumbles.

No-Work Compost

The laziest composting method of all requires nothing more than patience. If you are willing to wait a year for compost, just heap everything on the pile willy-nilly and allow nature to take its course. Eventually all the leaves, weeds, grass clippings, and kitchen scraps will decay into a rich humus. The top layer will look unchanged, but burrow down several inches and you'll find your treasure.

To Bin or Not to Bin

You certainly don't need a bin to make compost. An out-of-the-way corner of your yard will serve just fine if you'd rather not spend the money on a commer-cially made bin, or spend the time on a do-it-yourself version.

When neatness counts. Compost bins make your operation tidier than an open pile and can also make the work of turning the pile easier, thus speeding up the end result. More than a hundred types of composting bins have hit the market, ranging from small systems suitable for pocket-size gardens (even rooftops and balconies) to large, triple-compartment bins that divide fresh, processed, and mature compost. Read the literature, ask friends for recommendations, and if possible try them out before you buy.

A pallet-able idea. You can find free wooden pallets (also called skids) at many businesses. (If you see pallets but don't see a "free" sign, just ask.) Load three in your car and tie them together to make an open-fronted square for a sturdy, serviceable bin. And, of course, it's free! If you'd like something more formal, you can add a fourth pallet in front for a door.

what will you save?

Make Your Own Compost to Save

Compost is the all-purpose soil amendment, improving every soil type from heavy clay to sandy soil. In addition, it is an excellent topdressing for lawns and beds, adding nutrients to the soil. You can even use it by itself as a loose-textured planting medium for potted plants. You can buy bagged compost at garden centers, but it takes little effort and no expense to make your own. For every bag you make instead of buying, you'll save about $2. Considering that a modest-sized compost pile can yield bushels of compost every year, you could gain a savings of $50 or more annually.

The Frugal Gardener's Workshop:
Budget-Wise Bins

Cinder Blocks

Stack inexpensive cinder blocks to make a two- or three-bin compost unit, leaving the front of each bin open. Stagger the blocks as shown in the illustration, and allow space between each for air to circulate.

Wire Ring

Attach wire fencing (4 feet high × 12 feet long) to stakes hammered into the ground. Close off the circle by wiring the two ends together. When it's time to turn the compost pile or to shovel out compost, unfasten the wired ends and bend them back. Or unfasten the fence from its supports, uproot the stakes, turn the pile onto the neighboring soil or fork it into a garden cart, then recorral with the wire.

Plastic Barrel

This cement-mixer–style composter is ideal for small gardens. You can make compost in containers such as these in as little as two to three weeks. Fill the barrel with garden and kitchen waste, and rotate it daily. When the compost is ready, empty the barrel and begin again. You must remove a finished batch before starting a new one.

Plastic Bin

This plastic bin is an excellent system if you have limited space. Add material to be composted in the top of the bin. Collect finished compost from the door at the bottom that slides up and down to open and close. Air slots along the sides provide the oxygen necessary to keep the composting process going.

Sniffing Out Manure Sources

You can purchase manure at garden centers packaged in 25- or 40-pound bags. It is dry and odor-free and screened so that it's fine-textured, not lumpy. Collecting manure yourself, however, is an even better deal for frugal gardeners. You can often get manure for free, or for a nominal price, from farms or stables. After one to two hours with a pitchfork, you'll have a season's supply.

Old Is Better

If you have a choice when you go to collect your own manure, opt for the oldest pile that has been exposed to the elements so that it has decomposed. Then you can put it to immediate use in the garden instead of composting or aging it first. Fresh manure is too potent to apply directly to the soil or around plants—it can easily burn plants with an excess of nitrogen.

Hefty Bags to the Rescue

Sturdy plastic bags are excellent for hauling manure. Fill them only halfway so that they don't tear from the weight when you lift them. Five-gallon buckets, available free for the asking from many restaurants, are also great for hauling manure.

Multipurpose Manure

What to do with your newfound riches? Dig it in around plants that need a boost or shovel it anywhere your soil needs improving. Chemical fertilizers give plants a quick boost of nutrients, but do nothing to improve the soil. Manure builds the soil at the same time it provides nutrients to plants. Who could ask for anything more?

Top-dress with manure. Use nutrient-rich manure as a topdressing around your trees and shrubs to give them a growing boost.

Make fertility tea. Steep a shovelful of manure for a few days in a bucket of water to make manure tea, an excellent fertilizer to apply when watering your plants.

Frame a piece of ¼-inch-mesh hardware cloth with 1 × 4s for a quick and easy screen to sift your aged manure. Screened manure has a fine consistency, so it's easy to incorporate into the soil or use as a topdressing for lawn and garden. A garden hoe makes quick work of sieving large quantities.

FRUGAL GARDENER'S GUIDE

Manure Connoisseur

Any manure is great manure as far as your garden is concerned, but some are easier to use than others, and some just plain smell better. Use this chart to become an informed manure connoisseur.

TYPE OF MANURE	COMPOSITION	APPLICATION	COMMENTS
Cow	0.5% nitrogen	To avoid scorching plants, allow to mature for 8 or more weeks	Likely to contain weed seeds that may germinate
Horse	Slightly higher in nitrogen and phosphorus than cow manure	To avoid scorching plants, allow to mature for 8 or more weeks	Likely to contain grain and weed seeds that may germinate
Hog	Higher in key nutrients than horse manure	To avoid scorching plants, allow to mature for 8 or more weeks	Has an unpleasant odor
Sheep and goat (sometimes known as "goat berries")	Higher in key nutrients than hog manure	To avoid scorching plants, allow to mature for 8 or more weeks	No offensive odor
Chicken	1.5% nitrogen and phosphorus	Kills plants on contact when fresh; must be composted for at least a year	Use sparingly, even when well rotted
Rabbit	2.4% nitrogen	To avoid scorching plants, allow to mature for 8 or more weeks	Cover with carbon-rich mulch, such as shredded bark, to keep it moist while it decomposes

Build tilth in any soil. Dig manure into the soil to improve its texture and fertility. It improves the porousness of heavy clay soil and adds mass and bulk to light, sandy soil. That means that manure-enriched clay and sandy soils will both hold water better, and clay will be less likely to crack and dry out.

Stockpiling Manure

The more manure you gather and store so that it's on hand when you need it, the more likely you are to use it to amend the soil in the odd planting hole or to spread it around as a topdressing. While your manure is piled, it's undergoing important changes that make it usable in the garden.

15 Places to Find Free Manure

1. Riding stable
2. Livestock auction lot
3. Horse ranch
4. Sheep farm
5. Chicken ranch
6. Pet shop that carries rabbits
7. Rabbit ranch
8. Pig farm
9. Circus
10. Zoo
11. Wild animal park
12. Petting zoo
13. Cattle farm
14. Fairground
15. Rodeo

weeks (a year or more for chicken manure) so it has time to break down and mature before using it in your garden.

Weed seed kill-off. Cow and horse manure are commonly full of weed seeds waiting to germinate. To kill the weed seeds, you need to compost the manure at temperatures between 113° and 158°F. To generate that kind of heat, create a manure pile 3 feet wide and 3 feet deep. Use a compost thermometer with a long heat-sensitive probe to monitor the internal temperature, and turn the pile every few days to let in oxygen, which helps fuel the composting process. The hotter the better!

Green Manure

Green manure is using live plants directly to enrich the soil rather than having them pass through an animal's digestive system first. Called cover crops, they are an inexpensive and excellent organic way to improve the soil in vegetable gardens or beds of annuals that are empty in the off-season. In addition to adding

Nitrogen breakdown. Fresh manures are quite strong and will burn plants with their concentrated ammonia. Compost fresh manure for at least eight

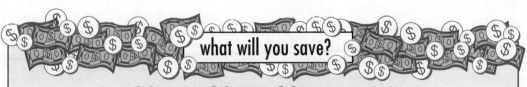

what will you save?

Manure Money Management

Free manure will save you money on fertilizer and soil amendments—anywhere from $2 to $8 or more per application of each couple of cubic feet. In addition, a garden rich in manure will be healthier and more vigorous than one grown without it. As a result, you'll reap greater rewards for all your gardening efforts.

organic matter, cover crops such as clover, annual rye, vetch, barley, and alfalfa keep down weeds while the ground is lying fallow. Sow the seeds in autumn and allow them to grow through the winter. In spring, use a rotary tiller to turn the plants into the soil before they have set seed. Wait three to four weeks before planting.

Nitrogen Boost from Legumes

Make green manure do double duty by choosing a cover crop such as clover or alfalfa from the legume or pea family. Legumes "fix" additional nitrogen in the soil by interacting with certain strains of rhizobium soil bacteria to release nitrogen in a form that's easily usable by other plants. Later when you till them under, your legumes will contribute their aboveground growth to soil improvement.

If you live in a warm climate, try heat-loving legumes like crimson clover and Austrian peas.

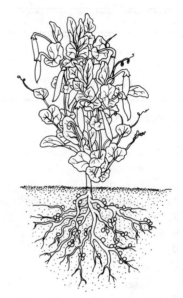

Legumes such as peas, beans, and clover pull nitrogen out of the air and add it to the soil by means of a bacterial relationship with nodules on their roots. Add these plants to your garden as crops or green manure to improve fertility, and follow them with leafy crops like lettuce to take advantage of the nitrogen boost.

Mulch: Reuse and Recycle

Mulch is a four-season wonder. In the winter it keeps roots warmer, reducing stress on many plants and helping to prevent plants from heaving out of the ground during freeze-thaw cycles. In spring, summer, and fall, it blocks out weeds. As the summer sun grows hotter, mulch helps to keep plant roots cool, especially if the mulch is a light color that doesn't absorb heat as readily as a dark color.

Mulch also helps the soil retain moisture by as much as 6 to 10 percent, and it encourages earthworms to take up residence. Mulches of organic materials break down to enrich and replenish the soil. This "garden blanket" is a boon to frugal gardeners everywhere—well, almost everywhere. Where slugs and snails are abundant, or where the growing season is very short, you'll get better results if you hold the mulch.

Organic Mulches Do Double Duty

Organic mulches are the best choice for thrifty gardeners because they contribute to soil fertility and tilth while suppressing weeds and conserving moisture. You can choose from compost, shredded leaves, newspaper, straw, pine needles, shredded bark, bark chips, and many other options. Straw is easy to apply and great for keeping in moisture. However, it's only moderately successful at weed control unless you pile it on really thick, and that is very expensive.

Black plastic is the worst option. Although it's useful for warming the soil in early spring so you can plant earlier, it is expensive, difficult to apply, and subject to cuts and slits that give opportunities for eager, vigorous weeds to sprout. In addition, it cuts off all oxygen to the soil, and at the end of the growing season it has to be removed, since it won't break down and improve the soil.

Newspaper as Mulch

For the frugal gardener, the ultimate way to recycle newspapers is in the garden. Newspaper is one of the most beneficial mulches available. It is also readily available throughout the country (in most homes bountifully so), inexpensive, and easy to apply. In mulch tests performed by Thomas D. Cordrey at Pennsylvania's Delaware Valley College of Science and Agriculture in the early 1980s, both shredded newspaper and sheet newspaper did as well or better at retaining soil moisture and keeping down weeds than more traditional mulching materials including straw, black plastic, or leaves.

Tear and soak. Where space around plants is tight, lay handfuls of wet newspaper strips around plants and cover with a thin layer of more attractive mulch.

Layer and anchor. For bigger areas, simply spread the sheets in thick layers around the plants in the bed. Soak with a hose, then cover the newspaper with a generous layer of nicer-looking mulch to keep the paper in place.

Fallen Leaves as Mulch

Shredded fall leaves are a wonderful, inexpensive option in regions where deciduous trees release bushels of the mulching material each autumn.

For a fast, free mulch, tear newspapers vertically into ½-inch strips, and then swish them around in a bucket of water to wet them thoroughly. Snuggle handfuls of the tangled strips around plants, then camouflage them beneath a thin layer of a more decorative mulch.

Use your lawn mower to chop leaves for mulch and composting. Remove the bagger and aim the chute toward the center of your cutting area so that you make several passes over the leaves as you concentrate them in a small area.

They're an attractive, practical mulch. Your lawn mower is the perfect tool for chopping fall leaves. Once they're chopped, apply a thick layer as mulch or add them to the compost pile.

Your tax dollars at work. In many communities, autumn leaves are collected by the municipality and dumped in a central spot where residents are free to collect all the leaves they can carry. This is a wonderful resource for the frugal gardener. If you want large quantities, check to see if the city is willing to deliver a truckload to your home.

Free Mulch from Tree Trimmers

Many tree service companies are more than happy to give away truckloads of shredded or chipped wood acquired in the course of cutting down and trimming trees. It saves them the time and expense of making a trip to the dump.

Let your fingers do the walking, and call around to locate a source. Call your local road department and the utility companies, too, to see where a tree clearing is planned and who is doing it. In many cases, a single phone call (or a stop by the side of the road if you see work crews in action nearby) is all it takes to get a nice big truckload of wood chips for absolutely nothing.

what will you save?

Mucho Savings from Mulch

Mulch saves you time on weeding and money on watering. It improves the soil, which means better, healthier plants. You can keep from losing perennials to "frost heaving" with a thick mulch. Also you can overwinter some plants that are borderline tender in your region if you protect them with thick mulch over the winter. Translated to dollars and sense, mulch can easily save you hundreds of dollars' worth of weeding and watering labor each season, plus a hefty chunk of change for mulch-protected perennials you won't have to replace after frost damage.

One Man's Trash…

Once you start composting and mulching, you'll always be on the lookout for new sources of raw materials. Many dedicated composting gardeners have been known to collect the bagged leaves and lawn clippings left by their neighbors on the curbside for trash collection—in many cases leaving their less fervent spouse mortified. But don't be shy. What the neighbor perceives as waste, the frugal gardener recognizes as a valuable resource.

Set shyness aside. Most folks are glad to have you cart away their bagged grass or leaves. All you need to do is ask. If you like, offer an exchange: Some of your overflow zucchini or tomatoes for a bag of grass clippings, for instance.

Untainted only, please. While you're asking, check to see whether the lawn was treated with pesticides or herbicides, which could affect the growth of your plants if you use the clippings as mulch, or infiltrate your chemical-free yard with some unhealthy or at least undesirable substances.

20 Money-Wise Mulches

1. Cocoa shells
2. Compost
3. Corrugated cardboard
4. Cottonseed hulls
5. Grass clippings
6. Ground corncobs
7. Hay
8. Newspapers
9. Paper towels or fast-food napkins
10. Peanut hulls
11. Pine needles
12. Rice hulls
13. Rotted manure
14. Sawdust
15. Seaweed
16. Shredded bark
17. Shredded leaves
18. Straw
19. Wood chips
20. Worn-out cotton throw rugs

Turn that old cotton throw rug from your bathroom or the thrift shop into a weed-killing, soil-enhancing mulch. Simply lay it over bare soil, or cut it into pieces for tighter quarters. It'll stop new weeds in their tracks and smother existing ones, keep the soil moist and cool, encourage earthworms, and gradually disintegrate as the soil community goes to work.

Frugal Feeding for Fabulous Crops

Healthy, fertile soil eliminates most of the need for supplemental fertilizers in your yard and garden. If your soil is rich in organic material, a once- or twice-yearly topdressing with compost or rotted manure provides all the nutrition most plants need.

Just like people, plants can overeat. If a plant is given too much nitrogen, for instance, it responds by growing an excess of weak, dark green leaves. All this energy channeled into producing unnecessary foliage can delay the production of flowers and fruit.

Read the Leaves

If your plants look healthy, grow well, and produce good crops, you're doing everything right. If you still have the urge to improve matters, turn to page 144 for lots of handy recipes for homemade food boosters to keep your plants flourishing in tip-top shape.

Occasionally a plant may cry out for an extra nutrient. It conveys its message of need primarily through the leaves. Here are some signs to watch for.

More Nitrogen Necessary

If a normally bright green plant begins to turn paler green, the lower leaves turn yellow, and the growth appears stunted, it probably needs additional nitrogen.

Phosphorus Feeding Needed Now

A phosphorus deficiency generally is indicated by stunted growth accompa-

nied by red, purple, or very dark green foliage. Manure and other organic fertilizers are excellent for providing phosphorus. The soil microorganisms that decompose the organic matter temporarily use the phosphorus and then release it back into the soil in a form accessible to the plants.

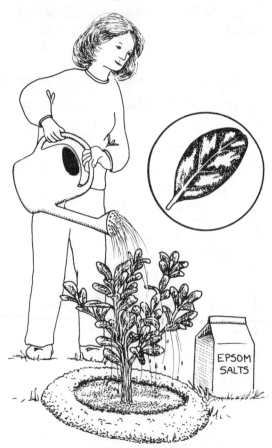

Plants that exhibit bizarre signs like discolored foliage, stunted growth, or twisted leaves may have a nutrient deficiency. Identify the problem and provide a supplement, then test the soil and amend as recommended to prevent recurrence.

Although phosphorus may be present in the soil, it isn't always in a form that is available to plants. It is most available to plants when the weather is warm and when the soil is kept moist. If phosphorus deficiency is an ongoing problem in your garden, check the pH. Phosphorus is more available to plants in soil with a pH level between 6.0 and 7.8.

Detecting Other Deficiencies

Boron. If new leaf growth is pale green at the base and twisted, it probably lacks boron. Add wood ashes or kelp meal.

Calcium. If new leaves and opening buds die back at the tips, the plant probably needs calcium. Apply lime to the soil to correct the deficiency.

Copper. Insufficient copper causes the young leaves to grow pale and eventually wilt. At that point, the tips turn brown. A vinegar drench will provide a short-term solution.

Iron. Iron deficiency is indicated by yellowing between the leaf veins and stunted growth. Choose a chelated iron, which maintains the iron in a nonionized, water-soluble form so the nutrient can be absorbed by the plant.

Manganese. A lack of manganese shows up as yellowing between the veins on young leaves, with brown spots scattered throughout the leaf. Douse the plant with a tablespoon of Epsom salts diluted in a gallon of water to solve the problem.

Potassium. Weak stems and leaves with yellow tips and edges that eventually turn brown are the signs of inadequate potassium. Greensand and granite meal are good sources of potassium.

Sulfur. A lack of sulfur is indicated by young leaves that turn light green. Add organic matter to the soil to increase the sulfur content.

Zinc. A zinc shortage is recognizable by yellowing between the leaf veins, thickened leaves, and stunted growth. Again, a vinegar drench may prove helpful.

As savvy frugal gardeners, it pays to watch for these signs and correct them ASAP. A dead plant is more than a disappointment—it's a waste of money!

Fabulous Fertilizers—Free!

Anything that feeds the soil, and thus the plants, qualifies as a fertilizer. Free fertilizers are all around us. Instead of throwing away grass clippings, throw them on the compost heap, use them as mulch, or mix them directly into beds when you dig them in the spring. It's even less effort to leave them on the lawn where they will decompose and return to the soil to provide nourishment: a perfect cycle of growth and decay. Other plants make good fertilizers, too.

Peas for the garden. Legumes from the pea family interact with soil bacteria to release and fix nitrogen in the soil. Meanwhile, their roots are penetrating the soil, aerating it. If you plow those same plants back into the bed, they will decompose, improving the organic content and soil structure.

Comfrey made its reputation as a healing herb, but its leaves are particularly high in nitrogen, so it's great for an impromptu fertilizer, too. This tough perennial plant thrives after being cut back to soil level, so don't hesitate to harvest the topgrowth and apply it as a nitrogen-rich mulch.

High-nitro herb. Comfrey leaves, in addition to their historical use as a medicinal herb for humans, are excellent as a high-nitrogen mulch. Cut back the plants occasionally and lay the leaves as mulch around other plants. They'll add a nitrogen boost to your compost pile, too.

Wealth from the sea. Seaweed washed up on beaches is an excellent material for mulch or for composting, since it's high in many micronutrients. If you're a frugal gardener who lives near the ocean, this is a great source of free mulch for your garden, or make your own liquid seaweed!

Create a Custom Blend

Store shelves are lined with fertilizers for every purpose you could imagine. Once you begin using organic matter to boost your soil fertility and tilth, you'll find you have surprisingly little need for auxiliary plant foods. Still, sometimes you may want to juice up your plants with a dose of high-power organic food—to help them over a difficult period, such as after transplanting, or to encourage bigger veggies or better flowers. Stock your shelves with a few basics, like fish emulsion and seaweed extract, and add that to your arsenal of stockpiled manure and compost, and you have all the makings for custom fertilizers, ready whenever you are and costing only pennies per application. Try these custom blends.

4 Fast Foods for Seeds and Seedlings

1. Once every two weeks, feed your seedlings with a weak mixture of water-soluble fertilizer made by mixing ½ cup fish emulsion with ½ cup seaweed extract. Store in a sealed container in a cool, dark place. To use, dilute 3 tablespoons of fertilizer in 1 gallon of water. Mist onto seedlings so you don't disturb the roots.

2. Water with manure tea made by filling a bucket one-eighth full of manure and topping off with water. Allow to steep for one to two days, stirring occasionally. Water seedlings and transplants with pure water first, and then follow with about 1 cup of manure tea diluted until it is amber colored.

3. Use compost tea to protect seedlings from fungi that cause damping-off. Mix 1 part well-rotted compost with 6 parts water. Allow to steep for a week, stirring occasionally. Strain the tea, and

then soak seeds overnight in the seasoned water before sowing.

4. Comfrey and nettle fertilizer is high in nitrogen and potassium, excellent for stimulating developing plants. Fill a bucket with comfrey and leaves from immature growth on stinging nettles (wear gloves and long sleeves to avoid nettle stings). Top off the bucket with water, and soak the leaves for three to four weeks. The unpleasant odor is normal, and you may want to put the bucket in an out-of-the-way spot. Strain off the liquid and use it to fertilize older seedlings.

10 Fast Foods for Veggie Gardens

1. Just as your potato tubers are beginning to enlarge, give them a boost of calcium by applying pelleted gypsum to the hill around the plants.

2. Nitrogen-hungry vegetables such as broccoli, peppers, and spinach thrive on alfalfa meal. Spread it liberally around the plants in your veggie garden.

3. Nourish potassium-hungry crops such as cabbages, carrots, beets, turnips, and parsnips with a midseason application of wood ashes. Keep stored wood ashes dry or their nutrients may leach away.

4. Top-dress high-nitrogen feeders such as corn and tomatoes with well-rotted manure.

5. Fish emulsion, diluted as recommended on the container, is an excellent foliar spray for vegetables needing supplemental nitrogen.

6. Make manure tea by filling a bucket two-thirds full of water and topping it off with manure. Allow it to steep for two to three days, and then pour off the liquid, leaving the solid material at the bottom. Dilute the seasoned water until it is the color of weak tea. Pour about 2 cups of the tea around any vegetable plant that might benefit from extra nitrogen. Do not use it on root vegetables—they need potassium, not nitrogen.

7. Make compost tea following the instructions above for manure tea, and use it in diluted form when watering the vegetable patch.

8. Apply fish meal to beds just before planting. As a fertilizer, it provides nitrogen and phosphorus.

9. Work seaweed meal (also known as kelp meal) into the soil in early spring before you plant. It is rich in nitrogen, potassium, and trace minerals.

10. Mulch around tomato plants and other heavy feeders with comfrey leaves. They are high in nitrogen and potassium. As the leaves decompose, those nutrients will be released into the soil.

10 Fast Foods for Flower Gardens

1. Starting in spring, scratch 1½ cups of alfalfa meal into the soil around each hybrid tea rose and water it in. Repeat the application every six weeks during the growing season. Perennials also thrive on alfalfa meal. Apply half a handful per plant.

2. Make an eggshell tea to give blooming perennials a calcium boost. Place crushed eggshells in a 1-gallon jug. Fill it three-quarters full with water and allow it to steep for a few days. Stir or shake the solution before you pour it on the plants.

3. When you clean out a fishbowl or aquarium, pour the old water onto the flower garden.

4. If your plants show signs of magnesium deficiency—yellowing of older leaves and curled leaf edges—water them with a solution of 1 tablespoon of Epsom salts (magnesium sulfate) diluted in 1 gallon of water.

5. When you plant bulbs, sprinkle bonemeal into the planting hole. It decomposes slowly, so the phosphorus will be released about the time the bulb begins to grow actively, giving it a helpful boost.

6. Use bloodmeal, which is high in nitrogen, to give blooming plants more energy. Follow the label instructions for the amount to use per plant, as this rich organic fertilizer can damage plants if they are given an overdose.

7. In early spring, encourage flower gardens to put on an extra growth spurt with an application of fish emulsion. Made from partially decomposed, pulverized fish, it is high in nitrogen as well as trace elements. Your garden will smell fishy for a few days, but the plants will flourish.

8. Place a nitrogen- and potassium-rich comfrey leaf in the bottom of a

Save the nutrient-rich water when you clean your fishbowl or aquarium. Pour into a bucket, then use to spot-feed garden plants. Your flowers will love it! Leafy vegetables, like lettuce and cabbage, will also flourish with a regular watering, courtesy of your fish.

planting hole. It will break down quickly, giving the new plants a boost.

9. Feed your flowers with a homemade organic fertilizer of 2 parts cottonseed meal, 1 part colloidal phosphate, and 5½ parts granite dust. Mix all the ingredients well. This fertilizer has a nutrient ratio of approximately 5 percent nitrogen, 10 percent phosphorus, and 10 percent potassium. You can find the ingredients at a farm supply store or garden center.

10. Apply aged manure to annuals as side-dressing in midsummer to give them a boost to get them through the dog days.

5 Fast Foods for Trees, Shrubs, and Lawns

1. When you mow, leave the grass clippings on the lawn. The clippings decompose quickly, adding nutrients to the soil.

2. Just as with flowers, if your shrubs show signs of magnesium deficiency—yellowing of older leaves and curled leaf edges—water them with a solution of 1 tablespoon of Epsom salts (magnesium sulfate) diluted in 1 gallon of water.

3. Acid-loving plants such as camellias, azaleas, and rhododendrons enjoy the nitrogen-rich boost they get from cottonseed meal. Apply it **following package directions** to the shrubs three times a year, timed to key summer holidays: Memorial Day, Fourth of July, and Labor Day.

4. Top-dress trees and shrubs with well-rotted manure. You'll be amazed at how fast they grow.

5. Use a spreader to broadcast a fine layer of screened manure over your lawn as a slow-release nitrogen fertilizer and soil amendment.

5 Fast Foods for Problem Soils

1. Add limestone to neutralize acidic soil. For most plants, you want to raise the pH to a neutral range—somewhere between 6.1 and 7.5.

2. Improve the structure of clay soil by adding pelleted gypsum (calcium sulfate). Choose pelleted gypsum over ground gypsum because it dissolves more readily. Start with 20 to 30 pounds of pelleted gypsum per 1,000 square feet of garden.

3. Add shredded oak leaves or a vinegar drench (pure vinegar on wet soil, or a vinegar and water solution on dry soil) to increase the acidity of your soil for plants such as azaleas.

4. To boost nitrogen, plant a cover crop such as alfalfa, clover, annual rye, hairy vetch, Austrian winter pea, or barley in the autumn. Till it into the ground the following spring before it goes to seed.

5. Spread wood ash from your winter fires onto the garden beds. Also known as potash, it will gradually build the soil, adding potassium as well as 32 trace minerals.

The Lazy Way to Great Soil

Frugal gardeners spend their time as well as their money wisely, which is why labor-saving techniques are so valuable to us. One of the easiest systems for amending the soil is to simply compost in place. Just pile on leaves, grass clippings, manure, and other compostables throughout the summer and autumn months, creating a 12-inch-thick layer of material. Leave it to decompose over winter. As the materials break down, the pile will shrink so that the 12-inch covering will be only a few inches thick by spring. In spring, dig or till in the top layer so it is well blended with the soil below.

How Much Is Enough?

It is impossible to add too much organic material to your soil. The minimum amounts you will need depend on the quality of the soil when you begin and how deep you plan to dig. Unless your soil is very heavy or very sandy, start by incorporating a 4- to 5-inch-thick layer of amendments spread over the top of the bed. Two wheelbarrow loads of organic matter and half a wheelbarrow of compost to enhance decomposition should be enough for a 5 × 5-foot garden plot.

Squeeze test for success. To check if you've incorporated enough organic matter, try this time-honored, simple soil test. Pick up a handful of soil and squeeze it. If it crumbles when you loosen your grip, you have good soil in your hands. If it doesn't, then you should add additional organic matter. You may groan at the prospect of digging the bed yet again, but every spading helps incorporate the material better, and in the end you'll be rewarded with a garden that grows well.

A Yearly Dose Does It

If you're preparing a permanent bed for perennials, it's wise to spend the extra time getting the bed right before you plant at all. After the soil passes the squeeze test, all your bed will need is an annual topdressing of organic matter, which earthworms will work into the soil for you. In the case of vegetable beds, you can repeat the digging-in process yearly so that your soil is in peak condition to produce bountiful crops.

Soil Test Sense

Many gardeners grow great plants without ever having their soil tested. They count on organic amendments to satisfy the needs of the soil community and the plants that grow there. But it can be a false frugality to skip having a soil analysis done. Linda McAleer, extension agent for Virginia Cooperative Extension in Fairfax County, tells the sad story of a woman who had a well-established hedge of azaleas. "They were beautiful," Linda says. "But someone told her she needed to make the soil more acid. Without having the soil tested first, she spread iron sulfate around the roots. She put on too much, giving the plants a toxic overdose, and killed them. A good-quality soil test report will tell you exactly how much lime or sulfur you need to adjust the pH of your soil to the ideal level for your plants. This woman's loss was unnecessary."

Changing chemistry. It requires serious chemistry to give an accurate breakdown of the nutrient content of the soil. Linda McAleer recommends paying the higher price to get a proper analysis from a reputable laboratory or through your local Cooperative Extension Service rather than buying a cheap test kit at a garden center. Have your soil tested every three or four years. Acid rain, leaf fall and decomposition, and other factors can change your soil's chemistry over time. With regular tests, you can keep up with those changes.

In addition to getting a comprehensive report about the chemical makeup of your soil, a good-quality laboratory will include information on what amendments—and how much—you'll need to make necessary improvements.

 **smart tips** 12 SMART SHOPPING TIPS

1. If you buy amendments by the bag, check the price per pound. As a rule, the larger the bag, the cheaper the price per pound.

2. Split a truckload of manure, wood chips, or other mulches and soil amendments with a neighbor. You'll both save big.

3. Become a champion scrounger. Keep your eyes peeled as you drive on your daily rounds, watching for curbside grass clippings, bagged leaves, and other grabbable goodies.

4. Rescue concrete blocks from a demolition site (ask permission first, of course) to make a quick compost bin that costs nothing.

5. Comparison shop by phone to save time and gasoline.

6. Borrow a pickup truck or hire a private hauler (check the classified ad section of the newspaper) when it's cheaper than the delivery fee from mulch or fertilizer suppliers.

7. Make "get it free" your motto. Before you shell out precious bucks for soil amendments or organic mulches, consider substitutes that you can get for little or nothing.

8. Post notices on community bulletin boards so people know what you're looking for. Be specific: Even the manure from a single backyard rabbit can go a long way, so advertise for "Manure wanted by the truckload" (or by the bucket) instead of just "Manure wanted."

9. Put out the word among neighbors, friends, and coworkers in case they have any contacts who can supply what you need.

10. Reserve a shredder in advance at the rental store so that you can process your materials when you want to, not when the machine is available. Nobody wants a mountain of black plastic trashbags sitting for months in the yard!

11. Before you buy any soil amendments—or add any freebies to your soil—have your soil tested. You may be surprised that your soil's pH level is just where it needs to be for the plants you intend to install.

12. Don't wait until spring to test your soil. Send your soil sample off early to beat the rush. You'll have your results in plenty of time for earlybird shopping specials.

✔ Frugal Gardener Checklist

- Nourish your soil to save money and avoid chemical fertilizers.

- Find free sources for soil amendments.

- Learn what, if any, supplemental nutrients your soil needs by testing it every three or four years.

- Build supplies of compost and manure and use them liberally to fertilize, mulch, and improve soil structure.

- Save time and money on weeding and watering by using mulch.

- Cover bare soil over winter with alfalfa, barley, Austrian winter pea, hairy vetch, or ryegrass to enrich the soil while the garden sleeps.

- Save money by making your own organic fertilizers.

- Mix batches of potting soil blends as you need them.

CHAPTER FIVE

CUTTING MAINTENANCE COSTS

Maintenance costs are measured more in time than in money, but as frugal gardeners know, the two are equally valuable. Avid gardeners would rather spend their time working in the garden than doing anything else, but repetitive chores like weeding, watering, and mowing the lawn are about as much fun as doing dishes.

Time is valuable, and we'd all rather be fooling around with plants than spending hours on must-do duties. After all, we could be out looking for bargains or sitting in a comfortable garden chair with a cool drink by our side, enjoying the beautiful scene we have created. Low-maintenance gardening to the rescue! These commonsense ideas will keep your yard looking beautiful while freeing you from hours of the labor that once consumed most of your garden time.

10 Commandments
of Low Maintenance

A low-maintenance garden is designed so that care is simplified and stream-lined. Follow these ten basic steps, and you'll find yourself with enough free time to actually sit on that inviting bench and sip lemonade while patting yourself on the back for your maintenance-saving garden smarts.

1. Reduce Lawn Size

The standard American lawn is a major time-waster, and if you use store-bought fertilizers, it's also a money drain. Rethink the size of your lawn and reduce it bit by bit until you have only the lawn you need—enough for a game of catch with kids or dog, enough for a picnic with friends, enough to be a living ornament for your gardens. You'll learn lots of tricks in this chapter for gaining a new perspective on your own version of the American lawn and how to live with it.

2. Mulch with Abandon

Mulching is fundamental to a low-maintenance garden. No other gardening technique accomplishes so much in one fell swoop. Mulch cuts down on water evaporation, reducing the need for wa-tering. It keeps roots comfortably cool on hot summer days and encourages earth-worm populations. It also blocks out

most weeds and improves the soil as it decomposes. So much from one simple practice! Look for more on mulch in the weed-control section on page 172, and in Chapter 4, "Save Money with Soil Amendments."

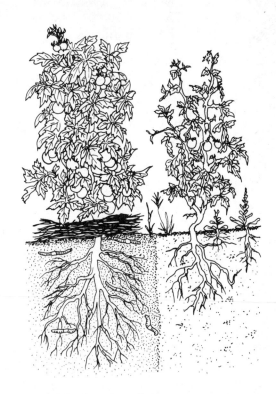

The mulched plant at left is growing in cool, moist soil that's well aerated by earthworms and is untroubled by weed competition. The unmulched plant at right is in hot, dry, compacted soil that needs frequent watering, and it's stunted be-cause neighboring weeds are stealing nutrients and moisture.

3. Invest in Soil Improvement

Healthy plants start with healthy soil. Make yours the best it can be by digging in liberal amounts of manure and other organic amendments. By improving the soil, you'll also correct drainage problems, cut down on watering chores, eliminate extra fertilizing, and grow sturdy, vigorous plants that are less susceptible to pests and disease. Chapter 4, "Save Money with Soil Amendments," has all the information you need to create top-notch topsoil.

4. Grow Appropriate Plants

For a garden that will save you time and money, opt for plants that are native to your region and conditions or for adaptable imports that grow easily in your area. Nurturing finicky exotic plants and making them grow in a less-than-ideal climate imparts a sense of satisfaction and control, but it's an expensive and time-consuming occupation. Enjoy your prima donnas if you choose, but fill your gardens with more dependable plants that don't require such cosseting.

Besides, keep in mind that the local plants that are mundane to you are exotics to people from other areas. Agapanthus, for instance, a South African native that is so well suited to life in California that it is used to landscape the freeways, is a prized and pampered fussbudget in English gardens. Enjoy what grows easily in your region, and use the money you save to travel to see the exotics in more ideal habitats.

5. Water Wisely

Knowing when and how to water will save you hours of time and improve your water bill, too. With proper watering practices, you can even train your plants to develop deep roots that search for water in the soil, so they aren't so vulnerable to drought. For ultimate labor saving, install a simple irrigation system with automatic timers that waters your garden for you. All you do is set the timer or flip the switch. You'll find all the how-tos on page 165.

6. Win the Weed Battle

Weed smarter and less often with easy techniques for keeping these gardener's nemeses in check. Mulching alone can eliminate nearly all your weed problems in flower and veggie gardens and shrub plantings. What's left is easy to eliminate with light hoeing and hand-pulling. Discover how to do it on page 172.

7. Enlist Nature's Allies

What your mama didn't tell you about the birds and the bees is that they—and other friends from the wild side—are your best allies when it comes to fighting pests in the garden. They clean up caterpillars, siphon up aphids, and otherwise keep the natural balance in your yard. Besides, they're fun to watch. Instead of initiating a wholesale campaign against anything that creeps or flies in your garden, learn how to attract beneficials and how to recognize some of the best pest fighters on page 176.

8. Group Plants by Need

Shade lovers in shade, sun lovers in sun—that much is just plain common sense. Take it a step further and group plants that prefer morning sun rather than steady afternoon rays, plants that do best in lean soil, or plants that flourish in gravelly soil. It also makes maintenance sense to group plants with similar care requirements in the same area. Then you can water all the plants at once, instead of just the extra-thirsty ones, and feed everything at the same time with the same fertilizer. It's a time-saver that will lead to a better garden that needs less intervention from you.

Your eyes are one of your best weapons when it comes to defending your plants against diseases, pests, and other problems. Watch for abnormal growth like curled leaves or insect infestations, and remove them as soon as you see them.

9. Practice Preventive Pest Control

We all know what an ounce of prevention is worth, so put the adage to work by monitoring your garden as you stroll through on your daily rounds. Watch for signs of potential problems—a curled leaf, a wilted stem, a mildewed branch, an influx of aphids—and literally nip them in the bud by removing the afflicted plant part. Get your protectors on the job, too, by attracting birds and beneficial bugs to your garden. It's easy to do, following the tips in this chapter, and it will save you hours of labor later by warding off serious outbreaks of pests or diseases.

10. Design for Durability

Keep the future in mind when you add features like decks, patios, walks, walls, fence, and arbors to your garden. Consider how much maintenance your selections will require, then weigh the investment in maintenance against the cost of the item. Durable materials such as stone or brick cost more initially, but in the long run will save you time and money on replacing rotted wood. Once built, a paved patio is virtually cost-free to maintain. It reduces your overall garden maintenance and gives you a place outdoors to relax and enjoy the fruits of your labor.

Buy the best-quality wood fence you can afford, even if you have to stretch your pocketbook a little. Thick boards and sturdy fasteners will hold up years longer than shoddy, inexpensive alternatives. When it comes to painted items, weigh prettiness against painting chores: That white-painted arbor may be appealing, but the unpainted wood one that will weather naturally is a better choice for less maintenance. Remember that metal furniture or trellises may also need periodic repainting.

Depend on Annuals for Constant Color

Perennials are great for frugal gardeners because they come back year after year, but annuals are a better bargain when it comes to maintenance—and they'll supply non-stop color from late spring through fall. They're plant-it-and-forget-it flowers that need no extra care once they're in the ground, other than occasional watering in dry spells. Annuals are inexpensive, whether you grow them yourself or buy nursery packs, and they brighten up a yard in a big way. While most perennials have a short season of flowering, annuals bloom continuously until the first killing frost. They are great fillers in a perennial border and make a spectacular display when massed together. Plant them close together and they'll choke out weeds. Choose trouble-free annuals such as cosmos, petunias, celosia, annual salvia, dusty miller, zinnias, and marigolds for sunny spots. In filtered shade, opt for wax begonias, torenia, coleus, and impatiens.

More Cost-Cutting Maintenance Ideas

If ten commandments aren't enough for you, here are a few more tips for low-maintenance gardening:

❖ Save on water bills by setting watering priorities. Trees, shrubs, and perennials planted within the past year are first on the list because they cost the most to replace. Vegetables come next so you don't lose the harvest, then annuals. Put your lawn at the bottom of the list. It will come out of dormancy after the first soaking rains.

❖ Throw a bedsheet over frost-tender vegetables and annuals in the early evening when nippy nights draw near. Frost-free Indian summers often follow light first frosts, giving you a few more weeks of good growing if you protect the plants from the earlier touch of chill.

❖ Stop deadheading annuals such as zinnias and cosmos late in summer so they can sow seeds for next year's bloom.

❖ Plant improved cultivars of petunias that need no deadheading or cutting back to keep looking good right through the summer. 'Purple Wave' petunia is hard to beat for sheer continual floriferousness.

❖ Get a longer growing season by taking advantage of warm microclimates in your garden, such as heat-radiating garden walls, south-facing beds, and protected corners of your house and patio.

❖ If you don't leave grass clippings on the lawn when you mow, empty your mower's bagger into the nearest garden bed, spreading the clippings out as a mulch. They'll quickly decompose while smothering weeds, holding moisture, and improving the soil.

❖ Don't fertilize flowers, veggies, shrubs, or trees when they are stressed from lack of water in the summer or when they're dormant in the winter.

❖ Plant deciduous trees near your house to cut your summer air-conditioning bill and winter heating bill. The leafy cover cools the house in summer, and the bare trees allow the sun to warm the house in winter. You'll spend less and conserve energy, too.

❖ Enlist birds in pest control by planting trees and shrubs that produce berries or fruit to attract them to your yard. Good choices include serviceberry, dogwood, hawthorn, holly, cherry, mountain ash, and birch.

❖ Design flowerbeds with straight-edged fronts and curved corners so that neighboring grass is easy to mow in a rectangle, with no odd-sized curves and strips left over.

For swift and easy lawn mowing, make the front edges of your beds a straight line and curve the corners so that the mower can make equal passes over the grass without backtracking to cut odd curves.

Taming the Lawn Tyrant

Once a week, every week, from spring through fall, a lawn demands your labor. Make the most of that investment of precious time by following these shortcuts. And if you find you're still spending more time than you'd like with your lawn, turn to the next section ("Mow? Just Say No!" on page 159) for lots of inspirational ideas.

Mow the Right Height

Most people mow their lawn too short. Mowing grass shorter than necessary invites disease problems and weed invasion. Taller leaf blades also shade the roots, preserving moisture and encouraging deeper root growth for healthier grass plants. The deeper roots will tap a greater area of soil for nutrients and water. Longer, more vigorous grass also discourages weeds by shading and crowding them out. Pull out a ruler to see if it's time to adjust the blade height: Your mower setting should be 2 to 3 inches (if your lawn is zoysia, cut 1½ to 2 inches high). Don't mow the grass again until it's grown a third more than the cutting height. For example, if you're cutting at 3 inches, mow when the grass tops out at 4 inches.

Let Clippings Lie

Repeat after me: Grass clippings do not cause thatch. Thatch is a layer of dead grass parts, including slow-to-decompose stem and root bits. Grass clippings decompose quickly, providing a layer of fine mulch that conserves soil moisture and provides some fertilizer. A season's worth of grass clippings gives nutrients back to the soil at a rate equivalent to one fertilizer application. If you don't need the clippings for mulch or compost, there's no reason to collect them, unless you've procrastinated on mowing chores and your newly mown lawn looks like a hayfield, with clumps of clippings strewn across it.

Train Your Lawn to Resist Drought

Frequent watering makes your grass grow faster. Light frequent watering is even worse: It trains your grass to grow a shallow root system since the moisture it seeks is in the top inch or so of soil. To cut down on mowing and reduce a lawn's water dependency, water less often. Infrequent, deep watering encourages deep root growth and less topgrowth. An inch of water every seven to ten days should serve most lawns well. Invest in a rain gauge to judge natural rainfall and sprinkler efficiency.

Feed in Fall

An overfed lawn will grow excessively, requiring more mowing, and it will be less resilient to stress and diseases. Also, too much fertilizing will upset the important balance of the soil's own hardworking bacteria. "Fertilize just once a year," recommends Joe Keyser, program specialist for the Montgomery County (Maryland) Department of Environmental Protection and an articulate activist on sound environmental gardening practices. "Fertilize in the fall, in October," he continues. He recommends organic fertilizer. "Don't be taken in by the conventional advice about 'controlled-release' synthetic fertilizers. Like watering, these fertilizers trigger the cycle of dependency," he explains. "A lawn that is fed more than once a year or with potent synthetic fertilizers is an overfed, hyperkinetic lawn. It will exhaust you."

Plant the Right Grass

If you're planting a new lawn or replacing an old one, start with careful selection of the grass you'll be using. Lawn grass has come a long way, with new research going on all the time into improved

Design for Easy Mowing

Sensible garden design makes mowing simpler by removing obstructions to the simple clean sweep of the lawn mower. Here are a few places to cut maintenance corners:

- Edge your lawn with mowing strips, such as brick, plastic, or metal lawn edgings laid flat in the grass so that the wheel of your mower can roll along them, eliminating trimming chores.

- Mulch around trees and shrubs in a wide band that keeps your mower from damaging trunks or branches and keeps you from getting poked by protruding twigs.

- Remove lower limbs of trees so you don't have to duck, or increase the size of the groundcover or mulch bed beneath them so that you don't have to walk below the branches when mowing.

- Design the shape of your lawn so it is easy to mow. Avoid having small, odd corners that are tricky to get into and turn around in.

- To avoid excess water runoff and to make mowing easier, make the lawn as level as possible.

varieties that resist disease, laugh at drought, tolerate shade, or exhibit other valuable improvements. Instead of buying the first bag of grass seed you see, check with your local nursery or extension service to learn the best varieties for your region. A few extra dollars invested up front for quality seed can save you years of problems later.

All Grass Is Not Alike

Match plant to site when you're choosing grass, and use even more care than when you're planting perennials or a shade tree—your weekends depend on it! Choose a grass variety that is suited to your climate and growing situation. For northern climates, choose cool-season grasses such as fescues and improved perennial ryegrass. In warm climates, choose heat- and drought-tolerant grasses such as zoysiagrass, Bermuda grass, and centipede grass.

Grass seed mixes combine grasses to get the benefit of several desirable features. For example, Kentucky bluegrass, known for taking foot traffic well, also tends to go dormant in extreme heat, so it's often combined with ryegrass and fescues to get heat tolerance as well as durability. In shady situations, opt for shade-tolerant grasses such as St. Augustine grass for warm climates and fine fescue for cool-season lawns. Hundreds of named cultivars are available for these grasses; consult a knowledgeable extension agent before you buy.

Mow? Just Say No!

The average American spends more time on his lawn than any other garden activity. Depending on the size of your lawn, you can easily use up a precious weekend afternoon mowing and trimming the edges of that tyrant lawn. If you're getting more resentful of the time you allocate to your lawn, the easiest solution is to get rid of some of your grass. Of course you'll want to keep some lawn for its usefulness and its beauty, but you can easily trim the edges here and there with alternative plantings that are more satisfying to look at and easier to care for.

in this manner provides horizontal open space and visual rest. A well-designed garden uses a lawn as a counterpoint to other landscape elements, not as the primary feature. To achieve this look, make beds of shrubs, perennials, groundcovers, and other greenery around the perimeter of the lawn, keeping the swath of lawn fairly narrow and occasionally allowing it to widen into a calming pool of quiet green. Or let a wide strip of lawn wend its way through your gardens.

Make a secret garden. Enclose a corner of the lawn with a shrub hedge, fence, lattice, or wall to create a private garden cut off from the rest of the open space.

Lawn as Ornament

Consider shrinking your lawn's size to a plot that serves a designated role in your overall landscape plan, rather than something that's there by default. Let your lawn serve a design function, providing an oasis of level green in contrast to a lot of vertical design elements. Like a pond, a lawn used

Use grass as an ornament in your garden to widen into a quiet pool of green as a focal point at the end of a narrower grassy walkway.

Meet Grandma's Mower

One of the delightful side benefits of having a small lawn is that you don't need a noisy electric- or gas-powered mower to keep the grass sheared. A small lawn is perfect for Grandma's mower, the old-fashioned push type with revolving blades, also known as a reel mower. Most have five blades, although for a finer cut such as on golf courses, there are seven- and nine-blade machines. Invest in a good-quality machine, and keep the blades sharp. Instead of enduring the weekly roar of a machine-powered lawn mower engine, enjoy the gentle whirring sound of the turning reel mower blades.

Save money and space. A reel mower will save you money on servicing and gas, and it takes less space to store. You can hang it by its handles on the garage or toolshed wall, thus saving floor space.

Lawn Alternatives

It's easy to slice the time you spend on lawn-mowing chores by replacing part of your grass with plants that will give you more satisfaction than a stretch of plain green. Replacing lawn with a wildflower meadow is a popular alternative and a rewarding one; you'll find details in the section "Low-Cost and No-Cost Meadow Mixes" on page 162. Here are some

other guaranteed great replacements to inspire your creative instincts:

Shrubs to the rescue. Replace a section of lawn with a border of mixed flowering shrubs. Old-fashioned forsythia, weigela, mock orange, lilac, and rose of Sharon will give you bloom throughout spring and summer.

Create a shady grove. Donate a portion of your lawn to a grove of small trees, such as redbuds, goldenrain trees, dogwoods, or serviceberries. Mulch under the trees with thick layers of newspaper topped with wood chips or shredded bark to keep the grass from growing through.

Plant rocks. Create a rock garden on a slope, with large rocks for accents and small shrubs and perennials planted between the stones. Mulch with attractive rounded river gravel or other locally appropriate stones.

Before you laugh, give it a try: You may remember the reel mower as an antique from another generation, but this well-oiled, sharp-bladed machine is a pleasure to use on a small lawn.

Use water wisdom. Replace lawn with a fish pond or reflecting pool. Site it in full sun away from shade trees, so leaves won't clog it up. Add a fountain to enjoy the relaxing and cooling sound of falling water.

Discover an island. Create or enlarge island beds in the lawn that can be enjoyed from all sides. Mound soil by adding topsoil or compost to raise the bed for better drainage and to give the planting more visual oomph.

Get tied up in knots. Take a level rectangle of lawn, especially if it can be viewed from upstairs windows or a balcony, and turn it into a knot garden. Plant the "knot" with low-growing boxwood, lavender, or other neat, evergreen shrubby plants. Fill in the spaces between the pattern of intertwining low hedges with different colors of gravel.

Make a conifer sampler. Replace a patch of your lawn with various low-maintenance, dwarf conifers of varying colors and textures to create a fascinating bed with year-round interest.

6 More Ways to Cut Your Lawn Down to Size

1. Replace lawn with groundcovers like vinca (periwinkle), pachysandra, or ivy in shady areas where grass is reluctant to grow.

2. Reduce the lawn size by digging additional flowerbeds.

3. Plant groups of shrubs in corners of your yard. They'll make your garden more appealing to birds while cutting down on mowing chores.

4. Pave an area to create an attractive place to sit.

5. Where shallow tree roots or dense shade make grass growing difficult, replace lawn with an attractive mulch such as cobblestones, colored gravel, or shredded bark.

6. Notice areas where the lawn is worn due to excessive foot traffic, and put in a path following the natural track.

Make the Most of Moss

Why fight to get grass to grow in damp, shady spots? Instead of rooting out the moss that naturally takes hold there, learn to appreciate it and turn that difficult lawn spot into a moss garden. Take a soil test to determine the pH; moss flourishes at an acidic pH level of about 5.5. If you need to make the soil more acidic, spread garden sulfur at a rate of 4 pounds per 100 square feet. Once the moss spreads, you'll have an attractive green groundcover that needs no mowing or fertilizing. Fill in gaps with clumps of moss transplanted from other parts of your yard in early spring. Keep your moss lawn tidy with an occasional sweeping with a soft, long-bristled broom.

Low-Cost and No-Cost Meadow Mixes

Since the early 1980s, seed companies have been perfecting the "meadow-in-a-can" collection of wildflower seeds, creating mixes that are suited to specific regions of the country as well as sunny and shady situations. Most of these mixes depend on annual flowers for their fast growth and almost instant color. That can lead to disillusionment the following year, when weeds outcompete the garden you planted. Follow these tips to create a satisfying, sustaining meadow.

Meadow Grasses Are a Must

Look for a mix that includes grass seed, which will provide soil stabilization, help support rangy wildflowers, and lend a more natural look to the planting. If the seed mix you want is grass-free or if you're making your own blend, add your own, nonaggressive grass seed or plants to the meadow. Native grasses suitable for your area of the country are a good choice; consult a catalog from a native plant supplier such as those listed in "Resources for Frugal Gardeners" on page 263. Never use aggressive pasture or grass such as annual rye or bluegrass for a wildflower meadow. They will quickly crowd out the wildflowers.

Collect Your Own Custom Mix

Wildflower meadow seed mixes are relatively inexpensive, and the cost per pound drops when you buy in bulk. Some frugal gardeners save even more money by creating their own seed mix with seeds they gather themselves (see "Flowers for Free" on page 76). Many commercial mixes include such "wildflowers" as Johnny-jump-ups (*Viola cornuta*), poppies (*Papaver rhoeas*), and bachelor's buttons (*Centaurea cyanus*), none of which are wild in America, but all

For a low-maintenance meadow garden that sustains itself year after year, depend on fast-spreading, tough-growing perennials that can compete with weeds and grass.

of which sprout and grow faster than the weeds they're competing with. You can follow their example, or you can use true meadow wildflowers that are native to your region, such as California poppies (*Eschscholzia californica*), purple coneflowers (*Echinacea purpurea*), and black-eyed Susans (*Rudbeckia hirta*).

Plants for Permanence

Instant meadow mixes are fine for fast color on bare, prepared soil, but to keep your meadow going year after year, you will need to take a different approach. Go ahead and sprinkle your seeds, but also add transplants of perennial wildflowers of vigorous constitution, such as bee balms (*Monarda* spp.), Joe-Pye weeds (*Eupatorium* spp.), perennial sunflowers (*Helianthus* spp.), native asters (*Aster* spp.), and blue mistflower (*Eupatorium coelestinum*). Your meadow will continue to be a true beauty for years after you've planted it.

Meadow Care

Keep the bed moist until the seeds germinate. Water the bed at least once a week the first year to help the plants become established. No fertilizer is needed. Selectively weed your meadow if necessary to eliminate any pernicious weed pests that threaten to take over. Then just enjoy the succession of plants as your meadow becomes self-sustaining.

Cutting Back Is Essential

In late winter, use a scythe or lawn tractor to cut back your meadow to a height of 6 inches. (You can rent a lawn tractor if you don't have one or barter with a neighbor who does.) This procedure will keep woody plants from invading and will allow light and room for the spring-sprouting plants. You may want to cultivate small areas of your meadow, baring soil so you can sow a new crop of annual flowers for extra color.

what will you save?

Less Lawn = More Free Time

Lawns are notorious time and money eaters. They require gallons of water to stay green, pounds of fertilizer, and regular mowing. The less lawn you have, the more time you will save to enjoy more satisfying aspects of garden and family life. Additionally, you'll save money on all the maintenance supplies and equipment you need to keep a lawn looking green and healthy. If it takes 4 hours to mow the lawn every week during a five-month season, that's 80 hours of time invested just in mowing. Eliminate just 20 percent of your lawn, and you've bought yourself two full 8-hour days of freedom from the mower. Congratulations!

Dollar-Wise Watering $trategies

Conservative watering is not just personally rewarding, it's absolutely necessary in these days of shrinking aquifers and population pressure. About half the water consumed by the average homeowner is used to water the yard and garden. As population density increases throughout the nation and summer droughts occur more frequently, water conservation has become an important issue nationwide, not just in arid regions of the country. Efficient watering means money saved as well as healthier plants—two great payoffs for the frugal gardener.

Train Drought-Tolerant Grass

Lawns are more drought tolerant if their roots go deep into the ground, where they can seek deeper moisture when rain is scarce. Encourage this deep root growth by watering slowly, deeply, and less often. Frequent, shallow sprinkling will give you a beautiful green lawn, but one good taste of drought will send it into a brown sulk much more quickly than deep-rooted turf. Never remove more than one-third of the grass height when cutting—a "scalped" lawn requires more water to recover. Aerate the lawn and dethatch if necessary so it's better able to absorb rainwater or sprinkling. If water shortages are severe, allow your lawn to go brown. Most lawns will turn green again once the rains begin.

Kill the Competition

Weeds in the lawn and garden beds compete for moisture and nutrients. Pull weeds as soon as you see them. If the weeds haven't yet set seeds, use their dead carcasses as an in-place mulch to preserve precious moisture in the soil around your desirable plants.

Prune to Reduce Watering Needs

One of the easiest ways to save water and to improve the appearance of your garden is to prune. A well-manicured plant, in addition to being more attractive, uses water more efficiently than an overgrown one because its roots don't have to supply water to unnecessary branches and foliage. Pruning an overgrown shrub or tree can dramatically improve its health, water efficiency, and overall appearance. Prune away all the dead or injured branches from your trees and shrubs, remove any weak or spindly growth, and thin out the tree or shrub to emphasize the beauty of its natural form.

Good Soil Saves Water

Sandy soil loses water because it flows through too quickly and evaporates easily. Clay cannot easily absorb water, so fast-flowing water usually runs off before it has a chance to soak in. Good-quality soil that includes plenty of organic matter saves water because the organic particles retain the moisture like a sponge. Adding organic amendments such as compost, shredded leaves, or aged manure to soil of any kind will increase its ability to absorb and maintain moisture. For more on soil amendments, see Chapter 4, "Save Money with Soil Amendments."

Stop Those Leaks!

An insidious source of water waste is leaks. Repair any hose connections, valves, or piping that show signs of dripping or seeping. Even a small leak can waste hundreds of gallons of water over a period of days. The simple task of replacing a washer or valve can solve the problem.

Irrigation Systems with Smarts

You can reduce your water use by as much as half—and water your plants more thoroughly—with a proper irrigation system. Though sprinklers are usually a waste of water, even they have an appropriate use. Lawns are best watered with the traditional sprinkler systems. Place empty tuna cans around your lawn to make sure that your sprinkler is delivering the right amount of water in all areas of the landscape. Soaker hoses, drip systems, and in-ground irrigation are other alternatives for using water wisely in your landscape and gardens.

Thrifty Sprinkling

Sprinkler systems that spray beyond the lawn onto pavements and paths or that are left to run too long are a prime source of wasteful runoff. Adjust your sprinklers so the spray falls where it will do the most good. Invest in automatic timers so you don't forget to turn off the water.

A useful attachment to an automatic sprinkler control is a shut-off device that turns the system off if it's raining. It works by sensing the weight of rain on a mechanical switch, which turns off the automatic system until the next time it is set to run. Tensiometers that measure moisture content in the soil also can be connected to automatic sprinkler timers; the timers only will kick in when water is needed. No more wasted water—or wasted money!

Invest in an automatic timer for your sprinkler or irrigation system and you'll never again forget to turn off the water.

Water the Roots

Trees, shrubs, flower borders, and vegetable gardens are more efficiently watered with either drip irrigation or soaker hoses. Water is delivered directly to the plants' root system, rather than being sprayed into the air where a surprisingly large percentage evaporates. The slow water delivery provided by soaker hoses and drip systems allows the water to soak in deeply, without wasteful runoff. As a result, plants tend to grow faster and more evenly, and their roots penetrate farther into the ground, increasing the plant's drought tolerance. Because water is concentrated exactly where it is needed, weeds are minimized, as are diseases that result from wet foliage.

Do-It-Yourself Drip

Drip irrigation systems are easy to install because lines don't have to be buried. Nurseries and home centers carry kits that come with all the parts you need, along with instructions for designing and installing your system. Drip irrigation systems are divided into zones based on the type of plants that need to be watered. A collection of trees and shrubs in one part of the garden would be on one zone, flowerbeds and groundcovers on another. The vegetable garden would merit a zone of its own, as would the container plants arranged on your patio.

In-Ground Irrigation

You'll save lots of money if you install an in-ground sprinkler system yourself—approximately 50 percent off the cost of an installed system. Granted, the installation is a lot of work because of the trenches you must dig to lay lines, but

Watch the Sun

The most thrifty time of day to water is at night or early in the morning when the temperatures are cooler. Then the plants can take up the water without the added stress of excessive heat and before it evaporates in the hot air.

your garden and pocketbook will thank you. Components and detailed instructions for designing and installing a system are readily available at home improvement centers. Some sprinkler manufacturers will even draw up a plan for you if you send your layout worksheet with a scaled drawing of your property including the house, driveway, sidewalks, lawns, trees, and garden beds to the manufacturer. The experts on their staff will send you a customized, detailed layout, including recommended pipe sizes, sprinkler-head designs and their locations, the number of zones your system should have, the number of zone valves, and the best piping route to take. If the thought of laying out the installation overwhelms you, call the manufacturer before you buy to find out if they provide this service.

Water Conservation in Containers

Containers can waste a lot of water. The confined roots can't stretch out into surrounding garden soil, so they're de-

Keep the moisture in your containers by sliding the smaller, planted pot inside a larger outside pot. Stuff the crevice between the two with moistened sphagnum moss. Use more moss over the soil in the inner pot as a water-conserving mulch.

pendent on frequent watering. The pots dry out fast, thanks to evaporation. To help your pots hold water, group containers together so they lose less moisture through their sides, and keep them out of drying winds that can desiccate leaves and speed evaporation. Use plastic pots alone or as liners inside clay pots, which are notoriously prone to evaporation through their porous sides.

During hot spells, move containers to a spot where they get more shade to save extra watering. Another way to minimize evaporation is by sinking potted plants into the ground or placing a pot into a slightly larger one and filling the gap with sphagnum moss for insulation and good looks.

Reuse Runoff

Runoff out of the bottom of a container is wasted water, unless it runs into soil where other plants have roots. Move portable containers onto the lawn or a garden bed before you water them so the excess water does some good. To minimize runoff, submerge containers in a large, water-filled tub, allowing the soil to absorb water until the bubbles stop rising. Then move the container to another tub to collect the runoff drips.

Become a Mound Builder

Build basins around your trees and shrubs to prevent water from running off before it seeps into the ground. Make the rim of the basin around the dripline of the plant, below the tips of the outer branches, the area within which most of the feeder roots are located. For large, deep-rooted trees, make the basin walls about 6 inches high; 3- to 4-inch berms will work for smaller trees and shrubs. You can fill the basin, knowing you've applied adequate water, and then move on to other chores. This technique really speeds up the task of watering.

Reach under the Eaves

Foundation plants growing along the walls of your house may not get much water if overhanging eaves prevent rainwater from reaching them. Make channels from the dripline of your roof or your downspout to the thirsty foundation plants to send water their way.

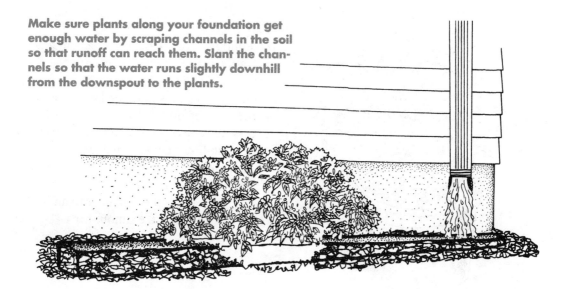

Make sure plants along your foundation get enough water by scraping channels in the soil so that runoff can reach them. Slant the channels so that the water runs slightly downhill from the downspout to the plants.

It's Raining, It's Pouring

Not all water comes out of your hose. Keep track of the amount of rain that falls during each storm, and use that information as a guideline for how often you need to supplement with irrigation. For example, a drizzle that drops just ¼ inch of water on the garden is not as valuable as a deluge that dumps 2 inches. Rainfall can be highly localized, so don't depend on your TV meteorologist to tell you how much fell on your property. Invest in a rain gauge, which you can buy for as little as $3, and you'll know exactly how much water you're getting from the sky.

Dry Shade Solutions

Maples are notorious for creating one of the most difficult gardening situations: dry shade. Their dense canopy of overlapping leaves prevents rainfall from reaching the ground below, unless it's a genuine deluge, and their multitudinous feeder roots quickly suck up any raindrops that do make it to the soil. Few ornamental plants will do well in such dim, thirsty conditions. Those that will tolerate dry shade include brunnera (*Brunnera macrophylla*), vinca or periwinkle (*Vinca minor*), dwarf mondo grass (*Ophigeogon japonicas*), mahonia or Oregon grape holly (*Mahonia aquilifolium*), ivy (*Hedera helix*), liriope, wild columbine (*Aquilegia canadensis*), epimediums, and *Geranium macrorrhizum*.

Roll Out the Barrel

Pure rainwater is excellent for watering plants both indoors and outside. A lot of rainwater flows off the roof, where it is funneled to downspouts and into underground drains. Instead of letting that water go to waste, catch it by placing plastic tubs or wooden barrels under the downspouts. It's a time-honored technique of saving valuable water. You can easily fill a bucket or sprinkling can from the barrel.

Some garden supply catalogs carry rain barrels, including a model that comes equipped with a hose fitted at the bottom of the barrel with an on/off valve for drawing water. Other features include a safety grid fitted into the top to prevent children from accidentally falling in and a screen to keep out leaves and other debris. If you can live without the fancy features, you can save money on a rain barrel by looking for an old wooden barrel at flea markets. An old wooden screen can be used on top.

Attach a rubber sleeve to the bottom of your downspout, and place the end of it in a large watering can. When it rains, your can will be filled with fresh water and ready to use.

Slow Down Runoff

Runoff is wasted water. If your soil is heavy clay, which absorbs water slowly, fast-flowing water will run off the surface and be wasted. As much as 50 percent of water can be lost due to runoff from clay soil. Amending the soil will solve the problem, but you can also alter your techniques to retain the water. Apply irrigation water very slowly so it has time to seep in, and build catch basins around the driplines of trees and shrubs to hold the water until it can soak into the ground.

Every Drop Counts in a Drought

If water is scarce in your area, in times of drought or naturally, turn to recycling to make the most of your household water. Instead of letting the shower water run down the drain while you're waiting for it to get hot, catch the cold flow in a bucket or watering can and use that water for houseplants or in the garden. Put a plastic bin in your sink for rinsing the dishes, and use the rinse water on your plants—you might even kill a few pests!

Gray Water in the Garden

Gray water is water that has been used for baths, laundry, showers, or other nontoxic cleaning purposes. Most soaps and detergents, except products containing boron, borax, or chlorine, are harmless to plants in moderation, so it is fine to use this recycled water in the garden. If you use a water softener, don't recycle gray water because the sodium in the water can harm plants.

If you want to recycle gray water, it will involve making plumbing changes to divert the water to the place where you want it. Refer to a detailed reference book before you proceed.

When to Water, When to Wait

In times of drought, many plants will survive with less water than you might have thought possible. For example, many well-established trees and shrubs, except for shallow-rooted plants such as azaleas, should be able to survive a season without extra watering. If you must seriously conserve water, be alert for signs of stress in your plants to tell you which plants are most desperate for a drink.

Signs of Stress

A plant that wilts, curling and drooping its leaves, is already in dire need of watering. If you are alert, you can notice prewilting signs that allow you to water before the crisis point. Look for leaves that have lost their luster, growing dull without their normal reflective quality.

Leaves that are just beginning to roll their edges inward or leaves that have a grayish tint also indicate the early stages of extreme water stress. These signs are the result of the plants' natural mechanism to protect against drought. Leaf pores close to conserve moisture, and the drooping reduces the leaf's exposure to the drying sun.

Obviously, waiting until plants are water-stressed isn't the solution. But there are frugal ways to stretch your watering dollar.

What's "Well Established"?

"Well established" means that a plant has sent its roots far into the soil, anchoring itself with strong main roots and growing a network of fine roots to carry food and water. A transplanted tree or shrub can easily take two years to become established. By the end of its first season in your soil, a few roots will have grown outward from the rootball, but it won't be fully established until at least the following year, and sometimes not until year three.

Trees and shrubs are pricey plants, so don't let them suffer when water is scarce. You'll need to supply supplemental water to any that haven't been in the ground for longer than two years, and remain alert for signs of stress even in plants in their third year in your garden.

Trees and shrubs started from seedlings establish themselves much more quickly than older transplanted specimens. Those that were self-sown volunteers and have grown their entire lives in your garden are solidly established even in year one.

Even a severely wilted plant, like the impatiens shown here, will recover when given a good drink of water. But the stress of the drought may cause a plant to drop leaves, fruits, or flower buds, even after it revives. If foliage is completely dried up from lack of water, the plant's survival is iffy.

Watering Roses

Large rose bushes that aren't severely pruned each autumn develop extensive roots, allowing them to survive drought conditions with little or no extra watering. Hybrid teas are more sensitive to drought than shrub roses. However, as long as the green stems don't wilt, a rose plant that goes without water to the point where the leaves droop can still recover with a couple of good soakings.

Survival Tactics

Many established trees and shrubs will drop excess leaves as a survival technique to make it through periods of drought. Grass goes brown. Don't be alarmed. Once the rains begin and the plants get regular water, they will grow new leaves. If you want to be on the safe side and avoid weakening your plants through the stress of drought, give them 1 inch of water every two weeks during drought periods.

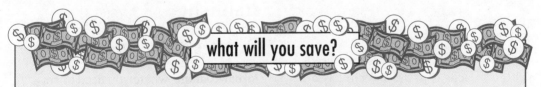

what will you save?

Set a Timer on High Water Bills

Wise watering and a comprehensive watering system for your garden will save you both time and money. An irrigation system with automatic timers will save you hours of holding the hose, as it waters the garden for you. Drip irrigation can save you hundreds of dollars a year on your water bill as well as help nurture healthier plants. As an additional frugal measure, train your plants to develop deep root systems by watering them deeply and less frequently. They'll be more resilient to drought and other stresses. By watering intelligently, neither too much or too little, you'll have healthier plants, another excellent way to save.

Beating Weeds

The bad news about weeds, the great survivors in the garden, is that they grow and flourish under incredibly adverse conditions. They tend to germinate and develop at a much faster rate than many cultivated plants, robbing the desirable plants of their moisture, growing space, sunlight, and nutrients.

In addition to these traits, many weed seeds are remarkably long lived. While the average vegetable seed has a storage life of only three to five years, weed seeds have been known to remain viable in the ground for decades, lying dormant until conditions are suitable for them to sprout.

The good news about weeds is that the frugal gardener has a great arsenal to use against them—and most of the weapons don't cost a penny.

Mulch, Mulch, Mulch!

The number-one way to stop weeds in their tracks is to use mulch. Lay a 2- to 4-inch layer around every plant in your garden, cover bare soil with the stuff, and renew it frequently, and your weeding chores will disappear. You can even use a generous layer of mulch to smother existing weeds. Don't overlook the value of using newspaper as a weed fighter. Lay it on thick, wet it to keep it in place, then cover it with a more attractive mulch. For more on this mighty labor-saving aid, see Chapter 4, "Save Money with Soil Amendments."

Hoeing and Tilling

If you're a mulch advocate, you may never need to drag out the hoe or the tiller to control your weeds. But these methods still have merit, especially in row-planted vegetable gardens where there is plenty of maneuvering space between the plants. Tilling the soil to uproot weeds has the additional benefit of aerating the soil, but be careful around shallow-rooted plants so that you don't disturb them.

Hand-Pulling

Use those excellent tools at the ends of your arms to get a grip on garden weeds. But don't save all your weeding for one long, tiring, discouraging session. Dandelion forks and other handheld weeding devices are useful, too. See Chapter 3, "The Frugal Gardener's Tools," for more on these gardeners' friends.

Wholesale Weed Removal

In situations where you need to cut down a slew of weeds in order to begin working the garden, a weed whacker is the perfect tool. Depending on the scale of the job, you either can use a hand tool such as a machete or scythe or a power string trimmer that cuts away unwanted vegetation with a spinning plastic string. Heavy-duty models with a metal blade will whack through even woody, thick-stemmed weeds. See Chapter 3, "The Frugal Gardener's Tools," for more on these tools.

13 Quick Ways to Stop Weeds

1. Mulch around plants to stop weeds. Thick layers of newspaper covered with more decorative mulch make an excellent weed block.

2. Work the soil for planting annual flowers or vegetables, water it, and then wait a seven to ten days for the weed seeds to germinate. Scrape off the weed seedlings with a hoe. If you have time, repeat the process once more before you plant.

3. Apply water directly to the roots of your cultivated plants, allowing the surrounding soil to go dry. Weeds will struggle under the drought conditions.

4. Mow or pull weeds before they set seed. One weed plant can produce as many as 250,000 viable seeds, multiplying your weeding problem exponentially.

5. Deeply buried weed seeds will not germinate until they are near enough to the soil surface to get some light. Avoid disturbing the soil so you don't bring new weed seeds to the surface.

6. Use pulled weeds to mulch around your plants. They will block the light to the soil, stopping the germination of additional weed seeds.

7. Hand-pull weeds for just 15 minutes a day. That's a short enough time not to get too bored or too sore, but long enough to make a noticeable dent in the job.

8. Plant hedges around your garden to minimize windblown weed seeds from the neighbor's yard.

9. Plant a cover crop such as clover, annual rye, vetch, barley, or alfalfa to prevent weeds in bare soil. Till the crop into the ground before it goes to seed.

10. Pull perennial weeds with extensive taproots such as dandelion, chicory, and curly dock and perennial grasses as soon as you notice them. A few a day should quickly get the population in check.

11. Make your yard attractive to birds, which eat multitudes of weed seeds.

12. Keep cheap dandelion diggers, which cost only about $1, stuck in the soil at various parts of your garden so you always have a weeding tool handy when the mood strikes you.

13. Use a shallow cutting tool, such as a Cape Cod weeder or scuffle hoe, to slice off weeds just below the soil surface without disturbing deeper layers of soil.

Solarize your soil by concentrating the sun's heat with black plastic to kill weed seeds in the top layer of soil. After four weeks, remove the plastic and plant, disturbing the soil as little as possible so as not to disinter viable weed seeds from deeper in the soil.

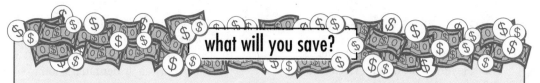

what will you save?

Fewer Weeds Means More Veggies and Flowers

In addition to being more attractive, a weed-free garden is a healthier place for your plants. If you are growing vegetables, you'll increase your harvest because you reduce competition from weeds. Your investment in flowering plants also will bring a better return if they don't have to share growing space with the weeds. By using organic weed-control techniques, you'll save money on chemical quick fixes that may harm the ecosystem.

Putting a Stop to Pests and Diseases

Warding off pests and diseases is one of the main aims of the frugal gardener. If pests attack your vegetable garden, you won't get much of a harvest. If disease ravages your fruit trees, you won't get apples this winter. Any plant in the garden is fair game for one or another pest or disease problem. Yet all is not dire: Most plants can tolerate a certain level of attack, and healthy plants are usually able to overcome such problems. Your aim, as a cost-conscious caretaker, is to do all you can to prevent problems in the first place and to step in swiftly if it becomes evident that they will not be quickly quelled by natural allies.

Prevention Is Cheap

Benjamin Franklin's adage that an ounce of prevention is worth a pound of cure is particularly apt in the garden. By following a few basic practices, you can go

a long way to minimizing the damaging pests and diseases in your garden.

Nourish the Soil

The best weapon a gardener has against both pests and disease is healthy, good-quality soil. Good soil will nurture robust plants that resist disease and that can handle being chewed on a little by pests. Healthy plants, thanks to healthy soil, are the first line of defense against pest and disease threats.

Plant for Diversity

Combine a mixture of plants in one bed or garden, rather than just a single type. A single crop, whether it is a fruit, vegetable, or ornamental, is easy prey for decimation if you get an infestation of the insect or disease that likes to attack it. Intermix your plantings to create healthy diversity. For example, rather than planting a rose garden, plant a garden that has lots of roses combined with various annuals and perennials. The garden will look more lush and floriferous when the roses are between bloom cycles, and the other plantings will distract rose pests. Or instead of the traditional vegetable garden where each vegetable type is planted in isolated rows, mix a variety of vegetables and flowers for a more interesting display and a healthier situation.

Introduce Garden Companions

Try companion planting, the art of planting neighbors that benefit each other. For instance, rue, which produces an oil in its leaves that causes a rash in some people, is believed to repulse rats and Japanese beetles. Plant rue near roses and other plants that are tasty to these voracious eaters. The roots of French marigolds (*Tagetes patula*) are proven to repel nematodes in the immediate area. Plant them among vegetables to help keep the soil free from the pests. Catnip attracts cats and discourages cabbage pests and aphids. It's a pretty plant that makes an attractive border around the cabbage patch.

Some say that basil growing next to tomatoes improves the flavor of the vegetable.

Depend on Decoys

In some cases, a companion plant is destined to act as a decoy. For example, aphids will suck the vital juices out of a wide variety of crops, both edible and ornamental. Plant a bed of nasturtiums, which aphids prefer above all other food choices, to protect roses, vegetables, and other plants. But be sure to keep decoy plants well away from those that share an attractiveness to the pest; otherwise, you're only inviting pests to a banquet.

No Hitchhikers, Please

Avoid introducing a problem into your garden. When you purchase a new plant, check it over carefully for any sign of insect or disease problems. Look at stems and both the tops and bottoms of leaves. Whitefly, spider mites, scale, and other insidious pests can sneak in on newcomers and infect other plants before you realize it.

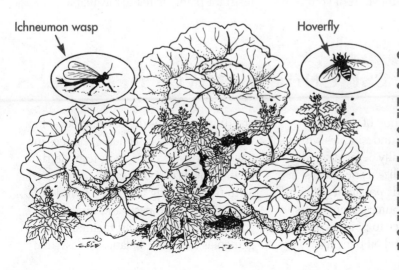

Ichneumon wasp

Hoverfly

Combine plants that provide apparently effective natural pest control. Catnip interspersed in a cabbage bed, for instance, is said to repel cabbage pests. At the very least, it'll attract beneficial insects to improve the balance of power in the garden.

Get a bug's eye view of the leaves of new plants before you introduce them to the garden. If insects or eggs are evident, remove them before transplanting.

Neatness Counts

A tidy garden usually has fewer pests and diseases than a messy one. Tall weeds and rampant growth are safe harbors for unwanted pests, including rats and mice. Anthracnose, a fungus that spreads by air or water, can be spread by infected leaves, especially when rain splashes off fallen, diseased leaves and back onto the plant.

Destroy or dispose of any diseased leaves or branches that you remove from your ornamentals or vegetables. Rake away unhealthy-looking leaves to prevent the spread of disease, and do your best to keep weeds at a minimum.

Buy Built-In Resistance

An easy way to prevent pests and diseases is to choose plants that aren't susceptible to them. Many plant hybrids that are listed as resistant to specific problems have been developed. For example, tomatoes may sport the initials F, V, and N, indicating that they have been bred to resist fusarium wilt, verticillium wilt, and nematodes. If you've had any of these problems with tomatoes in the past, or even if you haven't, you're wise to choose a variety that is less susceptible. Look for pepper hybrids—such as 'Bell Boy', 'Gypsy', 'Whopper Improved', and 'Yolo Wonder'— that are resilient to tobacco mosaic; apples like 'Liberty', which are highly disease resistant; and so on throughout the garden. With years of breeding behind them, a wide selection of pest- and disease-resistant plants is readily available.

Organic Pest Control $aves Big Bucks

The traditional method of pest control—zapping the undesirables with a toxic poison—is gradually being discredited as more people realize its negative side effects. In addition to the possibility of contaminating our water sources, many pests are developing resistance to poisons. Besides, a lot of poisons kill off beneficial creatures as well as the harmful ones. In a vegetable garden, insecticide residues may have hard-to-measure, long-term detrimental effects on our health.

In the following pages you'll find organic solutions to pests and diseases, so you can save money and maintain your garden as a healthy, balanced ecosystem.

Good Bug, Bad Bug

Of the billions of insects in the world, only a small minority feed on crops or ornamental plants. Using sprays against every insect in the garden is not only environmentally unsound but also bad economy because the beneficial insects are busy doing the work of the chemical poisons—for free. Know which insects you want to encourage and which you want to make disappear. Then enlist the help of your natural allies in the ongoing battle.

Meet Your Allies

Your garden will stay much healthier if you make an effort to include the natural inhabitants: birds, insects, snakes, toads, and other critters. By attracting animals that are higher on the food chain than plant pests, your garden will have a better chance of achieving its own natural balance more quickly, staving off pest outbreaks. Get to know your allies in the pest-control battle. They're more useful than any can of chemical spray because they keep working month after month. And of course, their help is free!

Befriend the Beneficial Bugs

Your first penny-wise approach to pest control is to encourage or introduce beneficial insects that will help bring your garden insect population into proper balance. Perhaps the best-known beneficial is the lady beetle, which feeds on aphids, mealybugs, soft scales, and spider mites, but there are many other good guys in the regiment of beneficials.

Feed the Beneficials

Many of the helpful insects, such as parasitic wasps, lacewings, and lady beetles, feed on pollen and nectar as adults, although their larvae devour insects. They have short mouthparts, so make their feeding job easy by providing small flowers with easy-to-reach pollen and nectar. Herbs such as fennel, dill, anise, and coriander all produce clusters of small flowers grouped together to form an umbrella shape. They're ideal for many beneficial insects, which can rest comfortably on the "umbrella top" as they feed. Grow yarrow, sunflowers, zinnias, and asters for later in the season. The beneficials will thank you by producing hundreds of offspring, which in their larval stage will devour multitudes of unwanted pests.

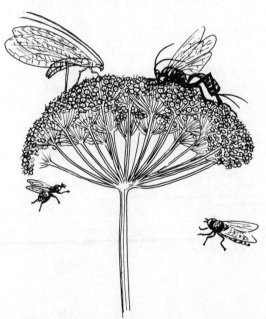

Adult beneficial insects, such as (*left to right*) the ichneumon wasp, hoverfly, lacewing, and tachinid fly shown here, feed on nectar, but their larvae dine with gusto on garden pests.

Good Guy Gallery

Learn to identify five of the super beneficial insects that will help protect your garden by controlling outbreaks of pests. Watch for them in your own garden. Their habits are fascinating. The adults feed on nectar, so provide plenty of nectar-rich flowers such as asters, mustard, and yarrow to attract them. Notice how the number of pests declines as the population of these protectors increases in your garden.

Hail the Hoverfly

Hoverflies, also known as flower flies, eat many species of aphids. You can recognize them by their distinctive flying style. They hover like helicopters over flowers, occasionally darting away like miniature hummingbirds and then returning to their post. They are sometimes mistaken for wasps; however, the hoverfly is stingless and harmless to humans. It's another story for aphids. One hoverfly larva can eat as many as 50 of them a day. Hoverflies commonly lay their eggs in young aphid colonies to ensure that the hatched larvae will have enough prey.

Many-Legged Predators

No respectable creature should have so many feet, but centipedes are a boon in the garden because they like to dine on slugs. You can encourage centipedes to settle down in your garden by providing lots of mulch. Spiders, whose eight legs show they're not true (six-legged) insects, are also great insect hunters, whether they're waiting patiently in a sticky web or stalking their prey on foot.

Learn the Larvae

The larval form of beneficial insects is very different from the adult form. For example, baby lady beetles have tapering, segmented, blue-gray bodies with black and yellow markings. "They look like small reptiles," says Susan Maguire, chairman of the Chichester Organic Gardening Society in England. "They're lovely—they swarm over my artichokes and runner beans, eating all the blackflies." Before you panic at the sight of unfamiliar "bugs" on your plants, try to identify just what it is you're looking at. Larvae are usually soft-bodied creatures. Refer to the pictures in a garden insect guide to see what the larval forms of beneficials look like.

Love Those Lacewings

Lacewing larvae prey on aphids, beetles, caterpillars, leafhoppers, mites, and scale insects. Their voracious appetite has earned them the nickname "aphid lion." Look for a white or pale green, delicate-looking insect that flutters erratically in a zigzag flight through the garden at dusk. To help lacewings overwinter in your garden, cut off the base of a 2-liter plastic soda bottle and push a rolled piece of corrugated cardboard inside. Hang the bottle in a tree or from a fence, with the open end facing down.

This Pirate Is an Ally

The minute pirate bug is easy to recognize because of its black and white harlequin markings. You'll find them in corn silks and stinging nettles. Collect them in a jar (carefully around stinging nettle!) and release them into your garden. Once situated, they'll feed on small caterpillars, leafhopper nymphs, spider mites, thrips, and the eggs of many insects. Encourage them to stay by growing pollen-producing plants such as goldenrod and yarrow.

Encourage Ichneumons

Most species of ichneumon wasps are tiny, although there are larger ones as well. They're harmless to humans. You can recognize them by the long, thread-like ovipositors that dangle behind. These bugs hunt caterpillars, sawfly larvae, beetle larvae, and other insects to feed their young. You can encourage these helpful wasps to come to your garden by planting pollen- and nectar-producing flowers.

Birds Are Music to a Gardener's Ear

Birds are just as valuable as beneficial insects when it comes to controlling pests. A wren, when feeding her young, can consume as many as 500 insects in an afternoon. Redstart young will eat almost triple that many insects in a day. Brown thrashers are hearty eaters, consuming as many as 6,800 insects a day!

Encourage birds to come to your property by providing them with an attractive habitat with plenty of sheltering shrubs and trees. Keep a birdbath filled with water, and set up an enticing feeding station if you don't already have one. Some birds prefer to roost in boxes, so if you want to attract bluebirds or purple martins—both insect eaters—install a house suitable to their needs.

Make Toads Feel at Home

Toads are also great insect feeders. At night they often sit by a garden walkway light, catching any unwary insect attracted by the glow. To encourage them to stay, you can buy charming, but expensive, terra-cotta toad houses, or you can make a reasonable facsimile yourself from a chipped flowerpot turned upside down. In fact, any damp, shady cover will satisfy the toads. Simply prop a board up on a stone to create a protecting cave for them, and put out a shallow container of water so they'll have something to drink.

This dish of water will also attract and nourish snakes and lizards. The lizards eat slugs and most insects and the snakes will dine on insects and small rodents. A small stack of wood or rocks will make an adequate shelter for a garter snake or a lizard.

Ernest Donchatz, who gardens on five acres in Clifton, Virginia, said that frogs moved in when he built several ornamental ponds in his formal, French-style garden. "When you step outside at night," he said, "it's like you are listening to a symphony." When they're not providing a serenade, the frogs are voraciously gobbling up insects.

Penny-Wise Pest Remedies

The first secret of penny-wise pest control is to catch the problem early. Once a pest takes hold, turning a minor nuisance into an infestation, it's much harder to get the situation under control. Walk through your garden frequently, taking time to enjoy the ever-changing beauty as well as to notice how plants are doing. If you detect any sign of pest damage or disease, take action immediately to nip the problem in the bud. A quick snip with your pruning shears and a borer-infested stem is history; a fast swipe with a paper towel and a hundred aphids meet their doom.

What's the Problem?

Learn exactly what is plaguing your plants. It's wasteful and environmentally unsound to spray a general poison without knowing whether or not it will solve your problem. If you don't recognize the insect or disease that is disfiguring your plant, then take a sample of the leaf or branch to a nursery or to your local cooperative extension agent and get an expert to diagnose the problem for you. Then choose an organic method of control that will specifically target the damaging pest.

Learn Life Cycles

Success is easier to achieve if you know the life cycle of the pest you are battling. Consider the stink bug, for example, which can do great damage to cabbage- and squash-family crops. They overwinter in weedy areas, where each female lays 300 to 500 eggs when weather warms. Within five weeks of egg laying, the new adults are ready to forage your crops and breed another generation. You can go a long way toward minimizing this pest by removing or mowing weedy areas near your garden beds. Better yet, replace the weeds with small-flowered plants, which will attract the native parasitic wasp that feeds on stink bugs.

Gypsy moth caterpillars can defoliate an entire forest. The caterpillars hatch in May, and that is the time to spring into action to minimize their damage. Band your trees with burlap strips, and pick off the caterpillars that take refuge during the day in the shade under the flap. By mid-July, the caterpillars have pupated, so after then burlap strips are useless and any remaining caterpillars will metamorphize into egg-laying moths. However, in fall and winter, keep an eye out for the brown egg masses attached to tree trunks, rocks, fences, or outdoor furniture. Each mass contains hundreds of eggs, so scrape them off and destroy them.

Fingers Are Fantastic Tools

Manual controls—your hands, that is—are the cheapest tools for controlling pests, although the process can be labor-intensive. Hand-picking pests also means that you'll have to overcome any squeamishness. Wearing rubber gloves may be helpful. You can also carry a jar full of soapy water to knock pests into a watery grave, a procedure best done in the cool of morning when insects aren't so fast-moving. Also, use your hands to aim a hard spray of water on shrubs and strong-stemmed flowers to wash off unwanted aphids.

Cute and Furry Culprits

Bambi, Thumper, Flower, and the rest of the four-footed gang may be irresistibly cute in the movies or in the woods, but they can munch through your garden in no time flat. Try these tricks to keep them away from valuable plants.

Don't Fence Me Out

The easiest solution to a rabbit problem is a fence. Use wire mesh no larger than ½ inch. Make a 2-foot-tall barrier and bury the bottom edge 6 inches under the soil.

Wire mesh is useful to deter mice from munching on bulbs, too. Either line the planting hole with fine wire mesh (useful if you're using the trenching method to plant the bulbs), bending the top over the planting before covering with soil, or cage the bulbs loosely in ½-inch wire mesh. You can also try tossing a handful of sharp gravel or crushed oyster shells into each planting hole with the bulb, on the theory that the sharp edges will hurt their noses.

High, black plastic-mesh fencing is easy to staple to trees and other supports, simple to handle, and definitely deer deterring. Tie white strips of cloth to the fence for a couple of weeks after you put it up so that deer know it's there and don't blunder into it.

When Moles Menace

Moles feed exclusively on insect grubs and worms in the soil, not plants or roots. However, their tunnels spoil the look of lawns, present an ankle-twisting danger, and are ready-made homes for mice and voles, which eat plants.

Flatten mole tunnels by walking on them whenever you see them (kids love this job). While you can use milky disease spore (see below) to eliminate grubs—one food source of moles—you may not get rid of the moles. They also snack on earthworms, which are a vital part of your soil community. You certainly don't want to eliminate them. In fact, the best approach to moles may be to congratulate yourself on having such nice worm-filled soil.

Dastardly Deer

If deer visit your yard, go the cheapskate route first and try the many deterrents that many people swear by: barbershop hair clippings, dried blood, hanging bars of soap, or store-bought deer-repellent sprays for prized plants. If none of those work, bite the bullet and erect a fence.

Plastic is great. Black or green plastic-mesh fencing, which biologists use for "deer exclosures" on public lands, works well and is unobtrusive, less expensive, and much easier to erect than wire fencing.

Call on Lassie. A free-running dog is a great deterrent, too, though you may have trouble getting Lassie to come home once she's off chasing after a deer.

BT Beats Bugs

An excellent nontoxic commercial solution to a caterpillar infestation is *Bacillus thuringiensis* (BT). A naturally occurring bacterium, it produces a protein crystal that is toxic to certain insects, paralyzing them. It seems to have no ill effect on birds or mammals. Different strains of BT are available for specific pests, including caterpillars, insect pests of vegetables, mosquitoes, Colorado potato beetles, and elm leaf beetles.

Lather 'Em Up

Insecticidal soaps have been proven effective on soft-bodied pests such as psyllids, whiteflies, mites, and aphids. Made from potassium salts of fatty acids, the soap is formulated to disrupt the external membranes of the soft-bodied insects by dissolving the waxy layer of their outer skins. The soap biodegrades quickly, so reapply it often, especially after rain. Manufacturers advise you not to try to mix your own soap sprays; some brands of soap have ingredients harmful to plants.

Grubs Begone

Milky disease spore kills grubs, which are the larval form of various beetles. Applied to the lawn, the powder infects more than 40 species of sod-eating white grubs, including Japanese beetle grubs, with a disease specific to them. The grubs quickly die. According to Theodore Reuter, director of St. Gabriel Laboratories in Gainesville, Virginia, where the product is produced, "Milky spore does not affect earthworms, birds, bees, fish, other animals, plants, or man, and it does not contaminate groundwater, ponds, or streams." Theodore adds that milky disease spore is the safest material produced for insect control—safe enough to eat on breakfast cereal. Although expensive to buy at the onset, once applied, the disease spores spread throughout the lawn, growing in effectiveness for 15 to 20 years. An application is a long-term investment to protect your lawn and plants that are food to the adult beetles.

Not all beetles are bad to have in the garden, however. Each has its own place in the ecosystem. Some frugal gardeners prefer to hold off on the milky spore and let the natural system take over.

6 Tips for Better Fruit

Encouraging beneficial insects can help control pests in all parts of your garden. Along with general pest-control strategies, try these tips to keep pests away from grapes and other home garden fruits.

1. Cover small fruit trees with netting to protect the fruit from bird damage.

2. Protect individual fruit on apple and pear trees by enclosing them in paper bags (plastic will overheat the fruit) tied to the branches with string or twist ties. Remove the bags just before harvesting.

3. Encase ripening bunches of grapes in old panty hose to protect them from birds and other pests. Cut the panty hose horizontally into sections long enough to cover a full-grown bunch of grapes. Tie a knot in one end, pull it over the unripe grapes, and then tie the open end to the vine.

4. Protect your fruit trees from flat-headed borers and sunburn by painting the trunk with diluted white latex paint (equal parts paint and water) or whitewash.

5. Agriculture researchers have discovered that the fire blight bacterium doesn't reside permanently in its hosts (generally fruit trees). Instead, it's attracted to the tender young stems and leaves, particularly of pears and apples. To avoid the problem, don't prune fruit trees heavily. The new growth triggered by pruning is the preferred environment for fire blight.

6. To keep rodents from nesting underneath fruit trees in the winter months, pull back loose mulch from beneath the fruit trees in early autumn. Later in the season, when the rodents have found winter shelter elsewhere, replace the mulch to a depth of about 4 inches. Arrange the mulch so it doesn't touch the tree trunk.

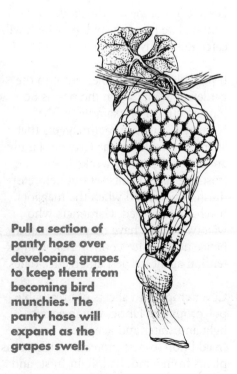

Pull a section of panty hose over developing grapes to keep them from becoming bird munchies. The panty hose will expand as the grapes swell.

6 Tips for Healthy Vegetables

Your vegetable garden will be healthier if you use the general pest-discouraging practices described earlier in this chapter, keep it tidy, and boost the population of beneficial insects and birds in your garden. When pests attack—and they will—try these quick and easy interventions if the balance isn't naturally and quickly restored by your garden allies.

1. When corn silk begins to dry and turn brown, apply ¼ to ½ teaspoon of mineral oil inside the tip of each ear of corn. That will stop most corn earworms from feeding on the cobs.

2. Leave a few stones in the garden to accommodate hunting spiders, which will catch destructive insects.

3. If possible, set vegetables out into the garden at a time when the pest is no longer active. For example, in the Northeast, cabbage root maggots that attack vegetables in the Crucifer family are active about two weeks before the frost-free date. Plants set out before or during this period when the maggots hatch are damaged. Gardeners who wait two weeks have no problem and hence no need for control. Ask your extension agent for pest emergence dates.

4. Cover crops with sheets of breathable polypropylene fabric, which admits light and water and keeps out insects. In addition to pest protection, it screens plants from wind, hail, light frost, and windborne weed seeds.

5. Improve the soil and discourage specific pests that have colonized an area by planting a cover crop (also known as green manure) such as alfalfa, barley, ryegrass, winter rye, hairy vetch, or clover. This approach can be part of your crop rotation schedule.

6. Erect a wren-size birdhouse near your garden. These little songbirds are fairly unafraid of human activity, so they won't mind raising their family in full view of your garden activities. When the nestlings hatch, the parents will look for a nearby source of food. Good-bye, pests!

10 Homemade Bug Sprays

When insect infestations get so far out of control that you can't wait for birds or beneficials to make a dent in them, you may yearn for a quick fix. Try these easy-to-mix, easy-to-use homemade recipes to control pest problems in your garden organically.

Pyrethrum Spray

When chewing or sucking insects such as mealybugs, thrips, or aphids are a problem, try this botanical spray to deter them.

   ½ cup powdered pyrethrum daisy
      flowers

   1 gallon water

   3 or 4 drops liquid nondetergent soap (to
      make the formula stick to the plants)

Collect pyrethrum flowers and dry them in the shade or in an oven set at the lowest setting. Store in an airtight, light-proof container in a cool place. Grind the flowers into powder as you need them.

Wear a dust mask when working with pyrethrum. Some people, especially those who are allergic to ragweed, may have a hay-fever reaction to the ground powder, so avoid breathing the pyrethrum dust. Use a coffee grinder, a blender, or a mortar and pestle to make the powder. Grind only as much as you plan to use, and then use it immediately.

Pour the powdered flowers into a gallon-size plastic milk jug. Add the water, cap the jug, and shake to combine. Use cheesecloth or a large coffee filter to strain the mixture into a bucket. Stir in the soap. Spray on plants, thoroughly covering both sides of the leaves.

Pyrethrum Spray Concentrate

This recipe makes a concentrate that you can store for future use.

1 cup tightly packed pyrethrum flowers

⅛ cup rubbing alcohol (70 percent isopropyl)

Pack the flowers into a 8-ounce jar with a lid. Pour the alcohol over the flowers, cover the jar tightly, and allow it to steep overnight. Strain the flowers out of the alcohol with a strainer lined with cheesecloth or a coffee filter, and discard them. Store the alcohol concentrate in a small, well-sealed container.

To make the spray, dilute the concentrate at a ratio of 1 part concentrate to 48 parts water. For example, to make 1½ quarts of spray, combine 1 fluid ounce of the pyrethrum concentrate with 1½ quarts (48 fluid ounces) of water.

Because the formula contains alcohol, test it on a few leaves before you do wholesale spraying. Don't use it on hairy-leaved plants, such as gloxinias and African violets, which it can damage.

Molasses Spray for Leaf Miners

1 part molasses

5 parts water

Stir to combine the molasses and water. Spray on plants infected with leaf miners.

Rodale's All-Purpose Insect Pest Spray

This spray is designed to discourage leaf-eating pests in the garden, such as snails and Japanese beetles. Keep the mixture away from your eyes and avoid contact with your skin; it may cause painful burning.

1 garlic bulb

1 small onion

1 teaspoon powdered cayenne pepper

1 quart of water

1 tablespoon liquid dish soap

Chop or liquefy the garlic and onion in a blender. Add the cayenne pepper and water. Steep for one hour, and then strain through cheesecloth. Add the liquid dish soap to help the mixture stick to the plants, and mix well.

Spray the mixture on your plants, covering both sides of the leaves. You can store the mix for up to one week in a labeled, covered jar in the refrigerator.

Ammonia Spray

Household ammonia is useful for controlling aphids, flea beetles, scales, thrips, and whiteflies.

1 part ammonia

7 parts water

Combine the ammonia and water. Apply as a spray.

It may injure some plants, causing a "burned" area like a fertilizer burn, so test on a leaf or two before you spray the entire plant. Do not apply during hot weather or on drought-stressed plants.

Garlic Oil

Garlic oil kills insects, both pests and beneficials, although adult lady beetles seem unharmed by garlic oil sprays. Use it to control aphids, imported cabbage-worms, leafhoppers, larval mosquitoes, squash bugs, and whiteflies. It has also proven effective against some fungi and nematodes.

3 ounces finely minced garlic cloves
2 teaspoons mineral oil
1 pint water
¼ ounce liquid dish soap

Soak garlic in mineral oil for at least 24 hours. Add water mixed with liquid dish soap. Stir well and strain into a glass jar for storage. When ready to use, combine 1 to 2 tablespoons of the concentrate with 1 pint of water to make a spray.

The oil and soap may damage some plants. Try on one or two leaves before you spray the entire plant, then wait two

Grow Your Own Pesticide

Grow your own insecticide—now there's an idea frugal gardeners take to heart! The dried, powdered flowers of easy-to-grow pyrethrum daisy (*Tanacetum cineraniifolium,* also called *Chrysanthemum cinerariifolium*) contain an active ingredient called pyrethrin, which kills insects on contact, particularly chewing and sucking insects such as mealybugs, thrips, aphids, and scales. Pyrethrin breaks down quickly in sunlight and heat, so you can spray and harvest on the same day. The benefits of this insecticide have been known since the late 1800s. You'll find the same active ingredient in many commercial insect sprays, but by making your own, you'll save money and avoid the additives in commercial formulations.

Grow pyrethrum, or painted daisies, in full sun. These short-lived perennials are easy to grow from seed or transplants and are hardy to Zone 6. Collect flowers to use as a natural insecticide.

to three days for any signs of ill effects. If all looks well, spray the plants thoroughly to ensure good coverage.

Starch Spray

This concoction will control cabbage moths as well as aphids, spider mites, thrips, and other small pests.

1 cup potato starch (available as a natural thickener in health food stores)

1 gallon water

½ teaspoon liquid nondetergent soap

Combine the starch and water, stirring well. Wait five minutes for the starch to soak up the water, then add the liquid nondetergent soap and mix again. Spray plants, covering them thoroughly so the water begins to run off. This spray does not keep, so you must mix a fresh batch each time you need it. It will leave a translucent, flaky residue that eventually will wear off, but if the look offends, rinse it off the day after you spray.

Tomato-Leaf Spray

Tomato leaves contain a range of water-soluble, toxic compounds called alkaloids. This spray is effective for controlling aphids. Research also indicates that it helps control corn earworms by attracting beneficial *Trichogramma* wasps that destroy corn earworm eggs.

1 to 2 cups tomato leaves (gathered from the bottom of the plant so you don't damage tomato production)

4 cups water

Mash or chop the tomato leaves in 2 cups of water and let the mixture steep overnight. Strain the leaves and add 2 more cups water to make a spray. For aphid control, thoroughly spray tips and undersides of leaves, especially lower leaves where aphids are

concentrated. To attract *Trichogramma* wasps to corn, spray the entire plant, especially around the forming ears.

Hot Pepper Spray

This homemade spray deters insects as well as cats and dogs.

½ cup hot peppers

2 cups water

Peppers may sting or burn skin and eyes. Wear rubber gloves while preparing and applying this mixture. Avoid getting the spray in your eyes or on your skin, and don't touch your gloved hand to your eyes. Puree the peppers and water in a blender. Strain the liquid through a cheesecloth and use as a spray. Apply every five to seven days until the pests are gone.

Soap Spray

This is a homemade version of the commercial insecticidal soaps on the market. Be sure to use pure soap.

1 teaspoon pure bar soap shavings

⅛ cup boiling softened water (if you have hard water, soften it by straining water through peat moss)

⅞ cup softened water

Dissolve soap shavings in ⅛ cup boiling water. Then add the remaining ⅞ cup water. For larger quantities, use a ratio of 1 part soap shavings to 50 parts water. To be effective, the spray must make contact with the insects. Spray both the top and undersides of the leaves to get the pests where they hide. Test-spray a few leaves first and wait two or three days for any signs of injury. Don't apply soap spray more than once a week to plants, and never use it on ferns or nasturtiums.

7 Low-Cost Pest Controls

1. Keep your plants healthy with good soil and adequate moisture. Pests are less attracted to vigorous plants than they are to weak ones.

2. Cover valuable plants with deer netting.

3. Spread diatomaceous earth—a mineral created from the remains of fossilized diatoms that punctures the bodies of insects such as caterpillars, slugs, snails, borers, leafhoppers, and thrips, killing them—on the soil around plants, and dust it onto plant foliage. Do not use swimming pool diatomaceous earth because it is treated with harmful chemicals.

4. Put out bait for snails and slugs by filling shallow dishes with beer and burying them so the rims are flush with the ground.

5. Leave a section of your garden a little untidy, with dead leaves, a few weeds, and hollow dead stems, to provide cover and hibernating places for beneficial insects.

6. Provide water to encourage frogs, lizards, toads, and other insect-eating creatures to settle on your property.

7. A feeding bat can consume as many as 500 flying insects per hour. Plant night-blooming flowers to attract bats; they'll come to the blooms to glean insects.

Defeating Disease

The same preventive-medicine methods that keep your plants protected against pests also work as disease defense. Here's a thumbnail refresher course; for more details about ways to use these practices, see page 174.

❖ Improve the soil.

❖ Practice sensible watering practices.

❖ Choose problem-resistant varieties.

❖ Practice good housekeeping.

❖ Locate plants close to beneficial neighbors.

Inoculate with Marigolds

African marigolds (*Tagetes erecta*) have been shown to inoculate soil against the fungi that causes verticillium wilt, a common soilborne disease. Sow the marigold seeds in the infected bed in spring after the last frost, and let them grow until September. Then till into the soil. Or, to avoid losing a season of harvest, start the marigolds indoors early, transplant them to the garden after the last spring frost, and till under in June. Follow with a planting of a quick-maturing veggie crop.

No Family Reunions

Plants lost to disease deprive you of a harvest and cost money to replace. Many diseases are specific to a certain family of plants. Rotating vegetable crops helps prevent these plant-specific diseases from building up in the soil. Don't follow one crop with another from the same family, since related plants generally are vulnerable to the same pests and diseases. For example, avoid following a cabbage planting with broccoli or kohlrabi, since all three are members of the cabbage family.

14 Dollar-Smart Disease Tips

1. Keep fallen leaves raked from around plants like camellia and mountain laurel that are susceptible to anthracnose and other fungal diseases.

2. Dispose of diseased leaves and branches that you remove from plants in the trash. If you compost them, you risk spreading the disease.

3. If you use pruning shears or loppers to remove diseased plant parts, disinfect them between each cut by dipping them in a solution of household bleach or another disinfectant.

4. When watering, avoid getting water on the leaves of plants. Wet leaves are vulnerable to sunburn and fungal diseases.

5. Prune off diseased wood as soon as you notice the problem to keep the disease from spreading. Cut several inches below the infected parts.

6. Avoid seedborne diseases by buying seed only from reputable dealers. If

Another Reason Not to Smoke

In addition to being bad for your health, cigarettes and other tobacco products can also wreak havoc with the health of your vegetable garden. If you smoke, keep cigarettes away from eggplant, peppers, tomatoes, and potatoes, and wash your hands before you handle the plants. Nicotine products may contain the pathogen that causes tobacco mosaic virus, which targets members of the Solanaceae family.

you save seed, save it only from healthy, vigorous plants.

7. Minimize fungal diseases by spacing plants so they get good air circulation.

8. Improve soil drainage to avoid the deadly disease phytophthora, which attacks the roots of plants growing in soggy soil.

9. If your soil is clay that stays wet in winter, plant shrubs high—with the top of the rootball slightly out of the ground—to avoid root rot.

10. Water newly transplanted seedlings, then when the soil dries, spray the transplants' leaves with manure tea. In addition to giving the plants a good feeding, the manure tea surrounds the

plants with good bacteria that keeps them healthy.

11. Avoid damaging your plants. Every wound provides an opportunity for disease to enter.

12. Disease organisms spread more easily in wet conditions. Whenever possible, stay out of your garden when the leaves are wet.

13. Nutrient deficiencies can stunt plants and make them less resistant to disease. Provide the best possible quality soil for your plants, and feed them well and wisely.

14. Garlic can prevent damping-off. Use a blender to puree one peeled clove of garlic in 1 quart of water. Let it sit for 24 hours, then strain. Drench the soil with the garlic liquid before you sow, or spray it on germinated seedlings.

4 Homemade Disease Sprays and Dusts

Keep these recipes at the ready in case disease problems crop up in your garden. They're inexpensive to mix yourself, easy to apply, and effective.

Sulfur Spray

Sulfur is an excellent fungicide, suitable to control apple scab, black spot on roses, and brown rot on fruit. As an added bonus, it acidifies the soil for acid-loving plants such as azaleas, rhododendrons, and heathers.

5 teaspoons powdered wettable sulfur (1 ounce)

3 gallons water

Combine the sulfur and about 2 cups of water in a bucket. Mix into a paste, and then add the rest of the water, stirring continuously until well mixed. Spray on plants and trees at ten-day intervals, as needed, to control fungal diseases. Agitate sprayer during spraying to keep well mixed.

Note: Do not use sulfur on cucumber and melon plants, and never use it within four weeks before or after any type of oil spray on foliage. Also, do not spray sulfur when temperatures are hotter than 80°F or you'll risk damaging sulfur-sensitive plants such as viburnums, tomatoes, raspberries, gooseberries, grapes, and blueberries.

Lime-Sulfur Spray

This spray is useful to control plant diseases such as mildew, anthracnose, leaf spot, and brown rot as well as some mite, scale, and insect pests on deciduous trees. Spray on the trees when they are dormant because the lime-sulfur will burn the leaves and growing shoots.

80 parts water

1 part commercial lime-sulfur concentrate

Measure the water into a plastic or enameled steel mixing container. Stir in the lime-sulfur concentrate, mix thoroughly, and spray. Typically home gardeners mix 1 cup of lime-sulfur with 5 gallons of water. Spray on wind-free days as drifting spray can stain and blacken house paint, especially white. Temperatures should be below 80°F when you spray, and the spray should be on for at least 24 hours before a rain.

Note: This spray is caustic. Wear rubber gloves, protective clothing, and goggles while handling this formula. If any splashes onto your skin, rinse off immediately with cold water.

At higher dilutions, you can use this spray during the growing season for diseases such as apple and pear scab, peach leaf curl, brown rot on plums, and black spot and canker on roses. However, you should never apply it when the fruit trees are in blossom. Do not use it on gourds. Finally, do not apply lime-sulfur within four weeks before or after a summer oil treatment on foliage.

Seedling-Strength Manure Tea

Manure tea used to water seedlings helps to prevent damping off, a fungal disease that kills developing seedlings.

1 shovelful horse, cow, or poultry manure (fresh or aged)

water

Fill a pillowcase or burlap bag with manure. Tie it shut and place it in a 5-gallon bucket. Fill the bucket with water and let it steep for two or three days. Remove the bag, and empty the manure onto the compost heap. Dilute the tea with 3 parts water for 1 part tea or until it looks like weak iced tea, then use to water seedlings and transplants.

Baking Soda and Horticultural Oil

Scientists at Cornell University have developed the following recipe as a nontoxic control of powdery mildew. It also is somewhat effective in controlling black spot on roses when applied on a weekly basis.

1 tablespoon baking soda (sodium bicarbonate)

2½ tablespoons of Sunspray Ultra-Fine Horticultural Spray Oil (available at retail outlets and in mail-order catalogs)

1 gallon water

Combine the baking soda and Sunspray Ultra-Fine Horticultural Spray Oil in the water. Spray the mixture on roses once a week beginning in April.

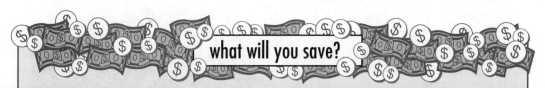

what will you save?

Keep Your Cash—Skip the Chemicals

Pests and diseases that get out of hand can cost you hundreds of dollars in lost crops and ornamental plants. Controlling the problem with chemicals could cost you hundreds of dollars in toxic materials. With chemical control, you would also risk killing off beneficial insects that can do the extermination job for you for free, and you also risk potentially damaging the environment. You will save lots of money and have a more environmentally safe garden if you use organic methods of pest control.

$tretching the $eason

Once you have your garden mainte- ·
nance under control, it's fun to
stretch the season to sneak in some extra
gardening days, especially when it comes
to vegetables. You can be the last gardener
in your neighborhood to harvest sun-
ripened tomatoes.

Scavenging for Cold Frames and Hotbeds

Cold frames and hotbeds provide a
sheltered setting for starting plants early,
hardening off tender seedlings, and extending the growing season in autumn.
Cold frames are glass- or plastic-covered
structures that work like miniature
greenhouses, protecting plants from cold
air and amplifying the warming effects of
the sun.

Hotbeds have a regular source of heat.
Originally, hotbeds were built over rotting manure that radiated constant heat.
Manure still works, but many gardeners
prefer to use electric heating cables.

Two-Hour Cold Frame

Make a utilitarian, almost-free cold
frame by arranging concrete blocks or
bales of hay in a rectangle. Top the blocks
or bales with an old window sash, or
storm window, or heavy, clear plastic
sheeting. On warm days, remove the lid or
prop it open to allow air to circulate and to
keep the plants from getting too hot. On
cold nights, provide extra protection for
tender plants by covering the lid with
blankets, canvas, or a thick layer of hay.

Don't Be Too Much of an Eager Beaver

It does no good to start to start
tomato seeds in January if it isn't warm
enough in your climate to transplant
them outside until May. For nearly five
months, you'll be stuck with plants
bursting from their pots and growing
leggier by the day as they seek light and
nourishment. Seed packets generally tell
you how many days you can expect
until germination. Allow a few extra
weeks for the seedlings to mature and
time your indoor seed planting so the
plants are ready to go outside at the last
predicted frost date in your area. If you
misjudge by a week or two and sow the
seeds later than the ideal, you're still
better off than if you start the seeds
too early.

Shep Ogden, who gardens in Vermont
and is the author of *Straight-Ahead*

**Fast, cheap, and useful—a straw-bale
cold frame goes together in minutes and
gives you a winter's worth of protection
to stretch the season. Sow spinach, lettuce, and other greens inside for fresh
winter salads and soups.**

Organic, explains, "All else being equal, you are better off with young, vigorous plants than older, rootbound ones. The best produce comes from plants that grow quickly, without what the pros call 'checks,' that is shortages of any nutrient, water, or temperatures to their liking. If the plants are a little small, all you've lost is a week or two in the garden; that is generally made up in the good growing days of early summer. Two weeks in March is only worth a couple of days in May."

Become a Weather Watcher

As the weather gets chillier later in the year, there are lots of tricks you can employ to extend the season for a tightwad timetable. But to be successful, you must have a good idea when the first frosty nights are likely to strike. Diane Relf, an extension specialist in environmental horticulture for the Virginia Cooperative Extension Service, gives these tips for recognizing when a killing frost might occur: "Daytime temperature is a strong indicator of an impending frost. When night temperatures have been consistently low but daytime temperatures have warmed things up nicely, watch for factors such as clouds or overcast weather that keeps the day temperature below 65°F. If this is combined with a clear, still night, a freeze is very likely.

"At night the heat that is given off by soil and plants escapes into the clear skies, whereas cloudy skies trap heat and

---

Indoor Sowing Timetable

Figure out when to start these seeds by counting backward from the last spring frost date for your area. (Call your county extension agent to find out that magic number, if you don't already know it.)

Annual herbs: 2 to 4 weeks before last frost
Basil: 6 weeks before last frost
Beans: 2 to 4 weeks before last frost
Broccoli: 6 to 8 weeks before last frost
Brussels sprouts: 4 to 8 weeks before last frost
Cabbage: 6 to 8 weeks before last frost
Cauliflower: 6 to 8 weeks before last frost
Celeriac: 6 to 8 weeks before last frost
Celery: 6 to 8 weeks before last frost

Eggplant: 8 to 10 weeks before last frost
Endive: 6 to 8 weeks before last frost
Leeks: 8 to 12 weeks before last frost
Lettuce: 4 to 6 weeks before last frost
Melons: 2 to 4 weeks before last frost
Onions: 10 to 12 weeks before last frost
Parsley: 8 weeks before last frost
Peppers: 8 to 10 weeks before last frost
Perennial herbs: 10 to 12 weeks before last frost
Tomatoes: 6 to 8 weeks before last frost

reduce the risk of freeze by mixing the warmer air back with the cooler air near the soil and plant surface." Diane explains that after enough hours of clear, still nighttime, plant temperatures will fall below freezing, usually just before sunrise.

So don't take chances when it's cold and clear. Get your crops under cover and bring houseplants indoors.

Rejoice in Indian Summer

Many early frosty nights are followed by lovely warm Indian summer days. You can save your tender plants for those few extra weeks of warmer weather if you cover them before a predicted nighttime frost. Collect old blankets, sheets, bedspreads, boxes, jars, baskets, and plastic sheeting, and use them to cover cold-sensitive plants.

Cold-Weather Veggies

Cabbage, cauliflower, peas, broccoli, and brussels sprouts can take some cold and generally taste better after a mild frost. However, they can't survive the constant cold that is typical of winters in northern regions of the country. Harvest them after the frost.

Other crops, including kale, spinach, evergreen bunching onions, lettuce, parsley, parsnips, carrots, and salsify are crops that can survive all winter in most North American climates. After the soil freezes, mulch them with 8 inches of coarse organic matter, such as evergreen boughs or cornstalks to prevent soil heaving due to freezing and thawing.

Avoid Uninvited Guests

Before the frosts hit, you'll want to bring houseplants and other tender growing things indoors if you plan to keep them through the winter. Prepare them for the change in climate from outdoors to indoors by cutting back the plants to a manageable size and putting the pots in a sheltered spot, such as a porch, for a few weeks before the serious cold sets in. Once the weather gets cold enough to risk the plants' lives, bring them indoors. Before bringing them inside, check the plants for insects or disease, and eradicate the problem before moving them indoors.

The Ultimate Season Extender

Some gardeners view a greenhouse as a luxury, but the frugal gardener can turn that investment to good account. With year-round growing, you can harvest salad greens and other delectables and enjoy the pleasure of gardening through every month of the year.

Greenback-Saving Greenhouses

For less-expensive greenhouse options, look for moderately priced Fiberglas designs, rather than the traditional glass. Be sure the Fiberglas is transparent or translucent and no heavier than 4 or 5 ounces per square foot. You can buy Fiberglas especially made for greenhouses that is guaranteed for 10 to 20 years.

Cheaper yet, but temporary, are greenhouses covered in plastic film. They are less attractive and more maintenance intensive than other styles, but the initial cost is significantly less than more traditional greenhouses.

Miniature Greenhouses

Cloches are light-permeable plant covers that keep cold air off sensitive plants. Early cloches were beautiful, hand-blown glass bell jars that fit over each plant. These are still available from specialty catalogs, but in addition to being expensive, they are heavy and breakable and don't have any ventilation. They make a charming garden accent, but the frugal gardener will opt for less expensive and more adaptable solutions for cloches to use in the garden.

Try these variations on the theme, but remember to remove or ventilate your minigreenhouses on warm days to prevent excessive heat buildup.

❖ Cut off the bottom of a plastic gallon jug, remove the cap, and place the jug over the plant. To keep it from blowing away, place a stake through the mouth of the jug and into the ground.

❖ Wrap a tomato cage with heavy-duty plastic and staple or tape the ends together. On cold nights, drape an extra piece of plastic over the top of the cage to keep cold air from dropping onto the plant.

❖ Prop an old window on bricks, logs, or cinder blocks to serve as a portable cold frame.

❖ Bend long strips of corrugated plastic into arcs over rows of plants to create an inexpensive, portable row cover. Hold the plastic in place with stakes spaced every few feet.

❖ Make a wire or PVC pipe frame sized to fit over a row of vegetables and cover it with transparent polyethylene plastic. Anchor the plastic to the ground with stones, bricks, or boards.

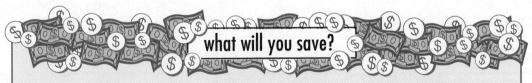

what will you save?

Season Stretching Saves on Grocery Bills

You can increase your vegetable harvest significantly by getting an early start on the growing season in spring and extending it in the autumn. In the case of vegetables that produce continuously throughout the growing season, the sooner you get them growing, the longer you'll be able to harvest. By extending the season, you can fit in one or two extra crops of quick-growing veggies. The longer you can harvest from your own garden, the less you'll need to depend on the grocery store for your food supplies, and that means you save money.

Frugal Gardener Checklist

■ Design your landscape so you can manage the regular maintenance with little or no extra help. Paying the neighbor kid to cut the grass adds up to a hefty sum over a season.

■ Choose low-care plants for your garden such as natives and sturdy plants that don't need a lot of feeding and fussing over to thrive.

■ Reduce the size of your lawn to save time and money on maintenance.

■ Choose drought-tolerant plants to save money and time on watering during dry spells.

■ Keep weeds to a minimum with mulch.

■ Walk through your garden regularly, keeping an eye out for any pest or disease problems that may be developing. Catch the problems in the early stages to make control easier.

■ Extend the growing season for vegetable crops with minigreenhouses made from readily available home supplies.

CHAPTER SIX

DESIGNING ON A BUDGET

A MONEY-SAVING GARDEN begins with good design. When you plan carefully before planting, you'll be able to make a bigger impact with fewer plants and create a more satisfying garden, too. It can be difficult to resist the urge to plant willy-nilly, but if you take some time to think about what you want before you plant, you'll be able to achieve the results you're looking for on a smaller budget.

That's because there are plenty of frugal design tricks to help you get a great-looking garden without an estate budget. One is buying smaller landscape plants, then filling in with inexpensive annuals or movable containers while your plants grow up. Not only is this approach cheaper, but also smaller transplants tend to thrive better. In this chapter, you'll find many more ideas to put to work in your landscape.

Garden While You Design

Designing first doesn't mean that you can't garden at the same time. A good design plan takes unhurried time to consider and draw up. Rather than waiting until you've finished the design, indulge in temporary plantings that will make it easier to concentrate on the big picture.

of your property. If you already have garden beds, let them stay until your design plan is finalized. With a few tricks of the trade, you can transplant perennials and even shrubs almost any time, even in summer, to fill in the niches you create later.

Plant Some Immediate Gratification

Satisfy those planting urges by creating a quick bed where you can enjoy a dose of colorful flowers while you consider the rest

Fill Containers for Temporary Gardens

Get a quick fix of gardening by filling large containers with colorful, long-blooming annuals. Reliable stalwarts such as geraniums, petunias, and impatiens will

Indulge your gardening urges while you redesign your gardens by creating a nursery bed where you can start cuttings, sow perennial flowers and herbs from seed, and coddle bargain-price "orphans" from the garden center. By the time their permanent homes are ready, your nursery will be full of healthy, rehabilitated shrubs and vigorous perennials and herbs ready for transplanting.

give you lots of return for a small initial investment. When your design is finished, you can move the containers to use their bright splash of color as an extra accent.

Start a Nursery Bed

Before you pull out a pencil and graph paper to begin, set aside a corner of your yard or existing garden for a nursery bed.

Sow perennial seeds or set out young plants there, and start cuttings of annuals, perennials, groundcovers, and shrubs. When you come across bargains on shrubs that are too good to pass up, plant them in the nursery bed. This way you can feed your hunger for more plants, yet keep them out of the way of your design. Your stock of plants will thrive, and when your plan is finalized, you'll have nice, large plants instead of puny youngsters.

Dreaming Is Free

Planning the perfect yard doesn't cost a penny. Take all the time you want to dream big. When your design is finalized and you're ready to start implementing it, you'll find ways to trim costs so that you stay on budget. Maybe you can't put in that brick patio right away, but you can still have a sitting spot for entertaining friends and family. Look for cost-cutting tips in this chapter and throughout the book. Chapter 2, "Save Money on Plants," for example, is chock-full of easy ideas for saving money on plants.

List Your Needs

Begin your design plan by making a list of the activities you want to do and the types of gardens you want to have in your yard. You may need space for a child's play area, a quiet retreat, entertaining, outdoor cooking, vegetable gardening, or your herb collection. Don't forget the

more mundane space needs, too: a corner for the compost pile, an area to walk the dog, or storage space for trash cans.

Calling All Non-artists

You don't need to be an artist to draw a rough outline of your yard. Measure it off, then make a proportionate sketch on paper. Draw outlines on the sketch for any existing buildings, driveways, fences, walls, shade trees, or other permanent elements. No need to be exact here—this is the rough plan.

Match Needs to Space

Take your list of needs and draw in areas on your rough plan where you think they might go. Use common sense as you work: If you have children, you'll want their sandbox to be in a part of the yard that you can easily supervise. Keep the compost pile

200   Designing on a Budget

near the garden for easy transport; place the patio near the kitchen door for convenient serving; put the herb garden in quick reach of the house so it's easy to snip parsley for dinner. Use a pencil to rough in these areas—making changes is guaranteed!

Coziness Counts

A sense of privacy is vital, especially if you live in a neighborhood, so draw in hedges or fences that will shield your property from the view of neighbors or the street. Then mark other places where a hedge, trellis, arbor, or fence can visually separate sections of the yard so that you end up with cozy enclosed spaces. Many designers call these "garden rooms," and that's an easy

concept to visualize. After all, outside space is just as important for living as indoors. Just as in your house, your property can hold separate spaces for eating, snoozing, and playing.

Paths Are the Key

Getting from one place to another in your yard and seeing beautiful plants along the way are the keys that hold your design together. But before you pick up the pencil to sketch them in, consider the various uses your pathways will serve.

Walls make us feel cozier than wide-open spaces. Adding simple, inexpensive plastic mesh trellises of annual vines around your patio makes it much more inviting. If there's an electric outlet nearby, you can decorate the greenery with strings of tiny white lights for nighttime magic.

Straight as an Arrow

Start by planning the utilitarian pathways: the swift route from driveway to house door, the straight walk to the mailbox, and any other paths that need to get you where you're going without wasted steps. A winding walk may be visually appealing, but when you're lugging bags of groceries or trundling a wheelbarrow, you need straightforward, no-nonsense paths. Children and dogs will make their own shortcuts to their play areas unless you do it for them. Keep utilitarian paths wide, well surfaced for sure footing, and straight as an arrow wherever possible.

Exploring Beauty

Now for the fun paths: those that guide your feet through the garden in a carefully calculated route so that you can admire the beauty along the way. These are the paths you'll see in garden design books, the ones that wend their way through concealing shrubbery or beneath an alley of trees or take you to a bubbling fountain or quiet pool. Put as many twists and turns in these paths as you like, but avoid dead ends. Exploring a garden is more fun if you don't have to double back the way you came.

7 Tricks of the Trade

1. It isn't necessary to draw each tree, shrub, and plant accurately on your design plan. Just give a general impression of the plants' shapes and mature sizes. Do your best to keep the drawings in scale.

Beat Traffic Noise with Water

If you live near a street, especially a busy one, the noise of traffic can be a constant presence in your garden. Plant hedges to absorb as much of the noise as possible, then add a splashing fountain to replace irritating car engines with soothing water music. You can install a small garden pond if you like, or go the penny-pincher route and use a large metal washtub or wooden barrel to hold water and a pump.

---

2. Keep an informal garden design from slipping from casual into chaotic by using linear elements such as paths, walls, or rows of trees or shrubs to provide a sense of order and control.

3. Lighten up a dark, shady corner with variegated foliage. Add a splash of light with hostas, ivies, aucuba, hollies, and Solomon's seal with variegated leaves.

4. Make a corner interesting by placing a statue, birdhouse, birdbath, or dramatic plant as a focal point.

5. At the end of a long view, such as the far end of a path, anchor the eye with a bench or other feature of interest.

6. Place shrubs at bends in the path to obscure the view beyond, creating a sense of anticipation.

A pair of columnar cedars flanks the opening to a prized garden of conifers framing the view. Notice how the contrast between the conifers and the small stretch of grass in front emphasizes the textures of the shrubs.

7. Draw attention to an attractive view by framing it between a pair of trees or shrubs, with an arbor, or between two urns or statues.

Design Aids

Paper and pencil work perfectly for many home garden designers, but if you have trouble imagining your landscape in two dimensions, you can turn to other widely available designing aids to help you think it through. One simple trick is to cut out photos of the plants you want from a catalog or magazine, then put them on your design and see how they look together.

Save Time with a Kit

Garden design kits come with a scaled garden-planning grid, reusable full-color stickers representing different plants, and detailed instructions and advice for planning a garden. They even include climate zone information and guidance on plant requirements.

Just Picture It

Picture your landscape with a disposable panoramic camera. If the ground is completely level or shrubs obscure the view, take the photograph from the top of a ladder. Enlarge the image with a color photocopier. Tape a sheet of tracing paper over the photo and outline the main features and existing plantings that you want to keep. Draw in your planned design. If you don't like how the final plan looks, simply start over with a new piece of tracing paper.

3-D Fun for the Family

Get your kids involved in planning a new garden by making a three-dimensional model of your proposed garden plan. You can move the components around like dollhouse furniture and experiment easily with different placements. It's great family fun and when it's finished, you'll have a very clear idea of how the final results will look.

Use a piece of foamboard or flat Styrofoam for the base. Fashion thin cardboard pieces into the house, fences, and other structures on your property. Felt can represent lawns, flowerbeds, paths, and patios. Snip bits of real, fine-leaved greenery to use for trees and shrubs. Experiment with different shapes and layouts until you're happy with the result.

High-Tech Gets Down-to-Earth

With the click of your computer's mouse, you can move a tree from one side of the garden to another, design and redesign a perennial border, or experiment with the placement and paving materials of a patio or terrace. The software grows more sophisticated with each edition. Most include a database of plants, information on their growth requirements and habits, and graphics that simulate garden features. Newer versions even show what the garden will look like after you install your selected plants. Some programs allow you to scan a photograph of your property into the computer, making your design in relationship to the house and surroundings easier to visualize.

Thrifty Plant Choices

So far, you haven't spent a dime on your design plan, except for the cost of graph paper if you used it. (Of course, if you bought a garden design kit or CD-ROM, you're out a few more bucks. But I'm sure you checked your local library before shelling out cash—mine has CD-ROMs!) Keep a tight grip on that wallet, though, because the budget-crunching part is coming up: the plants you use to fill your design. It's easy to go wild adding plants to your garden, but a few money-saving secrets can make fewer plants carry more weight.

Save Money with Specimens

One easy pitfall in the frugal approach to landscaping is to fritter away money on small, inexpensive plants. The result is a busy hodgepodge of plants with no visual impact or drama. Instead of yielding to such impulses, invest your money in a few major specimen plants that will make a strong statement in your garden. In addition to adding important stature and structure to your design, a specimen plant creates a striking focal point.

Less Is More

It's an interesting paradox: The more eye-catchers you add to a garden view, the less powerful they become. It's easy to see why with statues or other manmade objects—a single big urn draws the eye like a magnet, but six of them placed here and there lessens the impact because your eye doesn't know where to go first. Specimen plants work the same way. Use them sparingly, and follow the same rule for placing other ornaments in the garden.

Let specimen plants go solo for full stunning effect. Notice how your eye goes immediately to the single small tree in the garden shown above.

The trees in this garden, each eye-catching on its own, become part of a busy hodgepodge.

Let a Strong Plant Carry the Garden

Eye-catching plants, such as a weeping blue Atlas cedar with its graceful branches and lovely color, can carry a whole section of garden all by themselves. They can command your attention from across the garden. Only after you notice them do you take in the other plants around them.

Grass Makes a Great Specimen

A tall clump of ornamental grass contributes a lot of focal-point value to your garden for minimal price. A young plant in a plastic pot, which can cost as little as $5, will quickly come into its own once its roots are in your garden soil. By its second season, it will be close to mature size—4 feet or more in a large

species. Ornamental grasses wave peacefully in gentle breezes, adding movement and sibilant sound to the garden, and they continue to be focal points in winter, when their foliage bleaches to warm golds and tans.

Miscanthus is marvelous. For beauty and reliability, go with miscanthus (*Miscanthus sinensis* cvs.), also known as fountain grass. There are many adaptable cultivars that reach 4 to 6 feet in a single season. Some arch gracefully like a fountain of green, while others stand proudly upright. Their plumy flowers appear in late summer to fall and add visual interest in the garden over winter.

Invest in Trees

Money you spend on trees gives you a big return. These long-lived plants repay your investment with decades of cooling shade, visual beauty, and landscape value. Choose trees with more care than you

Great growth in a single season: Penny-pinchers love the big-time effects of inexpensive ornamental grasses. Miscanthus, which zooms from container size to specimen size in a few months, is hardy and adaptable. And it needs no irrigation or fertilizers to keep it looking great.

choose other garden plants. For one thing, they obviously cost more. But there's another reason. Once you get them in the ground, they're a permanent part of your landscape.

Trees on the Cheap

The thicker a tree's trunk and the taller it is, the higher the price tag hung on its branches. Yet older trees take longer to establish their roots when transplanted. Many younger trees catch up to and even surpass older trees within a few years, because they're quicker to establish enough roots to support more top-growth. Besides, the bigger the tree, the more likely you'll have to pay a professional to deliver and plant it!

Scout out seedlings. Seedling trees grow remarkably fast, so if you spot any desirables coming up in your beds, hedgerows, or sidewalk cracks, transplant them to permanent spots. Take advantage of those nut trees that squirrels planted for you. A tulip poplar, for example, can be 8 feet tall after three years, and a seedling Japanese maple can reach 4 feet in just two or three years.

Make friends with forest owners. Tree seedlings in local woods are usually abundant—and free if you get permission to transplant from the property owner. Learn to recognize the common native trees in your area, and you'll easily be able to find a no-cost source for maples, birches, and even hemlocks and other evergreens. Take

Slice the top off a plastic milk jug, leaving the handle intact, and fill the jug with a few ounces of water. Use it to keep bareroot tree seedlings fresh as you collect them with a sturdy trowel from a friend's woods. The young trees will transplant and establish easily if you keep them moist.

a bucket of water with you on your field trip and look for the youngest trees you can find. They'll transplant more easily and start adding growth quickly.

Watch for end-of-season sales. In summer and again in late fall, many nurseries try to entice buyers with rock-bottom prices to clear their stock. Watch for advertisements of such sales and become a regular at local nurseries and garden centers so you can be first on the scene for the most desirable leftovers.

Trees for Fall Color

Spreading, deciduous trees that provide shade in summer and burst into a flame of color in autumn offer delightful possibilities. Clothed in greenery, they add visual weight because of their size alone. When they color in fall, they become focal points in the garden. Adaptable trees with great fall foliage include sweet gum (*Liquidambar styraciflua*), red maple (*Acer rubrum*), sugar maple (*A. saccharum*), black tupelo, also known as black gum or sour gum (*Nyssa sylvatica*), Japanese zelkova (*Zelkova serrata*), ginkgo (*Ginkgo biloba*), and 'Marshall's Seedless' green ash (*Fraxinus pennsylvanica* 'Marshall's Seedless').

Trees with Unique Form

Trees or shrubs with unusual forms attract attention and are great for specimen plants. The Japanese maple (*Acer palmatum*) grows in wonderfully contorted forms that are especially striking in winter when the leaves have dropped. The foliage itself adds beautiful texture and color, especially in red-leaved varieties. Another attention-getter is Harry Lauder's walking stick, or contorted witch hazel

Take Fruits Out of the Orchard

Instead of choosing flowering or ornamental trees to provide the structure in their Del Mar, California, garden, Bill and Linda Teague opted for trees that produce flowers *and* fruit. They get a pretty floral display in spring—plus a crop of fruit! Cherries, apples, peaches, pears, and plums are all attractive enough for any ornamental garden.

Save space by choosing dwarf fruit varieties. Not only do they take up less room in your garden, but it's easier to reach the ripe fruit at harvest time. You can save even more space and create a striking feature in your garden by growing fruit trees against a fence or wall as espalier.

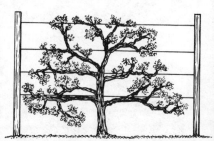

Make an edible, ornamental espalier that smells wonderful in spring by training an apple tree to a sturdy wire trellis. Select hardy young branches to tie to the wires and remove all extraneous shoots. Prune yearly in late winter to keep new growth tight to the trellis.

(*Corylus avellana* 'Contorta'), with branches that spiral and twist in fantastic shapes. Another contorted tree is the corkscrew willow (*Salix matsudana*), which sends its twisted branches reaching 50 feet into the sky at maturity.

Bare-Barked Beauties

Interesting bark is a particular asset in winter when there is less to look at in the garden. Paperbark maple (*Acer griseum*) has papery layers of bark that curl like rolls of chocolate decorating a cake. Other

Find Free Trees at the Florist

Willows of any kind are super easy to root from cuttings. Look for "cuttings" at florist shops, which commonly use branches of ornamental willow to add interest in arrangements. Pussy willow and corkscrew willow are usually available, and you should be able to acquire a few branches for only a $1 to $2, or even for free if you ask for twigs past their prime. Clip 1 inch off the end, stick the twigs a few inches into the soil, and keep them constantly moist but not sopping wet. By the end of the growing season, you'll have a new tree.

Collect freebie leftovers from a florist's shop, or scavenge your own florist bouquets to add to your shrub collection. Pussy willow and corkscrew willow are easy to root and are fast growing. Slice a bit off the bottom end of each branch and stick the branches in moist soil. They'll soon take hold and start putting out new growth.

If you can cut a privet hedge into a rectangle, why not cut it into a fun shape like a topiary rabbit for a child's play area? Use hedge shears to slice off anything that doesn't look like a bunny, then keep the lines of the creation clear with an occasional haircut.

excellent choices for beautiful bark include red-barked dogwood (*Cornus alba*) and its yellow-stemmed cousin (*C. stolonifera*), both multistemmed shrubs that are gorgeous against snow.

Birch trees are also great subjects for interesting bark, which may be papery, peeling, or colored, including the classic white birch. Some varieties of crape myrtle (*Lagerstroemia indica*) have striking, multicolored trunks, as do sycamores (*Platanus* spp.), which have the added fascination of peeling, and Scotch pine (*Pinus sylvestris*). Also consider striped maple (*Acer pensylvanicum*), which has bright green bark striped with creamy white, and Amur chokeberry (*Prunus maackii*), which has peeling, yellowish brown bark.

Fanciful Shapes

A shrub that's pruned as a topiary—whether it's shaped like a fanciful animal or pruned into a geometric form such as a cone, sphere, or tiered wedding cake—can become a useful focal point. This look is especially appropriate in a formal garden or in a place where two matching specimens flank the front door or a pathway leading to another part of the garden.

Trained topiary costs big bucks. Some garden artists support themselves exclusively by creating topiaries. But you can trim the cost by doing it yourself. Practice on fast-growing, inexpensive privet hedges or other shrubs before moving on to your prized boxwoods at your home's entryway.

Empower Your Plants

Plants have the power to make or break your garden design—and your budget. Make thoughtful choices so your plants can use their power to make a real impact in your design. The right plants in the right places can make a small garden seem larger or perform other *trompe l'oeil* tricks that work to fool the eye and make the most of your garden space. One neat trick is to choose plants with showy seedheads to prolong their season of interest. Variegated foliage can have the same effect. Consider these ideas for placing plants.

Warm Up a Winter Garden

Any bit of color is valuable on bleak winter days, and plants with yellow-tinged foliage are worth their weight in gold. Plant golden-colored evergreens such as 'Lane'

Lawson false cypress (*Chamaecyparis lawsoniana* 'Lane'), 'Goldcrest' Monterey cypress (*Cupressus macrocarpa* 'Goldcrest'), and golden Deodar cedar (*Cedrus deodara* 'Aurea') to provide "sunshine" to the garden, even on gray winter days.

Bring Blooms to Eye Level

Flowers at eye level pack much more oomph than those at your feet. Use iron shepherd's hooks to hold hanging baskets, plantings on tops of walls, or flat-backed containers on the sides of your house to bring plants into easy view. Decorate a tree with hanging baskets of blooming annuals.

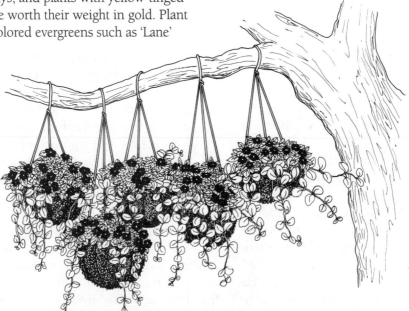

Add a layer of color at eye level by hanging plants from a tree. Stagger heights for a fuller effect, and fill the baskets with shade-tolerant flowers like these impatiens.

The Glories of Vines

Use these versatile plants to add height on trellises or to conceal eyesores in your landscape. Annual vines are fast growing and lush; slower-growing perennial vines take one or two years to achieve their purpose.

❖ Grow vines on bare, unsightly walls or privacy fences to soften their stark appearance.

❖ Disguise a chain-link fence by covering it with an evergreen vine such as ivy.

❖ Tack a strip of plastic mesh to the wall for an instant trellis next to your entry door. Night-blooming moonflowers (*Ipomoea alba*) are a nice touch to welcome friends and family going in and out of the house in the evening hours. Combine them with a trellis of morning glories to greet early risers.

7 Tricks to Make a Small Garden Look Bigger

1. In a long, narrow garden, break up the space with shrubs or trellises so that the entire length of the garden can't be seen at a glance. The garden will seem bigger and less confined.

2. Add variations in ground level, such as berms and raised gardens. Even in the smallest garden, you can add a small one-step-up terrace or dig out a sunken area for seating.

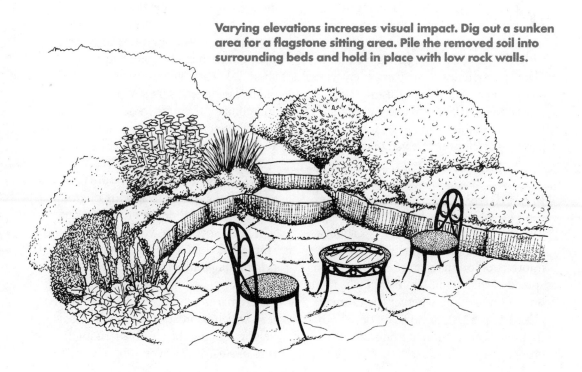

Varying elevations increases visual impact. Dig out a sunken area for a flagstone sitting area. Pile the removed soil into surrounding beds and hold in place with low rock walls.

3. Visually widen a narrow planting bed by adding height at the back to give an illusion of greater depth. Grow trellised vines or tall, narrow shrubs in the back, then continue to the front of the bed with plants of diminishing size. Finish off the front row with a low-growing plant along the edge to tie the bed to paving or lawn.

4. Put blue, lavender, or other cool-colored flowers in the back to make a garden look deeper. Warm-colored flowers such as yellow and red will pop forward, making the space feel shorter.

5. Break the visual monotony of a small, flat garden with a trellis or arbor covered with vines or climbing roses.

6. Plan winding paths to make the most of your space. Provide a sense of mystery and surprise by planting a tall shrub before the curve in a path so you can't immediately see where the path goes.

7. Fool the eye into perceiving more space by making a path more narrow as it moves farther away from the main viewing point. Your eye will interpret it as diminishing naturally because of distance.

The Frugal Approach to Planting

The most common mistake in garden planning is putting in too many plants. The garden may look good at first, but within a year or so, disaster begins to strike. The plants outgrow their space, encroaching on each other. The design ceases to be pleasing and becomes an unsightly tangle. Avoid that problem, and save money by planning carefully before you plant.

inches a year, but yew trees have been known to live for thousands of years. Leyland cypress will grow 3 to 5 feet a year, but then expire of exhaustion after about 20 years. The ultimate size of a plant also depends on soil, nutrition, site, and climate. If you're in doubt, consult a detailed reference book, or better yet, ask a local, knowledgeable nursery owner.

How Big?

Plant encyclopedias, nursery catalogs, and plant identification tags all provide information on the mature height and spread of each plant. Unfortunately, rarely does a source state whether the estimate is based on 5, 10, or 20 years of growth. In an ideal environment, the slow-growing yew will increase by 6 to 12

Give Special Plants More Space

When you plan the spacing of grouped plants, be careful not to crowd a plant that has a special growth habit. For example, the doublefile viburnum (*Viburnum plicatum* 'Tomentosum') has attractive, tiered horizontal branching. When mature, its spread can reach to 10 feet, which is broader than its 6½-foot height, making the shrub a striking feature in a garden. It would be a waste to plant this viburnum in a shrub border crowded up against other plants that obscure its unique beauty.

Use Color to Make a Splash

To make an effective display for less money, plant your flowers in large blocks of color instead of mixing colors in the garden. Three dozen plants of three different colors—12 white, 12 blue, 12 pink—will look pretty if you mix them all together. But they have more garden power if you plant them in masses of the same color, blending the edges of each group so it gradually melds into the next color. It also pays off in eye appeal to plant perennials in groups of three or five, instead of one here, one there.

White Multiplies Color Effect

White enhances neighboring colors, making them seem more intense. A scattering of white flowers throughout a garden or bed can create a sensation of shimmer, like white fairy lights strung in a tree, but you can get also too much of a good thing. Garden writer and photographer Derek Fell warns against planting white flowers in bold clumps. "They tend to create voids in the landscape," he says. "They make it look as though someone punched a hole in the garden."

No Disappearing Acts, Please

If you work during the days and are therefore most likely to be in your garden after sundown, stick to light-colored flowers to get the most pleasure out of your plantings. Blue flowers and those with deep, dark colors disappear from view as evening darkens the garden. It's the sunny yellows, pastels, and whites that continue to please at dusk.

Match Color to Climate

Regional differences in light intensity influence the colors that suit your garden best. In the tropics, flowers tend to be bold and flamboyant, both in form and color. Startlingly bold colors such as hot pink, fiery red, and glowing orange look great under a hot southern sun but garish in northern climates.

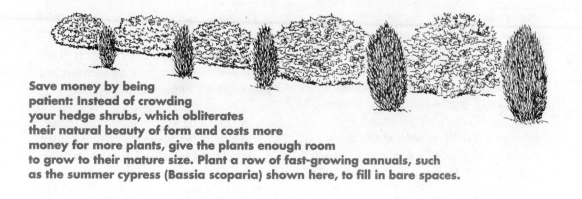

Save money by being patient: Instead of crowding your hedge shrubs, which obliterates their natural beauty of form and costs more money for more plants, give the plants enough room to grow to their mature size. Plant a row of fast-growing annuals, such as the summer cypress (Bassia scoparia) shown here, to fill in bare spaces.

In contrast, the softer colors—pinks, lavenders, pale yellows—that glow in northern light look insipid in a bright, sunny climate. Various shades of gray (silvery gray, grey-white, blue-gray, and green-gray) are easy on the eye in beachfront gardens where the glare of the sun and sea can be a visual strain.

Stir Emotions with Color

Color can also affect your mood. A garden filled with pastel pinks and blues or blues, grays, and silvers is more restful emotionally than a garden filled with lively reds, hot oranges, and vibrant yellows. Hot colors tend to be energizing, while pale colors create a calming effect. If you'd like to design a soothing retreat, don't fill it with fiery autumn colors. Instead opt for more subtle shades, such as pink, peach, lavender, and blue.

Color Makes a Selling Point

Flowers give a house that "curb appeal" that makes it attractive to potential buyers. If you're putting your home on the market, invest in instant eye appeal by planting annuals already in bloom in attention-getting colors. Yellow and red are the best choices because they jump forward and draw attention to your house and garden. Buyers will notice a bold bed filled with red or yellow flowers, and they will remember your house longer—hopefully, long enough to close the deal.

Durability Is Dollar Smart: Arbors and Other Garden Structures

Saving money is always the goal, but don't make the mistake of being penny wise and pound foolish. The least expensive option is not always the best, especially when it comes to major structures in the garden, such as a gazebo, deck, patio, arbor, or pergola. Look to the long term here, and make decisions that will give you years of good service from durable structures. Garden structures are big investments, even if you do all the work yourself. But choosing quality means you'll save money in the long run.

10 Ways to Shave Costs from Garden Structures

Do-it-yourself is the least expensive way to go when it comes to getting a well-made garden structure at a bargain price, but if you're not handy with hammer and saw, try these money-saving options.

1. Borrow a pickup truck from a friend or hire an inexpensive private hauler (check the classified ads service directory) to save on delivery costs.

2. Sketch the structure you like and show the picture to a woodworker in your neighborhood. He or she may be able to duplicate the design. But make sure you get a cost estimate first! The original may turn out to be cheaper.

3. Use recycled wood.

4. Check newspaper classified ads or the yellow pages, or ask neighbors to recommend carpenters. A competent carpenter can work from plans you supply (check the library for books of plans), with materials you specify. Be sure to get the price you agree to in writing before work begins.

5. Rural craftsmen offering arbors and other structures sometimes set up temporary business places along country highways. Prices may be flexible at the end of the summer.

6. Compare the costs of kits with finished products. If you have a few hours to invest in assembly, you can save a bundle. Be sure to include shipping charges when comparing costs.

7. Garden structures sometimes turn up at craft shows or flea markets. If you fall in love with one that's outside your budget, don't be shy about bargaining.

8. If a rustic look suits your garden, make a trellis, arbor, or pergola out of saplings and branches nailed together. Tree services can be a great source of free materials for rustic structures. Let them know what you're looking for, or stop and ask for trimmings if you see a truck in your neighborhood.

9. Pay for the materials for your structure, and trade your time and skill for the labor. Barter your specialty—homemade apple pies, weeding, engine tune-up, mending, sit-down dinner for six—with a willing carpenter.

10. If lack of power tools is what's holding you back from doing it yourself, check into rental prices. You may still realize a big savings, even with rental costs added on. Or ask your local lumberyard or home supply store to cut the wood to your specifications. Then all you have to do is fasten it together.

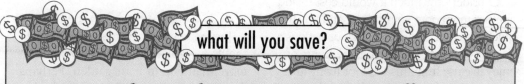

what will you save?

When Making Your Own Pays Off

The initial outlay on a major garden structure is high, but the added value to your garden can be immense, both in aesthetic appeal and in increased resale value. Doing it yourself can save you 50 percent off the retail cost—$50 to $100 or more in cold, hard cash, depending on the structure. Building from a kit may save you 20 percent or more off the retail cost. Hiring someone to do the work for you can save up to 20 to 50 percent off the retail cost.

Make a simple, low-cost patio by spreading gravel beneath a shady tree to accommodate a table and chairs. Light the pathway to the patio with inexpensive torch lights. Instant romance for the slimmest budget!

4

A Bargain in Extra Living Space

Consider how much it would cost to add another room onto your house, and you'll quickly see that building a deck or patio is a good investment. You'll get many hours of enjoyable use from this outdoor living area for much less than the cost of increasing your home's square footage. An inviting deck or patio provides a pleasant spot to sit and relax, to dine outdoors, to entertain, and even to work or study. In most cases, a good-looking deck or patio will also increase the value of your home. Certainly it will make your home more attractive and therefore more salable.

In addition to extending your living space, a deck or patio requires much less maintenance than most garden plants—a time-saver that cuts down on maintenance hours.

Why Stop with One?

Just as you may have several sitting rooms in your home, you may want more than one in your garden. Perhaps there's a secluded shady spot in the far corner of your garden that would be a pleasant place to sit on a hot summer day. Make a small patio there, defining the "room" with economical paving material such as gravel or wood chips.

Consider creating a patio in a spot where you have a view. Darrell and Trea Post of

Leucadia, California, had a patio immediately off their house, but they built another one on a hill at the back of their property so they could enjoy a view of the ocean. A deck sited at an alluring view can be anchored to the house by a path made of decking to create a truly delightful accent.

The Price of Whimsy

A charming gazebo is hard to resist. It hearkens back to a different era, a romantic time when lovers slipped away to its shelter. But most gazebos are too small to be truly useful, and they soon become consigned to the role of super-expensive garden ornament. Before you build or buy a gazebo, take a long, hard look at the space it provides. Will you actually spend afternoons lounging inside or enjoying romantic dinners, or will you soon give up its cramped confines in favor of a hammock or a table on the patio?

Choosing a Structure

Most American gardens have too few features, rather than too many. Even in a small garden, it may be possible to have an arbor framing a gate into the garden or as shelter for a bench at the end of the path. The same garden may have a patio or deck as well as a gazebo.

Harmonize Styles

Whatever structures you decide to put in your garden, make sure they're in harmony with the style of your garden and the design of your house. A gingerbread gazebo or fanciful arbor is perfect with a Victorian-style house, but next to a starkly modern house, it would be jarring. For a modern design, choose contemporary-looking arbors and garden structures with clean, uncluttered lines that echo the style of the house.

6 Reasons to Add an Arbor

Arbors instantly add solidity and height to a garden. Use them to accomplish these design aims:

1. Define entryways by using an arbor to frame a gate.

2. Create a transition from one garden space to another.

3. Make a small garden feel bigger by placing an arbor on the property boundary, thus creating the illusion that the garden continues on the other side.

4. Transform an ordinary garden entrance into a magical threshold by adding an arbor planted with flowering vines.

5. Create a focal point by placing an arbor at the end of a long view or path.

6. Make a sheltered place to rest and admire the garden by installing an arbor with an attached or free-standing bench inside.

smart tips | TWO DOZEN SMART SHOPPING TIPS

1. Check for landscape design software at your local library or on public-access computers at colleges. If it's not available, they may be willing to order it for you and others in the community.

2. Chip in with like-minded friends to buy a landscape design software package.

3. Trim design costs by substituting less expensive materials: gravel instead of brick, concrete instead of flagstone, wood chips instead of bark mulch.

4. Pots, birdbaths, and statuary are much cheaper if you eliminate the middleman. Check with your chamber of commerce or consult the yellow pages to see if there are manufacturers nearby.

5. Keep an eye out for outlet malls that include garden ornament stores or stores that sell mainly by catalog. Selection will vary, but prices can be as much as 50 percent off the retail cost.

6. Avoid impulse purchases at the nursery. Go with a shopping list and stick to it.

7. Watch for sales at nurseries, garden centers, and discount stores. Garden ornaments such as birdbaths, sculptures, and fountains are usually marked down significantly in late summer or early autumn.

8. Check the "chip and dent" area at your garden center, statuary seller, or container outlet. Clay pots and ceramics are highly vulnerable to damage, and you may find chipped or cracked pots for bargain prices—or even for free! If you don't see a corner for damaged merchandise, ask.

9. Early autumn is an ideal time to plant trees and shrubs because the cooler weather and ample rains help the plant to adapt to its new environment. It is also the time of year when plants go on sale.

Salvage a cracked pot by using duct tape inside the pot to hold the crack together and slipping a plastic liner pot inside to hold soil and plants. Make sure the inside pot applies no pressure against the walls of the outer cracked pot.

10. Be an informed shopper. Research the particular plant you want before you turn up at the nursery. Hold out for the one you want—or be absolutely sure that the recommended substitute will have the qualities you want.

11. Don't overplant. Research the projected mature height and width of each plant, and purchase only enough plants to fill in the space after a minimum of five years.

12. Use mail-order catalogs to get a wider choice of specialty plants such as fruit trees, berry bushes, and unusual varieties of perennials.

13. Buy small plants. They cost less and will establish a healthy root system faster than larger plants.

14. If you are hiring someone to install a deck or patio, remember that the cheapest bid is not always the best buy. Check references to make sure the person you hire performs quality work and keep to the budgets and schedules.

15. Don't cut corners on the quality of materials you use for a garden-building project. Use rot-resistant wood and buy heavy-duty, galvanized hardware to avoid rust streaks.

16. Ask for a discount if you're buying $100 or more worth of plants. Nurseries may be willing to trim a bit off the sticker price, or even waive delivery costs, when you buy in quantity.

17. A willing friend or neighbor with a pickup truck can save you lots of money in delivery charges.

18. Dress up a plain arbor with ready-made "gingerbread" trim. Reproductions are widely available, or check an architectural salvage yard for possibilities.

19. Use creativity instead of cash to accent your yard. Plaster or plastic columns from discount or craft stores are inexpensive. Spray paint them with faux stone finish and set a pot brimming with plants on top to add an air of expensive antiquity for less than $20.

20. Search out salvage yards in your region. It's worth a drive to save big money on all sorts of one-of-a-kind items. The treasure hunt is part of the fun, too. You may find wrought iron gates, concrete or carved stone finials, old porch post columns, and other great possibilities for dressing up your yard.

21. Instead of indulging in two or more poorly made arbors or trellises, buy or have one solid structure made. Cheap structures fall apart fast.

22. Strengthen prefab lattice by framing it in a sandwich of 1 × 4s around the edges. It will look better and will be less prone to twist in the wind and pop its staples or slats.

23. Use inexpensive substitutes where plants will hide the structure. A vertical strip of cheap wire fencing or sturdy plastic netting makes a fine trellis for lush annual vines, which will quickly hide their support.

24. Screw on decorative finials, available in many styles at home supply stores, to gateposts or the ends of your arbor for an instant deluxe touch.

✔ Frugal Gardener Checklist

▪ Allow yourself plenty of time to think through and plan your new landscape design. After you have the plan on paper, let it simmer for a week or so, then go back and look at it again to make sure you're still satisfied.

▪ Before you design a herringbone brick patio you can't afford, educate yourself about the cost of brick, pavers, and other hardscape items by window-shopping at home-supply stores.

▪ Implement your new plan in stages, beginning with the areas of your garden you'll use the most.

▪ Remember that good design is all about pleasing the eye. Take snapshots as your work progresses. They'll give you an objective distance that you may miss when eyeballing the real thing.

▪ Choose plants with more than one season of interest wherever possible. If you live in a cold climate, include evergreens, ornamental grasses, and deciduous trees and shrubs with appealing bark or form so that your garden is still a delight to the eye in winter.

▪ Depend on annuals for fast, cheap, long-lasting color. Buy them by the flat to save money.

▪ Instead of taking home whatever is available at the nursery, ask them to order any plants of special interest.

▪ Make fruit trees and other food plants a part of your ornamental gardens. Many edible plants are as attractive as their purely ornamental cousins.

▪ Be sparing with structures and ornaments. One good arbor can make a high-powered focal point for the whole garden.

▪ Use ingenuity to find garden ornaments. Specialty shops carry one-of-a-kind items, but the astronomical price tags reflect the time the owner invested in tracking them down. Spend a Saturday morning haunting junk shops or salvage yards, and you can easily find your own treasures for a fraction of the cost.

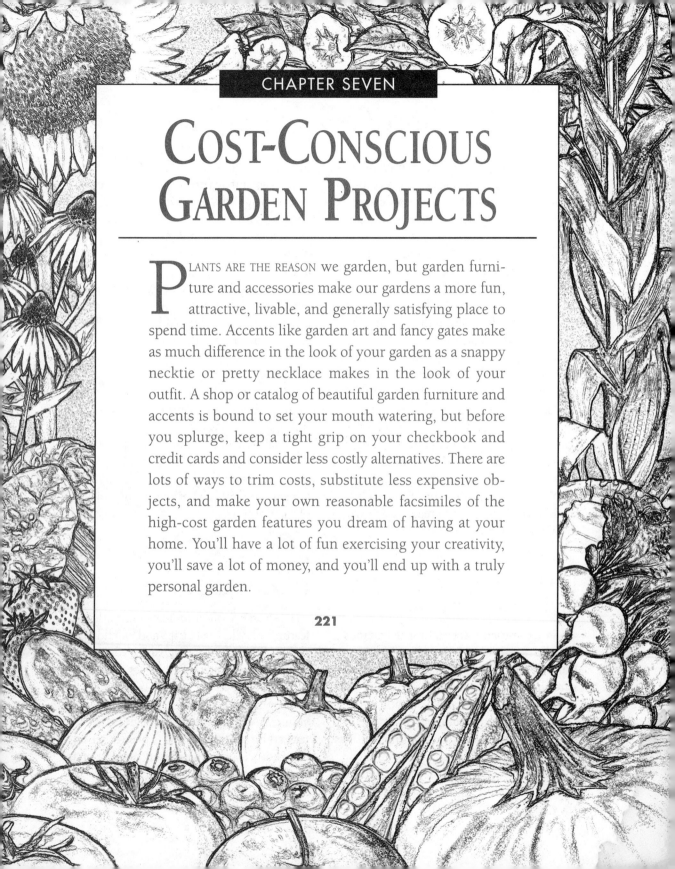

CHAPTER SEVEN

COST-CONSCIOUS GARDEN PROJECTS

PLANTS ARE THE REASON we garden, but garden furniture and accessories make our gardens a more fun, attractive, livable, and generally satisfying place to spend time. Accents like garden art and fancy gates make as much difference in the look of your garden as a snappy necktie or pretty necklace makes in the look of your outfit. A shop or catalog of beautiful garden furniture and accents is bound to set your mouth watering, but before you splurge, keep a tight grip on your checkbook and credit cards and consider less costly alternatives. There are lots of ways to trim costs, substitute less expensive objects, and make your own reasonable facsimiles of the high-cost garden features you dream of having at your home. You'll have a lot of fun exercising your creativity, you'll save a lot of money, and you'll end up with a truly personal garden.

Kick-Start Creative Thinking

Look at store-bought garden furnishings as a starting place, not as a purchase. Think about how you can create the same effect with less expensive materials or other objects. For example, what would that $600 sundial do for your garden? Can you get the same effect with a different object? A birdbath might create an equally striking focal point *and* bring in birds for color and pleasure (not to mention pest control!).

Look hard at the construction of the object—many are simply made out of ordinary materials. Their high price tags reflect an investment in time, not materials. If you've got more time than money, you can get the basic materials for most projects at your local DIY or builders' supply store, then dress them up at home. Get your inspiration from ready-made furnishings, then create your own individual interpretation.

Find Inspiration in the Recycling Bin

Gardening and decorating magazines are chock-full of gardening inspiration, but at $3 or more an issue, few frugal gardeners want to subscribe to every magazine that's available. But you can find plenty of inspiration free for the asking in the magazine recycling bin at your local drop-off site. Or ask your local library if they'd give you a chance to rummage through their stacks before they recycle their old issues.

Start a Neighborly Exchange

Suggest a magazine exchange to your nearby neighbors or coworkers. Everybody gets together, bringing their unwanted magazines, and you recycle them over and over as they go from one person to the next. Chances are, you'll discover magazines you didn't know existed, plus you'll find lots of photos to inspire creative thinking. And you'll have fun talking about your ideas with your friends.

Look Beyond the Obvious

Good garden furnishing ideas show up in just about every magazine you flip through. You may catch a glimpse of an unusual style of fence in the background of a portrait, for instance. Learn to keep your eyes open for the garden details that appear, no matter what the main subject of the photo is.

Become an On-the-Road Spy

Keep an eye out for interesting garden features on your daily trips and extended jaunts. Carry along a notepad so you can make a quick sketch of whatever it is that catches your eye. Feel free to borrow someone else's bright idea and adapt it to your own home grounds. A plain bench backed by a flowery trellis, a planter set on an upturned pot as a pedestal, an old porch post cut down and used as a birdhouse stand—you never know what will turn up on your travels.

Re-create a Reasonably Priced Facsimile

An outstanding garden accessory makes a garden memorable, whether it's your own private paradise or a public showplace. In many cases, a well-placed accent piece can be more attention getting than the plants around it. The rose-covered metal pergola that sheltered a path in painter Claude Monet's garden is as familiar to garden-loving fans of this French artist as his waterlilies, but unless you're a welder by trade, you're not going to be able to mimic Monet's arch without lying down a sizable bundle of cash. What's a cost-conscious gardener to do? Simple: Just follow the basic frugal commandment of using your ingenuity instead of your wallet.

Make a Functional, Fool-the-Eye Pergola

If you love the idea of a framework of roses above your garden path, create a similar effect by building a pergola out of PVC pipe instead of welded steel, as shown on page 224. The material is inexpensive and easy to work with, and it won't corrode or rot. Spray it with black paint to make it look like iron, or leave it white if you prefer that look. Or, to mimic a verdigris-encrusted copper pipe, paint your PVC trellis sea green and add touches of copper paint. The roses or other plants you grow over the frame will disguise the pipes enough so that casual observers will never guess that they're looking at PVC.

Draw Attention with Paint

An out-of-the-ordinary color is all it takes to give center stage to a garden accessory. At Huntington Library Gardens in San Marino, California, for example, nearly all visitors to this garden mecca remember the bright orange, steeply arched moon bridge spanning a pond in the Japanese garden. Paint is cheap, so have fun with it. Paint a plain bench cobalt blue, and you multiply its visual impact a hundredfold.

Depend on the Details

It's the finishing touches that make some garden ornaments so expensive—and so appealing. Try dressing up a less costly, more basic structure or ornament with details you add yourself.

The Finial Touch

Those fancy knobs that dress up the ends of banisters or perch atop elegant, pricey fence posts are called finials. Stroll the aisles of a well-stocked lumberyard or home supply store and you're bound to find them in an array of sizes, prices, and styles, from simple ball shapes to elegant curved and pointed spires. Prices start at just a few dollars. Place them at the corners of a trellis, on fence posts flanking the gate, or even alone atop a wooden post to add a charming finishing touch to your garden.

The Frugal Gardener's Workshop:
A PVC Pergola

C OVER A GARDEN PATH with an extended arbor (better known as a pergola) made of inexpensive PVC pipe painted black or dark green to look like expensive metal. Here's how to make a PVC pergola to cover a 4 × 20-foot walkway.

Materials

20 pieces of 2-foot-long, 2-inch-diameter PVC pipe for top rails

10 pieces of 8-foot-long, 4-inch-diameter PVC pipe for legs

10 T-shaped connectors (2 × 2 × 4 inches) for attaching legs

8 T-shaped connectors (2 × 2 × 2 inches) for attaching crossbars

4 pieces of 4-foot-long, 2-inch-diameter PVC pipe for crossbars

10 metal fence posts, 5 foot long × 3½ inches wide

Black or dark green spray paint

PVC glue

Newspapers or dropcloth

Tools

Sledgehammer for sinking fence posts

Measuring tape

Directions

1. Lay all pieces on newspaper and spray paint them black or very dark green.

2. Using a 2 × 2 × 4-inch T-shaped connector and the PVC glue, fasten two 2-foot pipes together for the top rails. Insert an 8-foot leg into the 4-inch opening of the T-shaped connector. Repeat this procedure nine more times for the other rails and legs.

3. Glue a 2 × 2 × 2-inch T-shaped connector at either end of a 4-foot-long crossbar. Repeat for the other three crossbars.

4. Insert a 2-foot-long top rail ensemble into either end of the 2 × 2 × 2-inch T-shaped connectors from the crossbars so that the crossbars are at right angles to the legs.

5. Measure and mark post locations, spacing them 4 feet apart on both sides of the walkway, exactly opposite each other.

6. Sink each 5-foot-long fence posts 2 feet into the ground at the marked locations.

7. With the aid of two helpers, carefully lower the legs of the structure over the supporting fence posts so that each end and the center of the pergola are supported.

8. Stand back and admire. Then plant roses or other climbers to cover your pergola.

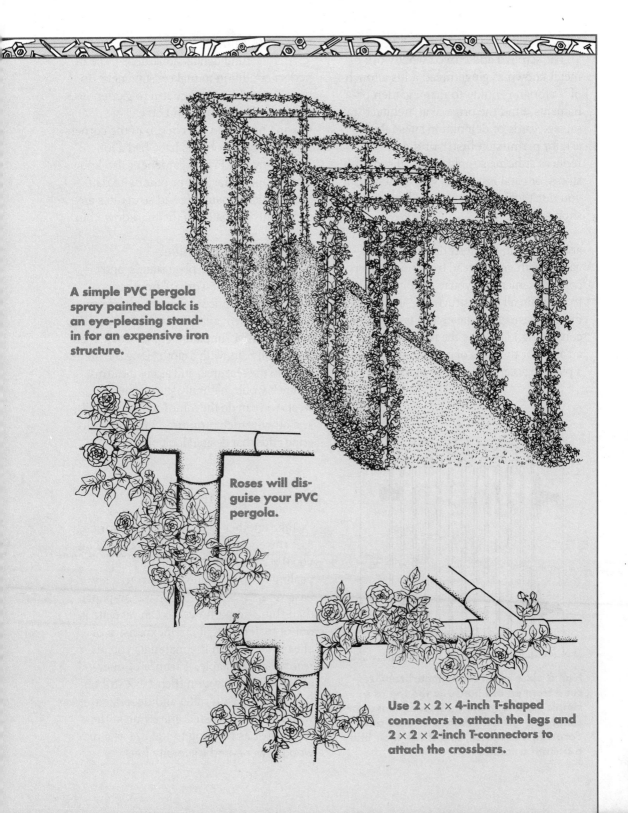

A simple PVC pergola spray painted black is an eye-pleasing stand-in for an expensive iron structure.

Roses will disguise your PVC pergola.

Use 2 × 2 × 4-inch T-shaped connectors to attach the legs and 2 × 2 × 2-inch T-connectors to attach the crossbars.

Gingerbread in the Garden

The scrolled and curved woodwork or metal known as gingerbread adds a touch of Victorian gentility to many garden ornaments. Find the original at architectural salvage yards or demolition sites (always ask for permission first!), or dig up replicas at home supply stores, discount stores, or catalogs. Prices vary widely, so if you don't feel you're getting a bargain, shop around.

A little goes a long way. Victoriana is all about overkill, but don't burden your garden with gingerbread trimming at every corner. (Remember, you're the one who has to maintain all these structures, and painting extensive gingerbread trim is very time-consuming.) Decorate the inside corners of an arbor or the sides of a plain trellis, or use a piece to accent the top rail of a gate.

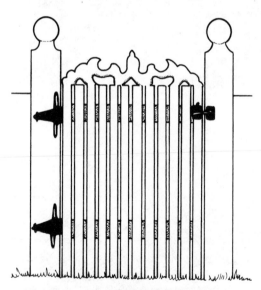

Nail a piece of scrolled gingerbread rescued from an old house to the top of a simple gate to make an instant, classy accent in the garden. Paint the fence and decoration to match, and it will look like a custom creation.

Celebrate Imperfection

Architectural details don't need to be in perfect condition to make a statement. In fact, flaws add a lot of charm to garden ornaments. Those chips and cracks or missing fingers on the cherub in the corner suggest that the objects have had a long and happy life. Frugal gardeners also know that chipped, cracked, or otherwise damaged garden ornaments and structures are commonly relegated to the markdown bin.

Make an Instant Antique

Wooden benches, plant stands, and tables with the paint worn off from years of use carry hefty price tags in antique shops. Make your own "antique" bench by painting an inexpensive, unpainted pine bench, then wiping off paint with a cloth along the front edge, in the seat area, and along the arms, where it would naturally show signs of wear. You can do the same for chairs, tables, and other garden furniture. Natural weathering adds that desired look of age, too.

Be a Copycat

Take another look at those high-priced rose towers and wooden obelisks, and you'll see that the design that's so appealing to your eye boils down to a few basic shapes. Sketch that shape on paper, then think about how you can recreate it out of materials that are inexpensive or cheap. Work with the materials you already have available. A teepee of interesting long sticks with their bark still on, tied together with raffia and decorated with a knob of twisted grapevine at the top, is just as pleasing to the eye as a redwood tower—and it's totally free!

Cheap and Free Sources

Materials for building projects can eat up a hefty chunk of cash. Trim costs by turning to creative sources of free or almost-free raw materials such as stone, brick, and lumber.

Join the Scavengers' Club

Building materials and decorative objects are all around you, once you begin opening your eyes to the possibilities. Demolition sites, city curbs, townwide cleanup days, the local dump, thrift shop castoffs, garage sale leftovers, classified ads—the world is full of opportunities for those who don't mind scavenging. Treasure hunting this way is wonderfully rewarding because you're guaranteed to make some great finds along the way.

Bulldozers Can Lead to Bargains

If demolition work is going on in a nearby neighborhood, you can sometimes find real treasures for free. Ask the supervisor on the site if you can have any porch posts, fancy banisters or railings, or other decorative possibilities you might find. The answer may be yes. Be sure to exercise caution when you work on such a site. Wear sturdy boots, long pants and sleeves, and stout gloves. Keep an eye out for machinery, and be sure the structure is sound before you enter.

If a house, church, or other structure has already hit the dirt, all is not lost. You may still be able to rescue goodies from the wreckage. Just be sure to ask permission first.

Need a Truckload of Free Brick?

Brick from old houses is less stable than outdoor brick, and it may begin to crumble in just a few years. It's also commonly available free from demolition sites or contractors looking to get rid of construction "debris." If new brick is beyond your budget, but brick pathways are what you yearn for, forget what you may have read about not using used brick, and snap up any used bricks you see. Even if you don't get a decade of wear out of it, you'll get to enjoy the look of your favorite material in exchange for a few hours' time laying it in place. And you may luck out and find that your free discarded brick is actually a sturdy, long-lasting type that gives you many years of service.

Just As Good As New

Check the yellow pages for junkyards (or architectural salvage yards as they're sometimes called nowadays) and you'll find a treasure trove of used decorative stuff that can make your garden truly one-of-a-kind at unbelievable bottom-dollar prices.. If you can't locate a source in the yellow pages, ask at your local hardware store or lumberyard, or call a builder or handyman for recommendations.

The Frugal Gardener's Workshop:
A $5 Gazing Globe

IF YOU HAVE an old pedestal from a birdbath hiding in your garage, or if you stumble across one at a garage sale, you can turn it into a stand for a gazing globe—all the rage among garden designers. And no one will ever know that yours is just a glorified fishbowl! Here's how to do it:

Materials

Round glass fishbowl

Metallic spray paint

Pedestal-type birdbath base

Scrap plywood, if necessary (see Step 3)

Aquarium glue

Tools

Paintbrush

Saw

Directions

1. Spray the inside of the fishbowl with metallic paint in your color choice.

2. Check the size of the fishbowl opening by inverting it onto the top of the pedestal. If it's too big and slips over the top of the pedestal, go on to Step 3.

3. Trace around the fishbowl opening on a piece of scrap plywood, and cut out the circle. Then cut a hole in the center of the plywood disk so that the top of the pedestal protrudes at least 1 inch. Slip the disk over the pedestal, then invert the bowl onto the disk. A touch of aquarium glue will hold the bowl securely in place.

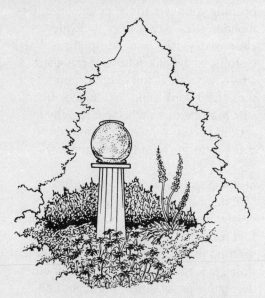

Gaze into the future and you'll see that you can make this garden ornament out of nothing more than a dimestore fishbowl and an old birdbath base.

Found Objects = Found Money

Look for money-saving recyclable building materials in dumpsters or on the curb on trash day. Linda Teague, who lives near the beach in Del Mar, California, is always on the lookout for found objects that may be of use in her garden. *Recycle* is a code word she lives by. "We use found lumber for benches and birdhouse stands," she says. "We used the wood from an old chicken coop to make a picnic table."

Linda recommends walking your neighborhood, keeping an eye out for "free for the taking" signs. She has found unwanted railroad ties, a garden table, succulent plants, and broken concrete. Broken concrete?! Linda used it to make a wonderful drystone retaining wall, with shallow-rooted plants placed in the spaces left between the random-shaped blocks. Other members of her garden club have found picket fences and other weathered fencing for free.

Put Your Crop of Rocks to Use

Settlers in New England harvested the stones out of their fields and used them to build the stone walls that characterize the northeastern landscape. Use found stone or rock for stepping stones or, if you have enough, to build a wall. In addition to being cheaper than buying or hauling stone, found stone can be beautiful. As a rule, locally indigenous stone is more attractive in a garden than imported stone because it belongs with its surroundings.

From Kitchen to Garden

Broken crockery and glass are more free resources for making garden accents. Use the pieces to make a mosaic tabletop or a colorful, decorative plaque to grace a bare expanse of wall or fence. Some Greek restaurants indulge in the old custom of dancing in a ring, throwing plates that shatter into the center. Find out if there's one in your community that would pass the shards on to you. As another possible source of broken pottery, check with local schools that offer pottery classes in their art departments. You could probably collect the pieces that break when being fired in the kilns.

Broken pieces of concrete sidewalk make a great—and free!— retaining wall and rock garden.

The Frugal Gardener's Workshop:
A Mosaic Tabletop

Recycle an old metal snack table into an object of art by covering the surface of the tabletop with bits of pretty broken pottery, china, ceramic, or mirrors. If you don't have broken glass or china laying around, collect appealing colors and patterns of dishes at thrift shops, slip them into a pillowcase, and whack lightly with a hammer to break them.

Materials
Old metal table top

Tile adhesive

Broken china, pottery, or glass

Tile grout

Tools
Putty knife

Sponge

1. Cover a clean metal tabletop with a ½-inch-thick layer of tile adhesive, smoothing it with a putty knife.

2. Arrange bits of broken pottery, china, or other decorative flat shards into the tabletop, pushing them into the adhesive so that all sharp edges are covered.

3. Apply tile grout over the tabletop, making sure all crevices are filled. Wipe off any excess grout with a sponge.

what will you save?

Recycle Materials for Projects

You can save hundreds of dollars on building materials if you're creative about using free raw materials or found objects for your garden projects. Use old porch posts from a demolition site or salvage yard instead of 4 × 4s for the legs of that arbor you're building, and you save at least $50 on the cost of the project. Spiff them up with a little sanding and a new coat of paint, and you have a unique garden furnishing that will remind you of your own ingenuity every time you stop to sniff the roses growing on it. Mosaic tabletops cost $100 and up, but you can make one yourself for less than $10. The trick is to keep an open mind and to be inventive about seeing new uses for old, rejected items.

(Almost) Free Face-Lifts

Before you throw something away, see if there is something you can do to restore, refurbish, or transform it, giving it a new lease on life. Try these tricks:

❖ A wire brush, some rust-removing "naval jelly" (originally used for refurbishing ships, but today widely available at discount and home supply stores), and metal scouring pads, followed by a fresh coat of paint, can remove years of age from old metal garden furnishings.

❖ Fresh paint and bright new cushions can make a shabby garden chair look new. Zip up the cushions yourself: It's simple to sew the straight seams for pillows. Recycle the fiberfill from flattened bed pillows for stuffing, and shop the remnant table at the fabric store for the cloth to cover them.

❖ Instead of ripping up a rotting fence, arbor, or other wooden structure, replace the damaged wood and then paint or stain the structure to protect it from further decay.

Treasures Out of Trash

We frugal gardeners have an eye for potential. Lisa Kindig, a bargain hunter and shrewd shopper, still savors the day she found a rusty metal garden furniture suite selling for just a few dollars at a garage sale. She scooped up the shabby-looking chairs, small table, and bench. Once she cleaned off the rust and repainted them, they were transformed. Her reward was a beautiful, quite valuable set of garden furniture.

Old Is In

Wood furniture with peeling paint or signs of wear is all the rage, but don't shell out cash for the "faux old" look. Find the real thing at yard sales, garage sales, thrift shops, or auctions—or sitting on the curb on trash day. An old wooden chair or table from indoors is a cinch to turn into a piece for the garden.

Put Paint to Work

Have fun with paint colors to give recycled wood furniture extra panache. Paint a chair bold red to match the geraniums or purple to go with your eggplant. The impressionist painter Claude Monet painted all his garden furniture and accents a deep green. Shades of blue blend beautifully with gray foliage. A low indoor table that's past its prime can enjoy a new life outside as a display table for containers or a backless bench. Paint it with durable outdoor paints, and then stencil a leafy design motif around the edge of the top surface.

New Tricks for Old Dogs

Fresh uses for old, worn-out items are a frugal gardener's best trick. A wheelbarrow pocked with rusted-through holes may not be much use any more for carrying heavy objects around the garden, but it can make a charming planter. In its new incarnation, the holes are an asset, providing drainage. Lay a piece of quarter-inch hardware cloth in the bottom for stability before filling it with soil and plants.

A leaky watering can or bottomless bucket also makes a fun plant container, and so do worn-out leather shoes and punctured rain boots. Plant a small-leafed ivy inside an old wire birdcage for an unusual hanging basket. Don't throw away your leaky old aquarium. Save it to use as a cloche to protect frost-tender seedlings in the early spring. Or use it to create a beautiful terrarium to adorn your porch, deck, or patio. Discarded household items can also make striking lawn art—so consider the possibilities before you trash them!

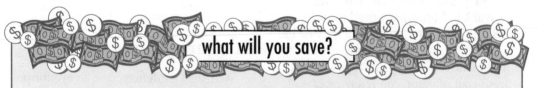

what will you save?

Be a Curbside Collector

First, give yourself a pat on the back for reusing items that otherwise would end up in the landfill. Then consider how much healthier your budget is when you give a wornout object a new lease on life instead of buying new. Of course, your savings will vary depending on what you restore. A recycled yard-sale kitchen chair may set you back $5 compared to $30 or more for a similiar new "old" chair. Clay firepits cost $200 and up, while an old wire shelf from a refrigerator laid across a circle of rocks serves the same purpose and costs nothing.

smart tips A DOZEN SMART SHOPPING TIPS

1. Before you buy, try to find a similar item used or free.

2. Get in the habit of reading the classified ads in your local newspaper. They're a great source of garden furniture bargains.

3. Learn the fine art of haggling. After you check out the furnishings you find at garage sales or through classified ads, ask "Will you take a little less?" Then make an offer about 20 percent lower than the asking price. If the seller balks, raise your offer to a 10 percent discount, and you still save.

4. Prices for homemade garden accessories such as benches, tables, and garden sheds are generally less expensive in rural areas where overhead is lower and where many people enjoy turning a woodworking hobby into a profitable cottage industry. Enjoy a day trip in the country and look for bargains.

5. Buy in the off-season. Many shops and catalogs offer garden accessories at a discount between the Christmas gift-giving season and spring.

6. Shop end-of-season clearances for garden furniture, when shops are clearing out this year's styles to make room for new ones.

7. Search out architectural salvage yards for doors, windows, and other architectural elements from buildings that you can recycle in a structure for your garden. Even if you have to travel a couple of hours to get there, the savings will pay off.

8. Before you begin a project, visit your local library to scour magazines and books for design ideas and plans for projects.

9. Mail order can be cheaper than buying retail. But be sure to include delivery costs and shipping when weighing prices.

10. Kits will save you money over assembled furnishings. Send for catalogs and compare styles and prices.

11. A good deal goes fast. If a garage sale ad mentions something you're interested in, visit the location the afternoon before the sale. Arriving early on sale morning may or may not work—sellers are usually frantically pricing items then, and your early-bird tactics may alienate them. But if you show up the afternoon before, chances are the seller won't mind letting you take a peek—or even buying—before the crowd arrives.

12. Open your eyes to the possibilities of recycled materials, and you'll soon find yourself spotting them everywhere: plywood packing crates, stacks of repairable fence sections, piles of broken concrete sidewalk that's perfect for stacked "stone" walls. Don't worry if lumber isn't the right size for this project: It may be perfect for the next.

Building Basics for the Tight-Fisted

A simple miscalculation or a lack of planning can turn your homebuilt garden project into a frustrating and expensive experience. Save yourself time, money, and aggravation by planning garden structures on paper before you make a trip to the lumberyard or home supply store. Then lay out your design on the site where you plan to build it to make sure what works on paper works in the actual situation. You can use garden lime to draw the outlines of paths and patios.

If you're working from plans, read through them the same way you'd peruse a recipe to make sure you have all materials on hand and understand the step-by-step directions. It's better to head back to the store before you start than to have an unplanned return trip in the middle of the project—especially if it involves concrete!

Find an Expert—Free!

Home supply stores, lumberyards, brickyards, and stoneyards are staffed by experts in their field. They're happy to give you all the advice you need on price and basic procedure—for free. Go to the hardware store or home center to see what's available at what price. Talk to the salespeople to get an estimate of the final cost of the project as well as their recommendations for the best material for the job. You'll learn which materials are easiest to work with, which are the most durable, and which are the most economical.

Measure twice, then ask an expert. It's easy to make a slip with figures when you're calculating dimensions or quantities of material. Most building supply

---

Two Tools Add Up to Savings

Two fairly inexpensive power tools add up to major savings in time and money. You'll quickly recoup their cost on the first project or two you put together.

■ **Circular saw.** Easy to operate and portable, this sturdy blade zips through boards in nothing flat. You can buy a basic serviceable model for less than $50. Use it to reclaim recycled lumber and to saw odd-sized scraps into usable pieces.

■ **Power screwdriver.** Setting screws for fasteners is a cinch with the power of electricity behind you. No predrilling is necessary because the screws push right in. You'll save big on time with this tool. Basic power screwdrivers cost about $30 on up; cordless models, which are wonderfully convenient, start at about $25. You can also buy a screwdriver bit for an electric drill to achieve the same labor-saving results.

stores will be happy to figure the amount of materials for you. If you decide to make your own calculations, always have them double-checked by an expert before you buy or build. The extra few minutes of time you spend will pay off with the first averted mistake.

Do Your Own Price Shopping

Prices of paving materials swing widely depending on where you live, so don't depend on price estimates quoted in wide-market publications. Although it's generally true that tile is most expensive, followed by cut stone, brick, slate, fieldstone, and paving blocks, prices may vary if you're in an area that produces any of these materials. In slate-quarrying areas, slate is cheap, especially if you buy at the quarry. In granite country, rocks to build a wall can be had for a song, relatively speaking. In limestone areas, gravel and landscape rock are a bargain-hunter's dream. The prices quoted in national publications may be way off base from the real prices you discover when you call for local quotes.

Compare Costs Before You Finalize the Design

No sense planning an elegant herringbone brick patio if the price is outside your budget. Plan the patio, by all means, but only in terms of its size. Once you decide on square footage, call building supply stores, brickyards, or other sources for quotes on various paving materials until you find one that satisfies both your aesthetic sense *and* your financial sense.

Shop Locally

Paving materials are heavy and hard to handle, so the farther you get from the source, the higher the price. Get to know what your area has naturally available, and take advantage of it. No sense buying New England slate in New Mexico, for example, when just a stone's throw from your backyard is a dealer in local sandstone.

Take a trip to the quarry. Whether you're in the market for sand, gravel, slate, or rock, you'll find the cheapest prices right at the quarry entrance. While it might cost $50 to load a pickup truck with these paving supplies at a home supply store, it can cost as little as $10 at the site—a difference that's certainly worth the trip. If you need a large quantity of heavy material, ask a contractor about hiring a truck and driver. Chances are, the price will still be significantly cheaper than buying on the retail market.

Go Rot-Resistant

For outdoor wooden items, especially for the parts where the wood will contact the ground, use rot-resistant wood such as red cedar, redwood, or cypress. Your initial cost will be more, but you'll save in the long run because these special woods last years longer than rot-prone varieties.

Save High-Priced Materials for Small Areas

Use your budget wisely by reserving expensive paving materials for small areas. A tiny circle of glazed tile can sit like an heirloom necklace in the center of a

Use costly glazed tile to make a medallion around a focal point such as a fountain or urn and cheaper, utilitarian concrete pavers to fill up the larger space around it.

garden, or surround a fountain. For more utilitarian and much larger areas, such as a patio, turn to less costly alternatives such as gravel or concrete pavers. Or trim costs by using luxury materials like tile as an accent in the center of the large area, in corners, or along edges.

Labor Savers

Saving effort is important when it comes to garden projects. Unless you enjoy carpentry or masonry as much as you do gardening, you may find yourself becoming frustrated with projects that take longer than an afternoon or, for big jobs, a couple of weekends. Put your thrifty nature to work when it comes to reducing labor: Few easy tricks will make projects a time-efficient pleasure.

Trade Work Time with Friends

Four hands are better than two when it comes to handling lumber and paving materials. When you have a helper for a project, the work flows smoothly and the materials are easier to move into position, so you save time and aggravation. If you don't have children handy to help out, barter with a friend or neighbor. Your friend comes to work with you on a Saturday project; you switch to your friend's place next weekend. It's a win-win deal.

Have Lumber Cut to Length

Many home supply stores and lumberyards will be happy to cut your boards to the length you specify for a small cost per cut—perhaps as little as 25¢. Calculate your cuts ahead of time, then confer with the store's staff to let them know what you

Do a Two-fer Deal

It's just as easy to saw the boards for two simple structures as for one, so enlist the help of a friend and spend a day making identical twins: one arbor for you, one for your friend. The work will go faster and be more fun with a helper, and at the end of the day, you'll both have a nice addition to the garden. If you want to introduce assembly line tactics to your workday, round up a few more friends and assign each a specific part of the process: One person saws, another attaches crosspieces, and so on. The work will fly!

need. With their professional equipment and experienced skills, the work will be done swiftly and accurately.

Easier hauling. Asking the shop to cut the boards to length means that for many projects you'll be able to haul the lumber home yourself, even if you drive a compact car. You'll save on delivery costs!

How's Your Back?

Projects involving laying brick or stone require a lot of heavy lifting and frequent bending. Be considerate of your back if it isn't used to this kind of work. Instead of one marathon session, spread the work out in easy one- to two-hour chunks. If you work until your back begins to ache, you can bet the discomfort will be several times more intense by the next morning.

Aggravation Avoiders

Simple carpentry is all that's called for in many garden projects. If you can hammer a nail and measure a board, you can learn any of the other basic skills needed to produce an arbor, trellis, or bench. Plan to work when you're calm and focused so you won't make careless mistakes that affect the outcome. And it's no fun and no savings, either, when your result is unusable because pieces are sawed to the wrong length or nailed together incorrectly.

Haste Makes Waste

The old saw is true indeed when it's carpentry projects that are on the table. The number one rule for any building project is *Take your time*. Think the project through before you start. Measure and plan with care every step of the way. Make cuts as precisely as you can. Most of all, allow yourself plenty of time to finish a project. An arbor can take six hours or more to build. You don't have to do it all in one day! Pace yourself, and be aware of when tiredness or frustration set in. When that happens, clean up shop and put the project aside until your next free block of time.

Make a List and Check It Twice

When you're down to attaching the last leg, it's terribly frustrating to realize that you don't have the necessary final six screws to finish building that bench. It also wastes time (and gas) to make repeated trips to the hardware store. Before you start a project, make a list of all the hardware you'll need to finish it. Always buy a few extra of the items on that list. Having extras on hand will save you lots of time searching for that nut or bolt you dropped.

Stock Up

Experienced project makers usually have a stock of assorted nuts and bolts, not to mention screws, washers, and other hardware sundries. If you're a beginner, spend a few dollars for a general assortment of such items to keep on hand, just in case you need them. Sooner or later, you will. The amount of time you'll save by having your own stock on hand can add up quickly, more than offsetting the small investment in dollars that an assortment of hardware will cost.

Make Use of a Magnet

Lost bits of hardware may not cost much in terms of replacement dollars, but their price in aggravation and wasted time can be dear. To avoid losing nails, screws, and other metal sundries, buy a strong magnet, attach it to a 3-foot-long string, and keep it handy when you're working. It will make it a cinch to collect dropped nails or other bits of hardware from the grass or the workshop floor.

Rug rats to the rescue. Collecting dropped hardware after you're finished with a project for the day can be frustrating to grownups, but children love the challenge of the treasure hunt, especially if you equip them with a magnet. When the power equipment is put away, turn them loose on the work area and you'll never have to bend for a bolt again.

Be in Awe of the Saw

Safety and *focus* are the watchwords when you work with heavy materials and power tools. Protect your eyes by wearing safety goggles or shatter-resistant glasses when you are working with power tools or metal, concrete, or stone. Wear protective gloves when you are doing heavy construction or working with caustic materials. Pull on steel-tipped boots when you're hauling stone, brick, or other things that could make you say "Ouch!" if you drop them on your toes. Here are other guidelines that will help you avoid accidents:

- Use deliberate motions around power tools: To avoid mishaps, think before you move your hand or fingers.

- Stop working if you get tired or distracted, or if the daylight fades.

- Keep children and pets away from the work area to avoid distractions and accidents.

- Keep your hands away from blades, bits, and sharp moving points.

- Never override safety fences or guards.

- Never wear loose clothing or allow hair or jewelry to hang where it can get caught in moving parts. Tuck your shirt in, button your sleeves, and pull your long hair into a clip.

- Unplug a power tool before you change a blade or bit.

Get Every Penny Out of Your Pavers

When you invest in brick, flagstone, or concrete pavers, you're banking on a permanent, beautiful effect for your garden. It's a good investment that will pay off year after year. Although the cost for these materials is high, you can save a pretty penny by laying the path or patio yourself, setting them into a bed of gravel and sand. The job is time-consuming, but it is not too difficult and the results are very satisfying.

Define the Borders

Laying paving is precision work. Begin by laying out the space you plan to pave. Use stakes and string to mark the straight edges. The garden hose is useful for marking curved lines, and if you don't like the initial look, you can experiment as you work with different possibilities. Once you've got the curve exactly as you want it, mark it on the ground with lime or sand.

Algebra to the Rescue

Here's your chance to "dust off" that high-school algebra you always wondered if you'd actually get to use. If you're planning a straight-bordered area of paving, design it according to the size of the pavers you're planning to use. You want the paving you choose to fit in evenly, with no leftover pieces. Remember to allow for the desired spacing between the paving units when you're calculating. For example, if you want a 12-foot-square patio, and you're using 12-inch paving blocks with 1 inch between the blocks,

you'll need 11 rows of 11 blocks each— not 12 rows of 12 blocks each.

Number of pavers in row (width of paver + desired spacing between pavers) – 1 (desired width of spacing between pavers) = length of row

$$
\begin{aligned}
\text{length of row} &= 12\,(12" + 1") - 1(1") \\
&= 12\,(13) - 1" \\
&= 156 - 1 \\
&= 155"
\end{aligned}
$$

Here's another option:

$$
\begin{aligned}
\text{length of row} &= 11\,(12" + 1") - 1(1") \\
&= 11\,(13) - 1" \\
&= 143 - 1 \\
&= 142"
\end{aligned}
$$

If you can adjust to a square patio that's 2 inches narrower than the 12 feet (or 144 inches) you had planned, you'll save the cost of 23 paving blocks. At a rough price of about $3 per paver, this tiny trim job adds up to big savings.

Slope for Drainage

When water lingers on paved surfaces, it can cause cracks, uneven settling, and all kinds of other structural unpleasantries, not to mention sopping feet. Avoid the problem by building a slight slope into your paved surfaces so rain and irrigation water can drain off quickly. Slope a patio away from the house at a rate of $\frac{1}{4}$ inch per foot. If the patio is 15 feet deep, the slope should be $3\frac{1}{2}$ inches higher near the house than at the other end. Here's how to make a slope guide for a patio so you can build in good drainage:

1. Calculate the correct number of inches of slope.

2. Using a pencil and straightedge, mark two stakes at the same place to indicate ground level, at least 6 inches above the base of the stake.

3. Measure the amount of slope you calculated on one stake, and make a second mark above the ground level mark.

4. Hammer the stakes into the ground at each end of the patio, installing them the same depth, and making sure the ground level mark is visible.

5. Tie string between the stakes, from the ground level mark on the far stake to the slope mark on the stake nearest the house.

6. Excavate soil from patio area, following the string as a slope guide.

Elevate to Keep Your Paving Clean

To keep soil from washing over the surface of your paved area, elevate the finished surface about 1 inch above the ground level of the surrounding area. Dig out the space to allow for a 4- to 6-inch-deep layer of gravel (check with your local authorities to find out what depth the local codes require, if any), a 1½-inch subbase of sand, and the depth of your paving material. To determine if the depth and slope are cor-

rect, measure from the string to the bottom of the excavation. To check the depth in the middle of the excavation, lay a straight board across the width of the hole and place a level on top. If the ground is even, the board should be flush with the soil and the level bubble should float in the center.

Installation Shortcuts

Installing a patio or a walkway is a simple job, but it does take some planning and a healthy dose of hand labor. You'll save big bucks by doing it yourself, though, so if you have the time to spare, teach yourself the simple skills and learn the steps to success.

No Room for Shiftiness

Paving set in sand and gravel may shift if it isn't held in place by edging. The least expensive and easiest edging to install is a strip of rot-resistant wood. Slices of pavers set on end are more expensive, but they are also more attractive and durable.

Edging that won't budge. Anchor wood edging in place with support stakes driven deeply into the ground. Cut the edging to the depth of your sand base plus the height of the paving itself. Nail the wood edge to the stakes. If you prefer paving as edging, lay brick or concrete strips on top of the gravel base.

Plain or fancy brick edging. Lay bricks on edge on the gravel subsurface, so that they are perpendicular to the length of the paved surface, or stand them on end in a tidy row. A fun variation for paths is to set the bricks on end at an angle, making a serrated edge known as dragon's-tooth brick edging.

Recycle Your Lawn Roller

Use a short-tined metal rake to spread ½-inch to 1-inch diameter of gravel or crushed stone evenly in your excavated area to a depth of 4 to 6 inches. Use a lawn roller to tamp it down thoroughly, or rent a hand tamper or a machine compactor if you have a large area to compact.

Use Pipes as Levels

To ensure that you level the sand evenly, sink 1½-inch outer-diameter pipes into the sand to the gravel level on both sides of the patio. Use these pipes as your leveling guide. Don't forget that a path or patio should have a slight slope for drainage as explained on the opposite page. Spread a 1½-inch layer of coarse builders' sand, smooth it with the back of your rake, and then drag a straight board, known as a screed, across the sand to level it.

Start in a Corner

Doing the same work twice wastes valuable time and energy, so begin laying your paving material in a corner to avoid disturbing the smoothed sand. Set each piece on the sand—don't push or wiggle the pavers into place. Settle the pavers as you work by tapping each one several times with a rubber mallet. Check periodically with a level, and tap again on any pavers that are sitting too high.

Avoid Depressions

If you need to kneel on the sand subbase, lay down a board or sheet of plywood. This trick will distribute your weight across the board so that you don't create low spots in the sand and gravel.

Quick Cuts for Brick and Stone

Simple is better when it comes to frugality, but if your design requires that the pavers be cut to fit properly into the edges and corners, making straight cuts is a job that you can become proficient at with a little practice. Mark the paver for cutting with a pencil or chalk. Then score a line on your mark on all sides of the piece, using a wide chisel called a brickset. Be sure to wear gloves and safety glasses or goggles when you make the cut. Lay the paver on a solid surface, center the chisel on the scored line, and then tap the flat chisel end firmly with a small sledgehammer or mallet, repeating until the brick or paver breaks. In most cases, it will split along the score lines. Rent a water-cooled masonry saw or wet saw if you need to make precise angled cuts.

Edge a brick path by laying bricks along each side for a neat finish.

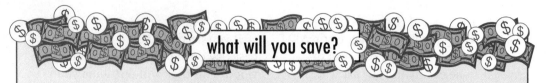

It Really Does Pay to Do It Yourself

Labor costs vary across the country but generally represent as much as half the price of the final project. Or to put it another way, doing the labor yourself saves you roughly as much cold hard cash as the price you paid for materials. Depending on the amount of paving you're putting in, that figure can easily mount into hundreds of dollars. Another financial payoff is that an attractive patio or pathway is likely to add more value to your home than the price of the materials.

For the final step, sweep fine dry mason's sand into the joints. Start in the center and work outward, sweeping in all directions to get as much sand worked into the joints as possible. Water the pavers thoroughly with a fine spray, and wait for the surface to dry. The water will help the sand to settle, so if necessary, sweep more mason's sand across the surface until all joints are completely filled.

Quick, Easy Repairs

If a brick or paver cracks or chips so badly that it needs replacing, you can either settle another paver into its place or create a planting pocket with a few inches of soil and adaptable plants such as sedums, hens-and-chicks, low-growing thyme, or other creepers. To replace a paver, simply pry it up and put another in its place, using the same procedure you used to install it.

Penny-Wise Paths

Paths play an important design role in the garden, plus they give you sure footing and keep your feet out of the mud. There is an extensive variety of possible paving materials for paths, ranging from options that cost nothing, such as free wood chips from your local tree-trimming company, to expensive possibilities such as tile, brick, and imported stones. Gravel, another inexpensive option, is a versatile material that looks fitting in both formal and informal situations. Stepping stones are charming in many settings and are less expensive because the area that's paved with them is smaller—you're not trying to cover the whole space. However, stepping stones are trickier to walk on than other surfaces, something to bear in mind if small children or elderly people will be using the path.

FRUGAL GARDENER'S GUIDE

Pathway Paving Choices

Choose a path material that suits the style of your garden, the style and materials of your house, and your budget. As you can see from the list below, there really is something for everyone. So if you can't afford flagstone or marble, don't despair. With a little ingenuity, you can dress up the most drab concrete block to look like high-priced pavers.

MATERIAL	COST
Brick	Expensive
Ceramic tile	Expensive
Cobblestones	Free if you collect your own, but heavy to carry
Concrete paving blocks	Midpriced
Crushed seashells	Free if you have a local source
Flagstone	Free to high-priced, depending on type of stone and source
Grass	Cheap in cost, high in maintenance
Gravel	Low- to midpriced
Interlocking paver	Mid- to high-priced, depending on quality and design
Marble	Expensive
Natural stone	Expensive unless local quarry is willing to sell flawed pieces at discount
Oyster shells	Free if you have a local source
Pebbles or cobbles set in mosaic pattern	Free if you collect your own, but labor-intensive
Pine needles	Free if you collect your own
Shredded bark	Low-priced, especially from a sawmill
Wood chips	Free or low-cost from local tree-trimming service
Wooden rounds	Free if you slice up a tree on your property, otherwise midpriced

Money-Saving Wood Mulch Paths

Shredded bark and wood chips are the easiest and cheapest paths you can lay. Shop at the source for material: tree-trimming companies or sawmills. To keep weeds from popping up in the middle of the path, put down a thick layer of newspaper (the thicker the layer, the longer it will be effective) and then spread the wood mulch on top to a depth of 6 to 8 inches. It will seem a bit high and soft at first, but in a few weeks it will compact. Renew the path about once a year with a 2-inch layer of new mulch, as it decomposes or compacts.

Start a Shell Path

In the colonial era, many homeowners near the coast paved their garden paths with clam and oyster shells. According to Gordon Chappell, landscape director at Colonial Williamsburg, in colonial days they'd simply shuck the oysters or clams, throw the whole shell onto the path, and walk it in. He recommends using a base material such as gravel, just as you would for a brick or stone path, with about 1 inch of crushed shells on top. At historic Williamsburg, the shells are crushed with a professional rolling machine to make a finer surface before they are spread on the paths. You can use a heavy lawn roller to start the crushing job. Once on the paths, normal foot traffic breaks them up more and compacts them onto the base. Such a path can last for a decade before it has to be renewed. And, as Gordon Chappell notes, "The only other way to get a white path in a garden is to use crushed marble, which I don't think is nearly as attractive as the shells."

She sells seashells. You can install a shell path bit by bit with souvenirs of seaside trips. For a bigger supply of shells, check with local seafood restaurants or seafood processing plant to see if you can take away their oyster and clam shells.

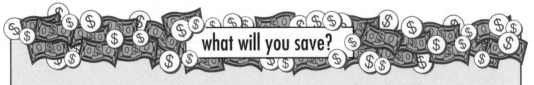

what will you save?

Save Money along the Garden Path

Finding a source for free materials is the name of the game for frugal gardeners. If you must have a more formal look or if you simply prefer pavers, you'll save plenty of money in labor laying the paths yourself. When deciding which type of path is best for you, weigh the cost against the look of the final product (to be pleasing, it must blend well with both the architecture of your home and the style of the garden), its durability, the amount of up-keep required, and the amount of money you realistically can afford. A 20-foot-long path of wood chips can cost you nothing but the easy work required to spread it; a 20-foot-long path with a fancy brick design can run $100, plus hours of labor to install.

Trim the Costs of Trellises and Arbors

Trellises and latticework are underused features in American gardens, which is a shame because they are quite easy and inexpensive to build. Building your own or adapting the ready-made designs on the market will give your garden a unique look, create privacy, and add height.

Tricks with Trellising

Trellising is so versatile it's worth adding to just about any garden. You can build free-standing trellises, or attach a trellis against a wall. It adds planting space, provides privacy, makes the garden look better, and gives fast-climbing vines almost as much visual weight as slow-growing trees. Try the following ideas to make the most out of this charming, inexpensive garden support.

Let Your Inner Artist Out to Play

Normally, we think of a trellis as a symmetrical pattern of diamonds or squares. A simple design is the cheapest to buy and the easiest to build, but it's fun to play with other possibilities. At Nemours, a DuPont family property in Delaware, an elaborate trellis painted pastel green covers an expanse of bare white wall, breaking the monotony of the wall with an intriguing pattern that creates the illusion of shutters around the windows with a recessed arbor in the center. The wall, which would be stark and imposing without the trellising, looks like a lath house or conservatory.

Create your own trellis masterpiece by playing with sketches on paper. Arch the top, add swags or curves, vary the height of various adjoining sections, decorate with finials, and you have a masterpiece instead of a mundane trellis.

Fool the Eye

In a small garden, use trellising to fool the eye into believing that the garden is actually much bigger than it is. At the far end of the garden, against a fence or wall, arrange the trellis pattern so that the slats narrow toward the center, suggesting a receding tunnel. Immediately, you'll have a sense that the garden extends into the distance. Plant a pair of trees on either side of the trellis to anchor the design, or train a hedge or vine alongside and across the top of the trellis. Not only will you create a greater sense of depth and space in your garden, but you'll also add interest to a ho-hum wall or fence.

Transform the Ordinary

Lattice is a very inexpensive way to dress up an unattractive structure in the garden. Use sections to hide an air-conditioning or heating unit from view or to screen a dog run. At his Cedaridge Farm in Bucks County, Pennsylvania, garden writer and photographer Derek Fell transformed an ordinary storage shed into a charming cottage by covering it with lattice. To dress up the bare window, he added shutters and a window box spilling over with flowers. Instead of an eyesore, the building is now an attractive focal point on the property.

Paint before you put it up. If you plan to paint trellising a contrasting color to the building, do so before you attach it to the structure or you'll spend hours doing tedious edging.

The Frugal Gardener's Workshop:
A Simple Arbor

THIS BASIC ARBOR is a versatile garden piece. Use it to mark a gateway into a special section of the garden.

Materials

Four 8-foot-long 2 × 4s (posts)

Six 8-foot-long 1 × 3s

One 5-foot-long 2 × 4

1 pound 1-inch drywall screws

1 quart paint or polyurethane

Paintbrush

One bag quick-setting concrete

One bucket gravel

Tools

Power screwdriver or electric drill fitted with Phillips screwdriver bit

Circular saw

Pencil

Tape measure

Square

Directions

1. Mark the 8-foot 2 × 4s with a pencil line at these intervals, measured from the bottom of the boards: 18, 24, 36, 48, 60, 72, 84, and 93 inches (the last mark should be about 3 inches from top of board). Write the measurement at each mark.

2. Mark and cut four of the 1 × 3s into twelve 30-inch-long sections. Cut the 5-foot 2 × 4 into two 30-inch-long sections.

3. Lay two 8-foot 2 × 4s parallel, 30 inches apart. Screw a section of 1 × 3 to a 2 × 4 at the 24-inch marking, using two drywall screws. Repeat at the markings for 36, 48, 60, 72, and 84 inches. Screw a 30-inch 2 × 4 at the 93-inch mark.

4. Repeat Step 3 for the other set of 2 × 4s.

5. Mark and cut each of the two remaining 1 × 3s into two 48-inch lengths.

6. Attach the four sections of 48-inch-long 1 × 3s across the top of the arbor with drywall screws. Allow each board to overhang 6 inches on each side of the arbor, creating an arbor with a 36-inch opening.

7. Paint or polyurethane the arbor.

8. Set your arbor in the desired location and mark the locations of the four posts. Move the arbor out of the way, and dig 2½- to 3-feet-deep holes for the poles. (Rent a posthole digger to make the job easier.)

9. Place a handful of gravel in each hole.

10. Stand arbor in holes. Fill with quick-setting concrete and hold in place until the concrete sets.

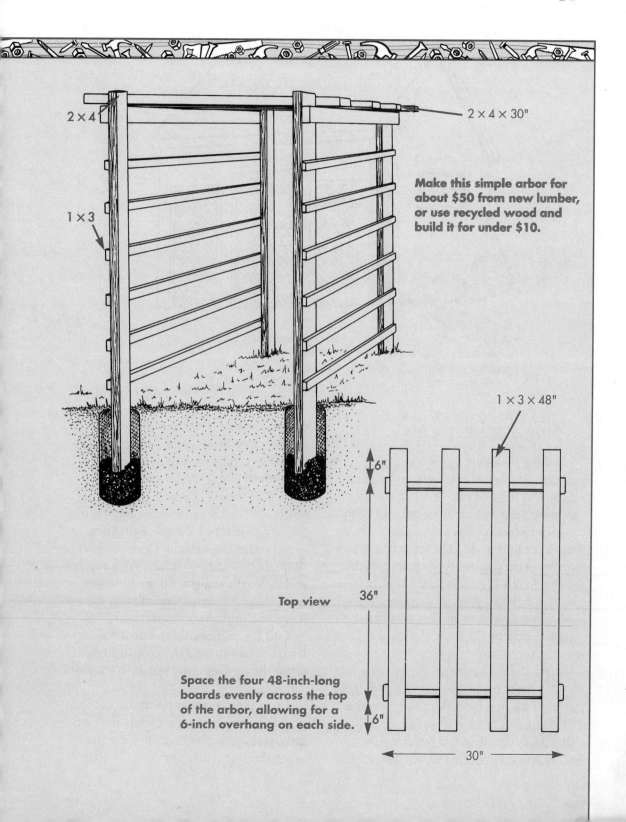

2 × 4

2 × 4 × 30"

1 × 3

Make this simple arbor for about $50 from new lumber, or use recycled wood and build it for under $10.

1 × 3 × 48"

Top view

6"

36"

6"

30"

Space the four 48-inch-long boards evenly across the top of the arbor, allowing for a 6-inch overhang on each side.

A plain garden shed is transformed when you add the cozy charm of trellis. Build your own from lath strips, or buy prefab sheets and frame them with 1 × 3s for a finished look. Paint and attach the trellis to the wall of the storage shed.

Arbor Arrangements

Arbors are another great asset in the garden, and they're relatively easy and inexpensive to build yourself. Use an arbor to mark the transition from one part of the garden to another, to create an accent over a gate, or to provide a sheltered retreat in a corner of the garden. If you place an arbor with a built-in bench on the property boundary, you'll give the idea that the arbor is a passage to another part of the garden, making the space feel bigger.

Make a Solid Anchor

The most arduous aspect of building an arbor is digging the holes to support the four posts. To anchor an arbor securely so that it stays in place under the weight of vines or the force of wind, you'll need to sink the posts 2½ to 3 feet deep in the ground. A posthole digger makes the job much easier, allowing you to excavate a narrow, deep hole without wasted effort. Put a 6-inch layer of coarse gravel in the bottom of the hole so that the bottom of the posts are sitting on quick-draining gravel instead of wet soil. Once the post is properly positioned, with its sides square and its length straight, fill the hole with quick-setting concrete and allow it to cure according to package instructions.

Call for helpers. Round up a willing friend or two to hold the posts upright while the concrete sets, usually a matter of minutes.

Erect temporary supports. Stake each post to keep it in position while the concrete gets a grip. Remove the supports when the concrete is dry.

Go Rustic

A rustic arbor, pergola, or trellis made of saplings or branches for the support posts and branches and twigs for the details is a winning accent in an informal garden. If you have the wood on your property or if you collect materials from friends or neighbors, it costs you nothing more than the time to build it. Scavenge after a storm for fallen branches.

Design around Your Materials

Plan the design of your structure according to the materials you can gather. An abundance of grapevine or supple willow branches is perfect for making a lightweight trellis attached to a wall of the house. If you have heavier branches, you can lash them together with raffia or wire or nail them together at joints to make a sturdier structure.

Dressing Your Arbor

Once you've built your trellis, arbor, or pergola, you enjoy the fun part of dressing it in vines. It's enchanting to see a tall structure in the garden smothered in flowering climbers, taking color and drama up toward the sky.

For strong structures, consider honeysuckle, climbing roses, clematis (mix varieties to get bloom from spring through late summer), wisteria, bougainvillea, and trumpet creeper. Don't overlook edibles such as grapes and hardy kiwi vines. (But if you want to sit under your arbor, remember that ripe fruit attracts bees and wasps.)

For lighter-weight woodwork that can't support much weight, stick to annual vines. Morning glories, scarlet runner beans, climbing nasturtiums, and cardinal climber are all good choices.

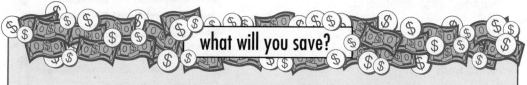

what will you save?

How to Trim Your Trellising Budget

Trellises, arbors, and pergolas can be as simple or as complicated as you like, depending on how much you want to challenge yourself. Keep in mind that the more wood involved, the higher the price, unless you're using tree trimmings or recycled scavenged lumber. In general, you can make an appealing arbor for about half the price of a store-bought one, saving you $50 or more. Assembling these structures from a kit also saves money, usually at least a third of the retail cost. Fancying up a prefab trellis saves you the time of building from scratch and gives you a more satisfying decoration for your garden. As you become more skilled in carpentry, you can build a more complex arbor for about $100—much less than the $250 to $300 price tags on ready-made ones..

The Frugal Gardener's Workshop:
A Rustic Trellis

SALVAGE TREE trimmings to make a rustic trellis for morning glories or scarlet runner beans.

Materials

2 poles of branches, 4 inches in diameter

2 poles of branches, 3 inches in diameter

Grapevines

Tools

Hammer

Staple gun

Directions

1. Use 4-inch-diameter poles for the supporting sides, and nail on 3-inch poles for the top and bottom crosspieces.

2. Fill in the interior of the trellis with grapevines looped from side to side or with branched twigs arranged in a pleasing pattern.

3. Secure the vines or twigs with heavy-duty staples in the side posts.

You can't beat grapevines for adding rustic charm to a garden. Simply wrap them around thick tree branches to make a quick and easy trellis for lightweight climbers.

Staple grapevines in place to secure them.

A Greenhouse Alternative

Lath houses made of slats that filter sunlight are popular as a greenhouse alternative in mild-winter areas of the country. That's because they allow gardeners to have permanent outdoor collections of sheltered plants, such as orchids and other tropicals, without the heat buildup of a greenhouse. But these structures also make sense for gardeners in any region because they're an ideal place to pot and propagate garden plants and houseplants.

The filtered sunlight of a lath house is ideal for fuchsias, begonias, ferns, and cymbidium orchids. It's also a safe nursery environment for seedlings and cuttings and a great place for a counter-high potting bench.

Lower Cost, Less Maintenance

Lath houses are much cheaper than greenhouses to build, and they're easier to maintain. You don't need to remember to run outside and open the door on a hot day or to install temperature-controlled electric window openers. Essentially a lath house is a building frame with lath strips for the walls and roof. Mounting the lath strips is a simple job requiring no more than a staple gun and a saw to cut the pieces to the correct length. Space the lath by the width of one piece, using an unattached strip of lath as a measuring guide. Run the strips north and south so the shade will shift evenly as the sun moves across the sky through the day. If possible, situate your lath house where it will get full sun; otherwise it may be too shady for your plants. Pave the area down the center of the house with stepping stones, concrete, or gravel to protect your feet from mud. A hose outlet near the lath house makes watering much more convenient.

Build the wood frame of your lath house or have it built, then attach the strips of lath yourself to have a viable and less expensive greenhouse substitute for the warm months.

Frugal Tricks with Fences and Hedges

Hedge plants may look puny when you first put them in, but if you're patient enough to wait two or three years for privacy, you can have a wall of pretty greenery for a fraction of the price of the fence. Start your own shrubs from cuttings, and you'll save even more. Fast-growing shrubs that are simple to root from cuttings stuck in moist soil include privet, forsythia, weigela, pussy willow, and rose of Sharon.

are easy to install yourself. Simply dig postholes for each upright support, bury them, and insert the rails in the slots. If the open design of post-and-rail fences doesn't provide enough security (small animals and people can easily slip between the spaces), cover the fence with wire fabric painted a dark color so that it is virtually unnoticeable. Rail fences are also an ideal support for roses and vigorous vines such as sweet autumn clematis.

More Wood, More Dollars

The amount of wood in a fence is the primary factor for determining cost, unless you're going for an elaborate fence with lots of fine detailing. A solid board fence costs more than open pickets; a taller fence costs more than a shorter one; and a wire fence generally costs much less than a wooden one. (Vinyl fences are the exception: They are much more costly than wood fences because they need no upkeep.) If a solid-wall effect is important to you for privacy or muffling street noise, consider combining hedge plants with the fence so that you can get by with a more open design of fencing or at least fewer sections of it.

Post-and-Rail Penny-Pinching

An inexpensive fencing option is post-and-rail because it costs less than solid board fences and it requires less precision to install—a bit of unevenness is part of the charm. Split-rail or whole-rail fences fit well into rural or casual settings and

Go Utilitarian

If your object is to confine pets or small children or to create a quiet background to enclose your garden, consider inexpensive wire fencing and posts. Substituting wire for expensive wood is an option that will bless your budget. Instead of five 8-foot-long sections of fence at $30 a pop, you can cover the same 40 linear feet with wire for $50—a savings of $100. Cover the wire with vines, and you'll have a functional barrier and a beautiful garden wall.

Even Heirs Are Frugal

On her 25-acre property in Washington, D.C., Post cereal heiress Marjorie Merriweather Post enclosed her elegant French garden with a tall metal-link fence. However, the fence is so densely clothed in ivy that it's invisible. Instead of seeing a jarring metal fence, all visitors are aware of is a muted dark green background acting as the perfect foil to the elements inside the garden. Thanks to the dense coverage of the ivy, you'd never know whether there was a costly wrought iron fence or a practical chain-link one beneath it. Even with plenty of money to spare, Ms. Post opted for a less expensive option that did the job perfectly.

Install It Yourself and Save

It's hard to build a simple wood fence for less than it costs on the market, but you can save money by doing the hauling and installation yourself. Find a strong friend with a truck (if you don't have one) to eliminate delivery fees. Dig the holes, set the posts, attach the sections of fence, and you can save a third to a half or more of the cost of installed fencing. At roughly $10 to $15 a linear foot, the final cost of an installed 48-foot-long fence can run $500. Install the same fence yourself, buying it at $30 per 8-foot section, and your total outlay of cash is only $180.

Sensible Spacing

You'll save a lot of time and money if you space your posts 6 to 8 feet apart to make the best use of standard lengths of precut fencing sections. Check the length of your selected fence-style sections before you begin setting posts. If the length of the fence doesn't divide up evenly into, say, 8-foot sections, make the final section shorter, or insert a gate in the space to make up the difference.

Solid Setup

To be stable enough to support the weight of fencing, you'll need to bury approximately one-third of the total length of the posts in the ground. Gateposts and end posts, which get more stress, should be even deeper. Use a posthole digger to make the holes to a depth equal to one-third of the post length, plus 6 inches. Fill the bottom of each hole with a 6-inch layer of gravel or large stones for drainage and to keep the concrete from seeping under the post. Set the posts in quick-setting concrete to prevent the wood from decaying from contact with the soil and to add stability to the fence. Taper the top of the concrete so that rainwater will run away from the post. Allow the concrete to cure for at last two days before you begin attaching the fence.

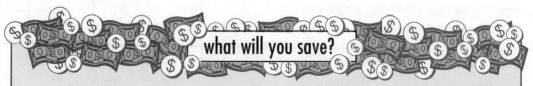

what will you save?

Do-It-Yourself Fence for Half the Price

Installing a fence yourself will save you bundles of cash, in many cases half or more of the installed price. For 100 linear feet of fence, that savings can add up to hundreds of dollars. It's a big job, but you need no special skills to do it. And think of the money you'll save on aerobics at the gym!

The Frugal Gardener's Workshop:
A Moon View in Your Fence

ADD AN INTRIGUING TOUCH to a plain board fence by cutting a peephole that you can use for viewing the rising moon. It can look Victorian, Japanese, or even contemporary, depending on your preference, fence style, and paint color.

Materials

Scrap plywood

12 lath strips, each 24 inches long

Nails

Paint

Tools

Staple gun and heavy-duty staples

Jigsaw

Paintbrush

Directions

1. Measure and mark a circle on a section of board fence so the circle is 18 inches in diameter. Place the circle so that it is at least 2 inches from any crosspieces.

2. Saw out and remove the fencing from the circle.

3. Measure and mark a 24-inch circle on the plywood, and then measure and mark a 16-inch circle inside of and concentric to the larger one. Cut out the plywood "doughnut" between the two marks.

4. Repeat Step 3, so you have two plywood doughnuts.

5. For one of the doughnuts, make a lattice design for the hole by attaching the lath strips across the face of the doughnut, and cut off the excess. You don't want any strips to extend beyond the doughnut.

6. Nail the plywood doughnuts around the circle of lath, one on each side of the fence. Make sure the lath is against the fence.

7. Paint the fence.

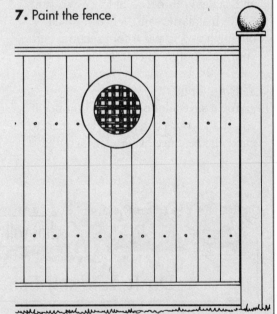

Customize a plain board fence by adding a "moon window" of lattice for a view through the fence. This project costs less than $10.

Penny-Pinching Planters and Window Boxes

Every spring the nurseries, garden centers, and home improvement stores offer beautiful, preplanted containers brimming with a pretty combination of flowering plants. The price may be high, but so is the temptation, and many gardeners succumb. The frugal gardener resists and instead uses these beautiful examples as inspiration. Enjoy the fun of planting your own containers with creative color and plant combinations, and pat yourself on the back for spending a fraction of the money charged by garden centers.

6 Quick Tricks to Dress Up Plain Pots

Simple plastic or clay pots are budget priced, but you can create rich effects with a quick spritz of spray paint or other easy decorations. Here are some ways to dress up plain pots:

1. Go for glamour with metallic copper, gold, or silver spray paint. Let some of the clay color show through for an antique look.

2. Spray a group of pots with cheerful primary colors, or with lime green, cobalt blue, and hot pink or orange-red for a South of the Border look. Plant the same flowers in each pot so that the effect doesn't get too busy. White daisies are pretty in primary-color pots; deep yellow or orange marigolds are perfect for Tex-Mex designs.

3. Paint a pot white or pastel, and glue seashells around the rim. Fill with gray-foliaged plants like dusty miller for a romantic, seaside effect.

4. Tie a bow of raffia or ribbon around a pot just below the rim, or rip a strip of calico and tie into a bow for a homespun look.

5. Cover a pot with plaster of Paris and stud it with broken bits of china, old buttons, or shards of mirrors and glass for a mosaic design.

6. Add stripes or polka dots to pots with bright paint as you would an Easter egg. Simple, primitive designs add childlike appeal.

Fancy up your flowerpots with a splash of paint and some glued-on decorations. Keep the plantings simple so that the containers get the attention they deserve.

The Frugal Gardener's Workshop:
A Picket Planter

THIS CHARMING PLANTER looks great on an old-fashioned porch, painted white and filled with ferns and ivy or cheerful red geraniums.

Materials

One 2-foot-long 1 × 3 (center picket)

Two 20-inch-long 1 × 3s (pickets)

Two 16-inch-long 1 × 3s (pickets)

Two 12-inch-long 1 × 3s (pickets)

Two 3-foot-long 2 × 6s (front and back)

One 3-foot-long 2 × 12 (bottom of planter box)

Two 12-inch-long 2 × 6s (sides of planter box)

Two 2½-foot-long 2 × 4s (front legs)

Two 4-foot-long 2 × 4s (back legs/uprights)

One 3-foot-long 1 × 3 (horizontal support for pickets)

Two 4-inch-long 1 × 6 (top caps)

Nails

Paint

Window-box liner, not more than 10 × 34 inches

Tools

Jigsaw or circular saw

Pencil

Straightedge

Measuring tape

Hammer

Drill

Paintbrush

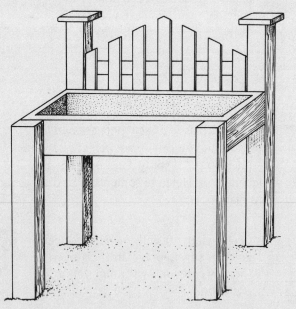

Dress up your porch with a cottage-garden planter. Make it yourself for about $20.

Directions

1. Cut the top of the center picket to a point. Cut tops of other pickets on a slant the same as the angle of the center point.

2. Build the planter box, nailing together the front, back, sides, and bottom. Drill ¼- to ½-inch holes in the bottom for drainage.

3. Attach front legs to the front of the box so that the bottom of the box is 2 feet above the bottom of the legs. The legs extend to the top of the box at the front corners.

4. Attach the back legs to the box so that the bottom of the box is 2 feet above the bottom of the legs. The legs extend 18 inches above the back corners of box.

5. Attach the central picket to the box so its bottom is flush with the bottom of the box.

6. Measure and attach other pickets equidistant between the central picket and back leg extensions. Make sure the angled tops are all going in the correct direction, with the highest side of the angle facing toward the center picket.

7. Attach the horizontal support across the pickets, nailing it to back leg extensions.

8. Nail the top caps on the top of the back leg extensions.

9. Paint the planter box, insert the window-box liner, and fill with soil mix and plants.

Thrifty Window Boxes

Window boxes bring charm to almost any house, and they give you a little more space for planting—always a plus. They're a great first timer's carpentry project. For the few dollars they cost to build, you'll get a big payback in extra appeal around the house. Care for window boxes as you do other container plantings, watering and feeding frequently to provide for the confined roots.

Just the Right Size

When you build it yourself, you can make a window box that's the perfect fit for your windows. Make the box the width of the window, including the frame with a depth that's proportionate to the height of your window. If your window is 3 feet tall or so, plan a box about 20 percent as deep, or a little more than 7 inches deep. For tall windows, make the box deeper, about 25 percent of the window height, so it doesn't look out of proportion.

Preserve Your Box

To use your window boxes year after year, seal untreated wood inside and outside with an exterior grade paint or polyurethane. Use a tiny brush to paint the exposed wood in the holes drilled for drainage. As added protection, you can line wooden boxes with metal sheeting or a plastic liner. Heavy-duty aluminum foil makes a decent makeshift lining as long as you overlap the edges of the sheets.

Allow Space for Moisture Control

Mount your box on brackets so that the back side of the box is ½ inch from the house. This ventilation space will help protect your home from moisture buildup. A filled window box is heavy, so be sure your brackets are sturdy and securely mounted. Position the window box so the top edge of the box is just below the windowsill.

Go for Eye Appeal

Think of your window box as a concentrated flowerbed that's meant to be seen from a distance. It will be most eye-catching if you keep the planting simple. Red geraniums with a ruff of gray, lacy dusty millers is a classic combo that flourishes all season. Save your complicated plantings for close-up flower gardens where your artistry can be admired. When you're planting window boxes, go for high-power zing. Here's the easy way to plant:

❖ Fill the box with mostly one type and color of long-blooming, low-care plant: pink impatiens, perhaps, or coral geraniums, red-flowered begonias, or lemon-yellow dwarf marigolds. Plant them close together, squeezing in plants for instant effect.

❖ Add an edging of sprawling plants, such as sweet alyssum or lobelia, to soften the front of the box and provide some contrast to the main bloomers.

❖ Stick in a few long, dangling vines or arching greenery. Variegated vinca vine is excellent because it will trail in streamers over the front of the box, making it look lush. Asparagus ferns or ornamental sweet potato vines are good choices, too.

Coordinate Colors

Be sure to consider the color of your house, the color of the box itself, and the color schemes of surrounding gardens when you choose plants. It's fun to paint boxes a bright color, like sunshine yellow, then use them as a focal point to play up coordinating or contrasting flower colors in the garden and at the window.

All-green, all-gorgeous. For a look of understated elegance, play with foliage instead of flowers in your window boxes. Look for houseplants with interesting foliage, like peperomia, philodendron, and ivies: They're perfect for a summer-to-frost window planting on the shaded side of your house. And prices of houseplants are generally no higher than those for annuals: about $1 to $2 a pot. Better yet, make your window boxes the summer home for your houseplants. Pop the pots into the box without transplanting, propping them up on stones or bricks if you need to raise them to the right height.

Don't Wait to Water

Replacing plants costs money, so keep your window garden flourishing with regular watering. You may have to water twice a day during the summer months. During cooler seasons, test the soil moisture by pushing your finger in about 1 inch. If it feels dry, it's time to water. If you wait for plants to wilt before you water them, the stress will slow their growth and flower production. To reduce the need for watering, add vermiculite to the soil. The plant roots can tap into the reservoir of water stored in the vermiculite.

The Frugal Gardener's Workshop:
A Frugal Potting Bench

MAKE A QUICK and easy potting bench from an old door and 4 × 4 legs.

Materials

One 2 × 10, cut to length of door

Old wooden door, hardware removed

Four 3-foot-long sections of 4 × 4s

Tools

Circular saw or jigsaw

Hammer

Nails

Directions

1. Nail the 2 × 10 to one edge of the door for a backsplash.

2. Lay the door flat, and mark the corners for attaching the legs.

3. Attach each leg by nailing through the door.

4. Stand upright on a level surface.

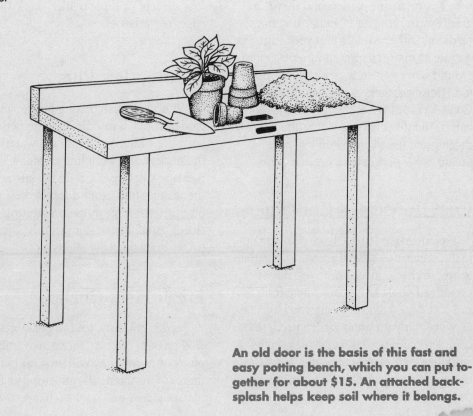

An old door is the basis of this fast and easy potting bench, which you can put together for about $15. An attached backsplash helps keep soil where it belongs.

Money-Wise Water Gardens

Water gardens add beauty and pleasure to any garden, and they're a great way to bring birds, butterflies, frogs, toads, and other wildlife into your yard. But despite its many charms and merits, an in-ground water garden is an expensive project. However, there is a frugal option. Consider creating a water garden in a pot or barrel. You don't have to worry about costly digging and installation, and it's space-saving, too—perfect for a deck or patio.

Cost-Conscious Containers

Preformed garden pools are showing up in discount stores as well as exclusive garden shops, so check prices before you buy. A preformed pool can cost anywhere from $80 to $300, depending on where you buy. The container for your water garden needs to be completely nonporous. Large plastic pots work fine for a small-scale water garden, as do "muck buckets" sold in houseware departments. Or, recycle a wooden half barrel

for a water garden by lining it with a 4 × 5-foot sheet of PVC pond liner, stapled to the edges of the barrel.

A Pump Is a Plus

Without a recirculating pump, a water garden is just a puddle. Fish do better with the added oxygen in the water, and the underwater bubbling creates a pleasing ripple pattern on the surface of the water. Shop around for the best prices on pumps—high-traffic home supply stores usually have significantly lower prices than specialty shops.

Fresh Fish, Cheap

Feeder goldfish, sold in pet stores to feed snakes, are very inexpensive. In an outdoor pond, they will grow as big as their environment allows. Guppies from a pet shop cost just pocket change and thrive in small water gardens, and minnows from a local stream or pond are free!

Guppies or Goldfish?

You risk losing goldfish when air temperatures go extremely high or low, so the experts at Van Ness Water Gardens in Upland, California, recommend mosquito fish (gambusia) or guppies for container ponds. For a 4 × 6-foot pond, start with ten goldfish; they will reproduce to the pond's capacity, eating any mosquitoes that venture nearby.

Great Garden Art for Next to Nothing

Much can be made of little if you're creative. Instead of buying garden statues like everyone else's, make a statement with one-of-a-kind objects.

Make the Most for Your Money

Not all garden sculpture is expensive, but many of the less expensive models look cheap. Cement cast statues can be pitted with air bubbles and clearly marked with a seam from the mold. Disguise flaws by painting the piece with buttermilk to encourage moss to grow, giving it an instant aged look. Then tuck your statue into the shrubbery, where it will look charming, only partially seen.

5 Inventive Ideas for Garden Art

1. Lay a broken clay pot, the bigger the better, on its side with the broken section along the ground. Add good-quality soil so that it spills out of the pot, and plant with blue pansies to create the illusion of a blue river of water pouring from the toppled pot.

2. Buy several tile chimneys or clay drainage tiles of different heights and arrange them in an attractive cluster. Top each with a different-sized clay saucer filled with water or birdseed to create a sculptural ensemble.

3. Showcase antique or worn-out tools as garden ornaments. Possibilities include an antique plow or wheelbarrow, a watering can, an old wagon wheel, or an old millstone.

4. Display pretty stones, shells, or driftwood in your garden as sculpture. Group smaller objects on a larger rock to give them more importance.

5. Spotlight driftwood or a gnarled vine for a nighttime display of curves and shadows.

✔ Frugal Gardener Checklist

- Instead of automatically throwing away worn-out items, consider how they might be restored.

- Do the labor yourself, whether it's paving a path or patio or building an arbor.

- Be on the lookout for thrown-away items that may be of use in your own garden. Somebody else's trash may be your treasure.

- If the fence you want is beyond your budget, use inexpensive wire covered with vines, or substitute the fence with hedge plants.

- Learn basic carpentry skills. You'll save an enormous amount of money on labor costs and get the satisfaction of creating your own beautiful and unique garden accessories.

- Trade free labor with a gardening friend or neighbor so you can each accomplish projects that require more than one pair of hands—without having to hire laborers.

- Go for big impact rather than big bucks. A simple PVC arbor dressed up with beautiful climbing vines or roses will make just as much of a statement in your garden as a three-times-as-expensive store-bought arbor.

Resources for Frugal Gardeners

Here's a selection of companies with great products for frugal gardeners. I've listed them by category for easy shopping. Prices and selection vary, so be a smart shopper by comparing catalogs before you buy.

Bulbs

Brent and Becky's Bulbs
7463 Heath Trail
Gloucester, VA 23061
Phone: (804) 693-3966
Fax: (804) 693-9436
E-mail: BBHeath@aol.com
Web site: www.brentand
    beckysbulbs.com

The Daffodil Mart
30 Irene Street
Torrington, CT 06790-6668
Phone: (800) 255-2852
Fax: (800) 420-2852

Van Bourgondien Bros.
P.O. Box 1000
Babylon, NY 11702-9004
Phone: (800) 622-9959
Fax: (516) 669-1228
E-mail: blooms@dutch
    bulbs.com
Web site: www.dutch
    bulbs.com

Flowers, Ornamental Grasses, and Water Gardening

W. Atlee Burpee & Co.
300 Park Avenue
Warminster, PA 18991-0001
Phone: (800) 888-1447
Fax: (800) 487-5530
Web site: www.burpee.com

Busse Gardens
5873 Oliver Avenue, S.W.
Cokato, MN 55321-4229
Phone: (800) 544-3192
Fax: (320) 286-6601
E-mail: bussegardens@cm
    gate.com

Carroll Gardens
444 E. Main Street
Westminster, MD 21157
Phone: (800) 638-6334
Fax: (410) 857-4112

Daylily Discounters
1 Daylily Plaza
Alachua, FL 32615
Phone: (904) 462-1539
Fax: (904) 462-5111
E-mail: daylily@earth
    link.com
Web site: www.daylily
    discounters.com

Goodness Grows, Inc.
Highway 77 N
P.O. Box 311
Lexington, GA 30648
Phone: (706) 743-5055
Fax: (706) 743-5112

Kurt Bluemel, Inc.
2740 Greene Lane
Baldwin, MD 21013-9523
Phone: (410) 557-7229
Fax: (410) 557-9785
E-mail: kbi@bluemel.com
Web site: www.bluemel
    .com/kbi

Lilypons Water Gardens
6800 Lilypons Road
P.O. Box 10
Buckeystown, MD 21717
(800) 999-5459

Limerock Ornamental Grasses, Inc.
70 Sawmill Road
Port Matilda, PA 16870
Phone: (814) 692-2272
Fax: (814) 692-9848

Milaeger's Gardens
4838 Douglas Avenue
Racine, WI 53402-2498
Phone: (800) 669-9956
Fax: (414) 639-1855

Niche Gardens

1111 Dawson Road
Chapel Hill, NC 27516
Phone: (919) 967-0078
Fax: (919) 967-4026
E-mail: orders@nichegdn.com
Web site: www.nichegdn.com

Nichols Garden Nursery

1190 N. Pacific Highway
Albany, OR 97321-4580
Phone: (541) 928-9280
Fax: (541) 967-8406
E-mail: info@garden
    nursery.com
Web site: www.garden
    nursery.com

Park Seed

1 Parkton Avenue
Greenwood, SC 29647-0001
Phone: (800) 845-3369
Fax: (800) 275-9941
E-mail: orders@parkseed.com
Web site: http://parkseed.com

Pinetree Garden Seeds

Box 300
616A Lewiston Road
New Gloucester, ME 04260
Phone: (207) 926-3400
Fax: (888) 527-3337
E-mail: superseeds@
    worldnet.att.net
Web site:
    www.superseeds.com

Roslyn Nursery

211 Burrs Lane
Dix Hills, NY 11746
Phone: (516) 643-9347
Fax: (516) 427-0894
E-mail: roslyn@concentric.net
Web site: www.cris.com/
    ~Roslyn

Southern Perennials and Herbs

98 Bridges Road
Tylertown, MS 39667-9338
Phone: (800) 774-0079
Fax: (601) 684-3729
E-mail: sph@neosoft.com
Web site: www.s-p-h.com

Van Ness Water Gardens

2460 North Euclid Avenue
Upland, CA 91784-1199
Phone: (909) 982-2425
Fax: (909) 949-7217
E-mail: vnwg@vnwg.com
Web site: www.vnwg.com

Wayside Gardens

1 Garden Lane
Hodges, SC 29695-0001
Phone: (800) 845-1124
Fax: (800) 457-9712
E-mail: orders@wayside
    gardens.com
Web site: www.wayside
    gardens.com

White Flower Farm

P.O. Box 50
Litchfield, CT 06759-0050
Phone: (800) 411-6159
Fax: (860) 496-1418
Web site: www.whiteflower
    farm.com

Herbs

Horizon Herbs

P.O. Box 69
Williams, OR 97544
Phone: (541) 846-6704
E-mail: herbseed@chatlink
    .com
Web site: www.budget.net/
    ~herbseed

Long Creek Herbs

Route 4, Box 730
Oak Grove, AR 72660
Phone: (417) 779-5450
Fax: (417) 779-5450
Web site: www.longcreek
    herbs.com

Nichols Garden Nursery

1190 N. Pacific Highway
Albany, OR 97321-4580
Phone: (541) 928-9280
Fax: (541) 967-8406
E-mail: info@garden
    nursery.com
Web site: www.garden
    nursery.com

Richters Herb Catalogue

Goodwood, Ontario
L0C 1A0 Canada
Phone: (905) 640-6677
Fax: (905) 640-6641
E-mail: inquiry@richters.com
Web site: www.richters.com

Sage Mountain Herbs
Rosemary Gladstar
P.O. Box 420
E. Barre, VT 05649
Phone: (802) 479-9825
Fax: (802) 476-3722

The Sandy Mush Herb
Nursery
316 Surrett Cove Road
Leicester, NC 28748
Phone: (704) 683-2014

Well-Sweep Herb Farm
205 Mt. Bethel Road
Port Murray, NJ 07865
Phone: (908) 852-5390

Pest, Disease, and Weed Control

Gardener's Supply
Company
128 Intervale Road
Burlington, VT 05401-2850
Phone: (800) 863-1700
Fax: (800) 551-6712
E-mail: info@gardeners.com
Web site: www.gardeners.com

Gardens Alive!
5100 Schenley Place
Lawrenceburg, IN 47025
Phone: (812) 537-8650
Fax: (812) 537-5108

Harmony Farm Supply
and Nursery
P.O. Box 460
Graton, CA 95444
Phone: (707) 823-9125
Fax: (707) 823-1734
E-mail: info@harmony
    farm.com
Web site: www.harmony
    farm.com

The Natural Gardening
Company
217 San Anselmo Avenue
San Anselmo, CA 94960
Phone: (707) 766-9303
Fax: (707) 766-9747
E-mail: info@natural
    gardening.com
Web site: www.natural
    gardening.com

Peaceful Valley Farm
Supply
P.O. Box 2209
Grass Valley, CA 95945
Phone: (530) 272-4769
Fax: (530) 272-4794
Web site: www.grow
    organic.com

Seed Starting and Season Extending

W. Atlee Burpee & Co.
300 Park Avenue
Warminster, PA 18991-0001
Phone: (800) 888-1447
Fax: (800) 487-5530
Web site: www.burpee.com

Gardener's Supply
Company
128 Intervale Road
Burlington, VT 05401-2850
Phone: (800) 863-1700
Fax: (800) 551-6712
E-mail: info@gardeners.com
Web site: www.gardeners.com

Harmony Farm Supply
and Nursery
P.O. Box 460
Graton, CA 95444
Phone: (707) 823-9125
Fax: (707) 823-1734
E-mail: info@harmony
    farm.com
Web site: www.harmony
    farm.com

Johnny's Selected Seeds
Foss Hill Road
Albion, ME 04910-9731
Phone: (207) 437-4357
Fax: (800) 437-4290
E-mail: customerservice@
    johnnyseeds.com
Web site: www.johnny
    seeds.com

Milaeger's Gardens
1838 Douglas Avenue
Racine, WI 53402-2498
Phone: (800) 669-9956
Fax: (414) 639-1855

Peaceful Valley Farm
Supply
P.O. Box 2209
Grass Valley, CA 95945
Phone: (530) 272-4769
Fax: (530) 272-4794
Web site: www.grow
   organic.com

Soil Care and Composting

Cook's Consulting
R.D. 2, Box 13
Lowville, NY 13367
Phone: (315) 376-3002

Gardener's Supply
Company
128 Intervale Road
Burlington, VT 05401
Phone: (800) 863-1700
Fax: (800) 551-6712
E-mail: info@gardeners.com
Web site: www.gardeners.com

Gardens Alive!
5100 Schenley Place
Lawrenceburg, IN 47025
Phone: (812) 537-8650
Fax: (812) 537-5108

Harmony Farm Supply
and Nursery
P.O. Box 460
Graton, CA 95444
Phone: (707) 823-9125
Fax: (707) 823-1734
E-mail: info@harmony
   farm.com
Web site: www.harmony
   farm.com

The Natural Gardening
Company
217 San Anselmo Avenue
San Anselmo, CA 94960
Phone: (707) 766-9303
Fax: (707) 766-9747
E-mail: info@natural
   gardening.com
Web site: www.natural
   gardening.com

Ohio Earth Food, Inc.
5488 Swamp Street, NE
Hartville, OH 44632
Phone: (330) 877-9356
Fax: (330) 877-4237

Peaceful Valley Farm
Supply
P.O. Box 2209
Grass Valley, CA 95945
Phone: (530) 272-4769
Fax: (530) 272-4794
Web site: www.grow
   organic.com

Timberleaf Soil Testing
Services
39648 Old Spring Road
Murrieta, CA 92563
Phone: (909) 677-7510

Wallace Laboratories
365 Coral Circle
El Segundo, CA 90245
Phone: (310) 615-0116
Fax: (310) 640-6863

Woods End Research
Laboratory
P.O. Box 297
Mt. Vernon, ME 04352
Phone: (207) 293-2457
Fax: (207) 293-2488

Worm's Way
7850 N. Highway 37
Bloomington, IN 47404
Phone: (800) 274-9676
Fax: (800) 316-1264
E-mail: info@worms
   way.com
Web site: http://worms
   way.com

Tools and Supplies

Alsto's Handy Helpers
Route 150 East
P.O. Box 1267
Galesburg, IL 61402-1267
Phone: (800) 447-0048
Fax: (800) 522-5786

A. M. Leonard, Inc.
241 Fox Drive
Piqua, OH 45356
Phone: (800) 543-8955
Fax: (800) 433-0633
E-mail: info@amleo.com
Web site: www.amleo.com

Dripworks
231 E. San Francisco Street
Willits, CA 95490
Phone: (800) 616-8321
Fax: (707) 459-9645
E-mail: dripwrks@pacific.net
Web site: www.dripworks
   usa.com

Gardener's Supply Company

128 Intervale Road
Burlington, VT 05401-2850
Phone: (800) 863-1700
Fax: (800) 551-6712
E-mail: info@gardeners.com
Web site: www.gardeners.com

Kinsman Company, Inc.

P.O. Box 357
River Road
Point Pleasant, PA 18950
Phone: (800) 733-4146
Fax: (215) 297-0450
E-mail: contact@kinsman
   garden.com
Web site: www.kinsman
   garden.com

The Natural Gardening Company

217 San Anselmo Avenue
San Anselmo, CA 94960
Phone: (707) 766-9303
Fax: (707) 766-9747
E-mail: info@natural
   gardening.com
Web site: www.natural
   gardening.com

Plow & Hearth

P.O. Box 5000
Madison, VA 22727-1500
Phone: (800) 627-1712
Fax: (800) 843-2509

Trees, Shrubs, and Vines

Carroll Gardens

444 E. Main Street
Westminster, MD 21157
Phone: (800) 638-6334
Fax: (410) 857-4112

Forestfarm

990 Tetherow Road
Williams, OR 97544-9599
Phone: (541) 846-7269
Fax: (541) 846-6963
E-mail: forestfarm@
   aonepro.net
Web site: www.forestfarm
   .com

Greer Gardens

1280 Goodpasture Island
   Road
Eugene, OR 97401-1794
Phone: (541) 686-8266
Fax: (541) 686-0910

Gurney's Seed & Nursery Co.

110 Capital Street
Yankton, SD 57079
Phone: (605) 665-1930
Fax: (605) 665-9718

Pickering Nurseries, Inc.

670 Kingston Road
Pickering, Ontario
L1V 1A6 Canada
Phone: (905) 839-2111
Fax: (905) 839-4807

Roslyn Nursery

211 Burrs Lane
Dix Hills, NY 11746
Phone: (516) 643-9347
Fax: (516) 427-0894
E-mail: roslyn@concentric.net
Web site: www.cris.com/
   ~Roslyn

Wayside Gardens

1 Garden Lane
Hodges, SC 29695-0001
Phone: (800) 845-1124
Fax: (800) 457-9712
E-mail: orders@wayside
   gardens.com
Web site: www.wayside
   gardens.com

White Flower Farm

P.O. Box 50
Litchfield, CT 06759-0050
Phone: (800) 411-6159
Fax: (860) 496-1418
Web site: www.whiteflower
   farm.com

Woodlanders, Inc.

1128 Colleton Avenue
Aiken, SC 29801
Phone/Fax: (803) 648-7522

Vegetables

Abundant Life Seed Foundation

P.O. Box 772
Port Townsend, WA 98368
Phone: (360) 385-5660
Fax: (360) 385-7455
E-mail:
    abundant@olypen.com
Web site:
    http://csf.Colorado.edu
    /perma/abundant

W. Atlee Burpee & Co.

300 Park Avenue
Warminster, PA 18991-0001
Phone: (800) 888-1447
Fax: (800) 487-5530
Web site: www.burpee.com

The Cook's Garden

P.O. Box 535
Londonderry, VT 05148
Phone: (800) 457-9703
Fax: (800) 457-9705
Web site: www.cooks
    garden.com

Johnny's Selected Seeds

Foss Hill Road
Albion, ME 04910-9731
Phone: (207) 437-4357
Fax: (800) 437-4290
E-mail: customerservice@
    johnnyseeds.com
Web site: www.johnny
    seeds.com

Ferry-Morse Seed Co.

P.O. Box 488
Fulton, KY 42041-0488
Phone: (800) 283-3400
Fax: (800) 283-2700
Web site: http://trine.com/
    GardenNet/FerryMorse

Gurney's Seed and Nursery Co.

110 Capital Street
Yankton, SD 57079
Phone: (605) 665-1930
Fax: (605) 665-9718

Park Seed

1 Parkton Avenue
Greenwood, SC 29647-0001
Phone: (800) 845-3369
Fax: (800) 275-9941
E-mail: orders@parkseed.com
Web site: http://parkseed.com

Pinetree Garden Seeds

Box 300
616A Lewiston Road
New Gloucester, ME 04260
Phone: (207) 926-3400
Fax: (888) 527-3337
E-mail: superseeds@
    worldnet.att.net
Web site: www.super
    seeds.com

R. H. Shumway, Seedsman

P.O. Box 1
Graniteville, SC 29829-0001
Phone: (803) 663-9771
Fax: (803) 663-9772

Ronniger's Seed & Potato Co.

P.O. Box 307
Ellensburg, WA 98926
Phone: (800) 846-6178

Seeds Blüm

HC 33, Box 2057
Boise, ID 83706
Phone: (800) 742-1423
Fax: (208) 338-5658
Web site: www.seeds
    blum.com

Seeds of Change

P.O. Box 15700
Sante Fe, NM 87506-5700
Phone: (888) 762-7333
Fax: (888) 329-4762
E-mail: service@seeds
    ofchange.com
Web site: www.seeds
    ofchange.com

Shepherd's Garden Seeds

30 Irene Street
Torrington, CT 06790-6658
Phone: (860) 482-3638
Web site: www.shepherd
    seeds.com

Southern Exposure Seed Exchange

P.O. Box 170
Earlysville, VA 22936
Phone: (804) 973-4703
Fax: (804) 973-8717
E-mail: gardens@southern
    exposure.com
Web site: www.southern
    exposure.com

Recommended Reading

Composting and Soil Care

Appelhof, Mary. *Worms Eat My Garbage*. Kalamazoo, MI: Flower Press, 1982.

Campbell, Stu. *Let It Rot: The Gardener's Guide to Composting*. Charlotte, VT: Storey Communications, 1975.

Gershuny, Grace. *Start with the Soil*. Emmaus, PA: Rodale Press, 1993.

Hynes, Erin. *Rodale's Successful Organic Gardening: Improving the Soil*. Emmaus, PA: Rodale Press, 1994.

General Gardening

Benjamin, Joan, ed. *Great Garden Shortcuts*. Emmaus, PA: Rodale Press, 1996.

Benjamin, Joan, and Deborah L. Martin, eds. *Great Garden Formulas*. Emmaus, PA: Rodale Press, 1998.

Bradley, Fern Marshall, and Barbara Ellis, eds. *Rodale's All-New Encyclopedia of Organic Gardening*. Emmaus, PA: Rodale Press, 1992.

Coleman, Eliot. *Four-Season Harvest: How to Harvest Fresh, Organic Vegetables from Your Home Garden All Year Long*. White River Junction, VT: Chelsea Green Publishing, 1992.

Costenbader, Carol W. *The Big Book of Preserving the Harvest*. Pownal, VT: Storey Communications, 1997.

Michalak, Patricia S., and Cass Peterson. *Rodale's Successful Organic Gardening: Vegetables*. Emmaus, PA: Rodale Press, 1993.

Herbs

Kowalchik, Claire, and William H. Hylton, eds. *Rodale's Illustrated Encyclopedia of Herbs*. Emmaus, PA: Rodale Press, 1987.

McClure, Susan. *The Herb Gardener: A Guide for All Seasons*. Pownal, VT: Storey Communications, 1995.

Sombke, Laurence. *Beautiful Easy Herbs*. Emmaus, PA: Rodale Press, 1997.

Landscape and Flower Gardening

Binetti, Marianne. *Shortcuts for Accenting Your Garden: Over Five Hundred Easy & Inexpensive Tips*. Pownal, VT: Storey Communications, 1993.

Bradley, Fern Marshall, ed. *Gardening with Perennials*. Emmaus, PA: Rodale Press, 1996.

Cox, Jeff. *Perennial All-Stars: The 150 Best Perennials for Great-Looking, Trouble-Free Gardens*. Emmaus, PA: Rodale Press, 1998.

DiSabato-Aust, Tracy. *The Well-Tended Perennial Garden: Planting and Pruning Techniques*. Portland, OR: Timber Press, 1998.

Ellis, Barbara. *Taylor's How To Grow North America's Favorite Plants*. Boston: Houghton Mifflin, 1998.

McKeon, Judy. *The Encyclopedia of Roses*. Emmaus, PA: Rodale Press, 1995.

Phillips, Ellen, and C. Colston Burrell. *Rodale's Illustrated Encyclopedia of Perennials.* Emmaus, PA: Rodale Press, 1993.

Sombke, Laurence. *Beautiful Easy Flower Gardens.* Emmaus, PA: Rodale Press, 1995.

Taylor, Norman. *Taylor's Guide to Annuals,* rev. ed. Boston: Houghton Mifflin Co., 1986.

Taylor, Norman. *Taylor's Guide to Perennials,* rev. ed. Boston: Houghton Mifflin Co., 1986.

Pest and Disease Control

Gilkeson, Linda, et al. *Rodale's Pest & Disease Problem Solver.* Emmaus, PA: Rodale Press, 1996.

Hynes, Erin. *Rodale's Successful Organic Gardening: Controlling Weeds.* Emmaus, PA: Rodale Press, 1995.

Michalak, Patricia S., and Linda Gilkeson. *Rodale's Successful Organic Gardening: Controlling Pests and Diseases.* Emmaus, PA: Rodale Press, 1994.

Nancarrow, Loren, and Janet Hogan Taylor. *Dead Snails Leave No Trails.* Berkeley, CA: Ten Speed Press, 1996.

Pleasant, Barbara. *The Gardener's Bug Book.* Pownal, VT: Storey Communications, 1994.

———. *The Gardener's Guide to Plant Diseases.* Pownal, VT: Storey Communications, 1995.

———. *The Gardener's Weed Book: Earth-Safe Controls.* Pownal, VT: Storey Communications, 1996.

Seed Starting

Bubel, Nancy. *The New Seed-Starter's Handbook.* Emmaus, PA: Rodale Press, 1988.

Ondra, Nancy, and Barbara Ellis. *Easy Plant Propagation.* (Taylor's Weekend Gardening Guides.) Boston: Houghton Mifflin Co., 1998.

Powell, Eileen. *From Seed to Bloom: How to Grow over 500 Annuals, Perennials, and Herbs.* Pownal, VT: Storey Communications, 1995.

Magazines and Newsletters

Birds and Blooms
  5400 South 60th Street
  Greendale, WI 53129

HortIdeas
  750 Black Lick Road
  Gravel Switch, KY 40328

Organic Gardening
  Rodale Press Inc.
  33 E. Minor Street
  Emmaus, PA 18098

Index